Awake, Emerging and Connected

Awake, Emerging and Connected

Meditations on Justice from a Missing Generation

Edited by
Victoria Turner

scm press

© Victoria Turner 2024

Published in 2024 by SCM Press
Editorial office
3rd Floor, Invicta House,
110 Golden Lane,
London EC1Y 0TG, UK

www.scmpress.co.uk

SCM Press is an imprint of Hymns Ancient & Modern Ltd
(a registered charity)

Hymns Ancient & Modern® is a registered trademark of
Hymns Ancient & Modern Ltd
13A Hellesdon Park Road, Norwich,
Norfolk NR6 5DR, UK

All rights reserved. No part of this publication may be reproduced,
stored in a retrieval system, or transmitted,
in any form or by any means, electronic, mechanical,
photocopying or otherwise, without the prior permission of
the publisher, SCM Press.

Victoria Turner has asserted her right under the Copyright, Designs
and Patents Act 1988 to be identified as the Author of this Work

Scripture quotations are taken from the following versions:
The Revised Standard Version of the Bible, copyright 1946, 1952 and 1971
by the Division of Christian Education of the National Council of the
Churches of Christ in the USA. Used by permission. All rights reserved.
The ESV Bible (The Holy Bible, English Standard Version), copyright
© 2001 by Crossway, a publishing ministry of Good News Publishers.
Used by permission. All rights reserved.
The Holy Bible, New International Version, NIV. Copyright ©1973, 1978,
1984, 2011 by Biblica, Inc. Used by permission of Zondervan.
All rights reserved worldwide.

British Library Cataloguing in Publication data
A catalogue record for this book is available
from the British Library

ISBN: 978-0-334-06543-2

Typeset by Regent Typesetting

Contents

Contributors   xi

Introduction: 'She who wants the world to remain as it is, doesn't want it to remain at all'   1
Victoria Turner

Part 1 Questioning Western Epistemological Hegemony: Rethinking Approaches to Justice

1. Christ's Being Beyond Time: A Theological Emancipation from the Acceleration of Time   21
   Samuel Efrain Murillo Torres

2. Against Western Cognitive Hegemony in Academic Theology: The Quest for Epistemological Justice in Liberation and Intercultural Theology(ies)   36
   Daniel Jara J.

3. Indigenous Queer Subjugation and Lessons from Nagaland   48
   Inatoli Aye

4. African Approaches to Transitional Justice   65
   Adam Randera

5. The 'View from Below' from Above: A Critical Genealogy of Settler Christianity in Oceania   77
   Andrew Clark-Howard

6. Restoring Wholeness in Creation: A Samoan Indigenous Spiritual Perspective on Climate Justice   93
   Iemaima Vaai

Part 2 Insiders and Outsiders: Struggling through History and Context

7 Palestinian Women: The Question Within the Question   99
   Muna Nassar

8 Justice for the Workers: Theologizing Trade Unions and Labour Movements   110
   William Gibson

9 'This is my Story, this is my Song': Queer Presbyterians, Provocative Questions, Practical Politics, and a Case for Church History in the Development of Theologies of Justice   122
   David Brandon Smith

10 The Myth of the Gospel: Trump, Politics and the Crisis of the Evangelical Church   138
   Nathan Dever

11 A Step Forwards or Backwards? Reflections on Homelessness, Housing and Politics in England from 1945 to the Present   148
   Ian Rowe

Part 3 Disrupting Theology, Theory and Thinking

12 An Essay That Is Already Belated: Some Notes on Holocaust and the Recovery of Witnessing   163
   Dave Korn

13 Reimagining Hindu Liberation Theology in India with Raimon Panikkar   175
   Shruti Dixit

14 Exposing Selfish Motivations Disguised as Justice: Questioning the Narrative of the Miracle of Cultured Meat   185
   Arvin Gouw

15 Discussing Human Dignity from the Peripheries: A Dialogue between *Buddhagotra* and *Imago Dei*   199
   Patricia Guernelli Palazzo Tsai

16 A Lived Theology of Belonging   212
  Amar D. Peterman

17 Technological and Theological Visions, Desires and Practices   222
  Michael Morelli

18 The Fallacy of Hopelessness: Constructing a Metamodern
  Theology of Hope   236
  Iona Curtius

Conclusion: Disengaging our Disengagement and Disconnections   248
Victoria Turner

Index   253

[S]he who wants the world to remain as it is,
doesn't want it to remain at all.
Erich Fried (1921–88)

Contributors

Adam Randera is a Programme Officer at the African Centre for the Constructive Resolution of Disputes (ACCORD). He holds an MPhil in International Peace Studies from Trinity College Dublin, with a focus on African approaches to transitional justice. He also holds a BA in Philosophy, Classical Studies and Linguistics, and a joint Honours degree in Philosophy and Linguistics and Applied Language Studies, both from Rhodes University. Adam's research interests include public policy, transformative justice, gender and identity, and the building of grassroots capacities for peace.

Amar D. Peterman has an MDiv from Princeton Seminary and is an author and theologian working at the intersection of faith and public life. He is the founder of Scholarship for Religion and Society, a research and consulting firm based in the United States. His first book, focused on the common good, neighbour love and faith formation, is forthcoming.

Andrew Clark-Howard is a PhD candidate in the School of Theology at Charles Sturt University. Originally from Aotearoa New Zealand, he currently lives and works with his partner Steph on unceded Burramattagal land in Western Sydney. His interests include modern theology, theological method, decolonization, and the theology of Dietrich Bonhoeffer.

Arvin Gouw (PhD) is working in the field of theology and science at the University of Cambridge Faculty of Divinity. His most recent book is *Religious Transhumanism and Its Critics*, co-edited with Brian Green and Ted Peters (2022), and his research has been published in academic journals including *Cell Metabolism, Nature Biotechnology, Science, PNAS, Zygon, Theology and Science.*

Daniel Jara J. works as lecturer at the Chair of Intercultural Theology and Physicality and at the Center for Religious Studies CERES of the Ruhr-Universität Bochum. He is project coordinator of 'UNIC-RESCUe:

European Research Network for Religion, Society and Culture' of UNIC (European University Cities in Post-industrial Transition).

Dave Korn is an American poet and scholar. He holds an MScR in US Literature from the University of Edinburgh.

David Brandon Smith is a Minister of Word and Sacrament in the Presbyterian Church (USA), a Doctoral Candidate in Church History at the Faculty of Protestant Theology of the University of Bonn, and a Research Associate at the Bonn Center for Dependency and Slavery Studies.

Ian Rowe is a caseworker for a leading homeless charity in London working with some of the most vulnerable people in the city. He started working in the sector in 2020 during Covid-19 and worked in one of the hotels set up by the government to ensure no one was rough sleeping during the pandemic. Since then he has moved into a more specialized team working with clients with complex needs and supports them in moving into or sustaining accommodation. In 2017 Ian completed a History degree at the University of Kent, followed by a range of jobs both in the UK and the Netherlands including working in community and homeless projects in Amsterdam.

Iemaima Vaai is of Samoan descent and is an environmental climate justice activist for the Pacific. She is currently working under the youth, climate change and conflict project initiated by Toda Peace Institute as a researcher. She has previously worked for environment and ecumenical organizations and has a BA in Environmental Management and a postgraduate degree in Climate Change from the University of the South Pacific.

Inatoli Aye is an indigenous woman from Nagaland, India. She is a PhD student at the University of Wales Trinity St David. Inatoli is rooted in the tradition of liberation theology and has published in the areas of feminist, queer and indigenous theologies.

Iona Curtius is a PhD candidate in Systematic Theology at the University of Aberdeen, with a background in theology and English literature. While Systematics is her homeland, she enjoys occasional excursions into other areas of theology. She is interested in truth and embodiment, stories and cultural developments, and sometimes becomes mildly obsessed with cyborgs.

CONTRIBUTORS

Michael Morelli is assistant professor of theology and ethics at Northwest Seminary and College, a founding member of ACTS Seminaries, and an affiliate of Trinity Western University. He is the author of *Theology, Ethics, and Technology in the Work of Jacques Ellul and Paul Virilio* and the editor of *Desert, Wilderness, Wasteland, and Word: A New Essay by Jacques Ellul and Five Critical Engagements*.

Muna Nassar, a Palestinian Christian woman from Bethlehem, advocates for justice for the Palestinian people and has worked as a project coordinator for Kairos Palestine. In 2021, she obtained an MPhil in intercultural theology and interreligious studies from Trinity College Dublin. In December 2022, Muna joined the World Communion of Reformed Churches based in Hannover, Germany, as executive secretary for mission and advocacy. As a writer, she aims to articulate and represent the diversity of Palestine and Palestinians, highlighting their voice and agency.

Nathan Dever is a PhD candidate at the University of Edinburgh where he is completing a project on American evangelical missionary work in the contemporary Middle East. He holds a BA in Political Science from the University of Louisville, and an MSc in Middle Eastern Studies and Advanced Arabic from the University of Edinburgh.

Patricia Guernelli Palazzo Tsai is a Buddhist scholar and practitioner from Mahāyāna tradition and a lay Dominican. She teaches at Instituto Pramāṇa, and is also Legal Director of the Buddha-Dharma Association in Brazil. She is a member of Sakyadhita International Association of Buddhist Women, and co-founder of the Sakyadhita Sao Paulo chapter. Her research focuses on Mahāyāna Buddhism, Buddhist Ethics, Christian Ethics, Latin America Liberation Theology, and Interreligious Dialogue.

Samuel Efrain Murillo Torres is in the final year of his PhD at the University of Aberdeen where he is applying Bonhoeffer's theology to the crisis of the disappeared in Mexico. A methodist minister, Sam works extensively with the World Methodist Council, the Global Christian Forum, and is part of the current efforts for the possible peace process in Mexico, mainly from the ecumenical accompaniment with families and victims that have experienced enforced disappearances, towards the search of our missing beloved ones, identification of found bodies and advocating for non-repetition considering the current national forensic crisis in Mexico. He is the founder and director of the Latin American Centre for Religions and Cultures, Public Theologies in Governance and Society.

Shruti Dixit is a doctoral researcher at the Centre for the Study of Religion and Politics, School of Divinity, University of St Andrews. Her research deals with rethinking revelation in Hindu–Christian dialogue while engaging with Raimon Panikkar's Opera Omnia. Shruti is the network coordinator of Network of Hinduism in Dialogue, which is affiliated with the Oxford Centre for Hindu Studies and also holds the Further Education Institution seat at the Interfaith Scotland's Youth Advisory Board.

Victoria Turner (PhD) is tutor in Theology and Mission at Ripon College Cuddesdon, a theological college of the Church of England. She is also co-editor, with Stephen Burns, of the *International Journal of the Study of the Christian Church*, and book reviews editor for the journal *Modern Believing*. Her PhD studies were undertaken at the University of Edinburgh in the field of World Christianity where she explored the Iona Community and the Council for World Mission. Victoria's own ecclesial belonging is with the United Reformed Church.

William Gibson (LLB) is in his final year studying Theology and Religious Studies (MA) at the University of Glasgow. He currently works for the Student Christian Movement as their theology and resources project worker but prior to this he worked at Apple and was a union organizer and rep in the first unionized Apple store in the UK. William is a member of the Church of Scotland and associate member of the Iona Community.

Introduction

'She who wants the world to remain as it is, doesn't want it to remain at all'

VICTORIA TURNER

I am supposed to be attending a friend's Christmas party the following night [of the UK 2019 General Election] but I cancel at the last minute, because I know I'll probably be the only Black person in a room full of white ones. I'm worried that after the requisite hand-wringing about the election results, someone will blithely suggest we talk about something less depressing 'because it's Christmas', and I will smash a plate against the wall because I don't think there's anything else we should be talking about, don't think it's fair that white people get to change the subject. So instead I stay home and cry. *Otegha Uwagba*[1]

I hate those quotes at the top of books/chapters – those clever ones from usually very clever philosophers. I find them pretentious – and more often than not do not understand whatever it was Hegel, or Foucault, or Augustine were trying to say in the 20–30 words that have graced the first page. These suspended words apparently, in their succinct wisdom, summarize the whole chapter but are never referred back to. Do others also just pretend to acknowledge their relevance, or think that it is their fault that these words have passed over their simple heads, then feel guilty for not having read the whole of Augustine's 13 Confessions (AD 397–400), and then wallow in self-doubt because they will never read all of Augustine's 13 Confessions and therefore will never be illuminated by this top-page quote, and probably will never be worthy of writing a kind of top-page-quote kind of book?[2]

So, I have used an unconventional, yet (hopefully) relatable, 100-word top-page quote. Uwagba is an impressive author, culture journalist and Black Millennial from south London. I love how the raw emotion seeps through the pages of her short 2021 book *Whites: On Race and Other Falsehoods*, and how seamlessly the plate throwing is weaved in – unquestioned and completely normalized. Is it not exactly the reaction of Jesus in the Temple? 'He overturned the tables of the money-changers and the benches of those selling doves. "It is written," he said to them, "'My house will be called a house of prayer,' but you are making it 'a den of robbers.'"'[3]

In an anthology of a friend, I wrote:

> Passion, feeling, energy, emotion, suffering, solidarity, sympathy, movement. I feel God's love when I feel … So, when I'm angry about suffering, I rejoice. Because being angry is the outworking of being so utterly connected to another person and their feelings. Protest is holy … This passion and energy and feeling flowing through us is the Holy Spirit reminding us of our connection to each other through Christ who became us too. These reactions are not to be quickly suppressed, to be replaced with rational thought. God's love is our ability to feel another's pain, stand in their shoes, fight their fight, just as Jesus did for us. When we register the power of this passion, sit with it, meditate on it, we are worshipping God and giving thanks for this immense privilege of being both so authentically human and so in touch with the Spirit's movement.[4]

My vision for this book was to collect the people I know who feel this raw kind of emotion towards the world. People who are frustrated with the absence of necessary conversations in their daily lives: worn-down from tip-toeing above the sea of false-peace from their lonely tightrope – their precarious footing ensuring their real thoughts (or even presence) do not disrupt the status quo of illusion-disillusion. People who not only desperately want change, but allow their minds to wonder and wander – release their meditations from the imposed inevitability of neo-capitalism's ruling elites, patriarchy's hard grip, whiteness' blinding 'purity' – and glimpse something more. I wanted people from different traditions, (non)religions, contexts and disciplines to articulate justice through their lenses to create a prophetic imagination[5] that disrupts how the world currently *is* by exposing its lies and inconsistencies, and expresses how it could be.

Young People are Being Sold a False Dream

In my context of the UK, the government has driven up the prices of education to the point where 'humanities – and the enrichment they give – are Mickey Mouse', and revenue-rich courses – law, medicine and accountancy – are prioritized.[6] This has gone beyond choice for individuals being lost from class inaccessibility, where the freedom of education, no longer being free, is not a risk easily taken, but a journey of debt to be entangled in.[7] These non-profitable courses, for the capitalist institutions that are universities, are even being cut by the management.[8] Kosuke Koyama (1929–2009), a Japanese theologian (and astute social critic), in 1975 lamented,

> How tragically the sense of values in the minds of children is destroyed because of the insidious greedy philosophy that the purpose of education is to enable children to make more money by getting good-money-earning jobs in the future. Education is subjected to the 'philosophy of more money'.[9]

Ways of thinking, social critique, relationship building across classes, nations and continents, and imaginations are being cut in societies. The paid university system has translated knowledge exchange into a purchasing exchange – degrees no longer transform, but are transacted, solely for the purchase of economic accumulation in the future.

This is exemplified in a recent statement made by the (publically unelected) Conservative Prime Minister of the UK, Rishi Sunak:

> The UK is home to some of the best universities in the world and studying for a degree can be immensely rewarding.
>
> But too many young people are being sold a *false dream* and end up doing a poor-quality course at the taxpayers' expense that doesn't offer the prospect of a decent job at the end of it.
>
> That is why we are taking action to crack down on rip-off university courses, while boosting skills training and apprenticeships provision.
>
> This will help more young people to choose the path that is right to help them reach their potential and *grow our economy*.[10]

To quote John Sutherland in response, 'The young have been reduced to a "precariat" – a precarious sector of society which has creature comforts no previous generation has enjoyed, but no distant horizon life prospects.'[11] The 'our economy' Sunak writes of is one in which he and his wife are valued at £730 million, with his multi-million pound fortune being kept in a 'blind trust' – a fund where the owner is kept ignorant of the investments to 'overcome' any ethical responsibility.[12] Perhaps it is not only the blind eye in voting, but in financing too, that Sunak turns to the murder of innocents. As an investor, previous bank manager and owner of a hedge fund company, Sunak and his government dream of increasing wealth – but wealth for wealth's sake – not needing to be concerned with the question: at whose cost?

Ha-Joon Chang, a South Korean economist at Cambridge University, outlines in his book 23 *Things They Don't Tell You about Capitalism* that the trickledown economics of making the rich richer actually do not make the pie bigger, and money and markets do not have moral values (who knew?!), so the trickledown is never guaranteed.[13] In fact, Chang recommends that downward income redistribution would help economic growth – the reason being that if the majority population spend more of their incomes, a base-increase in wages would increase the health and education of workers boosting efficiency and leaning towards social peace (decreasing crime and strike action), all of which might actually encourage investment.[14] So, in fact, the opposite of trickledown would benefit the country's economy. Increasing access to university courses, diversifying jobs, careers and interests, and increasing tax subsidy would benefit society (though research shows that the tax-payer paid less towards society's higher education institutions before students had to pay their own university fees).[15] Noam Chomsky explains: 'The nature of the [capitalist] system is that it's supposed to be driven by greed; no one's supposed to be concerned for anybody else, nobody's supposed to worry about the common good – those are not things that are supposed to motivate you.'[16] These larger questions of the common good stand outside of a politics that is controlled by the market.

The short-bite, fanatical, cut-throat social media-style statements are meant to scare those for whom university is already scary. Accessible education is scary for those who hold millions in assets because these are the people who benefit from a pool of unstable, precarious, nervous and seemingly competitive workers. Mark Fisher explains how the 'rigidity' of the Fordist production line gave way to a new 'flexibility', a 'word that will send chills of recognition down the spine of every worker today'.[17] For especially younger generations, 'work and life become inseparable' through constant precarity, the fear of having no contracted hours next week in their zero-hour contract, the lack of postdoctoral jobs in their field, or the pressure to form that side-hussle on the weekend. A raging 'psychological conflict' stems from the troupe of productivity that shames any kind of sabbath-mandated rest until the financial aim is reached.[18] Are we happy or unhappy in those hours of lost time spent in the void of social media? Are we really able to rest? Are we happy when we are rearranging the cushions of our new sofa to show off on Instagram? Are we trying to impress? Would having a friend come and sit on it not give enough pleasure?

And no matter how hard you work, society tells you (or sells you through self-help culture) that you are not doing enough – or maybe more accurately, you are not good enough. Young people are being sold a false dream. There's nothing to learn, only skills to earn. To use the theologian Mary Grey,

> In the shrinking of what life has come to mean, somehow we have stopped dreaming. Or rather, society has become a bad dream, a global theme park from which we cannot wake up. There is no space to escape to ... means have become ends: it is money itself that is desired, yearned for, dreamed of, money for which we have sold our collective soul. It is an addiction that in psychic and in psycho-spiritual terms has hijacked our imaginations, cheapened and vulgarized our aspirations of fulfilment, and the degree of mutuality and intimacy we could hope to attain in relationship.[19]

The myth of a better life with accumulation from the capitalist market is questioned beautifully by Koyama:

> Lord, we are citizens of the island Republic of Singapore. Our ethic ancestry is Malay. Over many centuries our life has been rooted in the soil and village community. We love to walk on the dark ground. We love to see chickens and cows (not hogs!), walk around freely in our front yard. But now suddenly change came to us ... We are living in one of 170,000 units of high rise Government housing projects ... We are 'away' from the ground to which we belong ... Our building has 120 units. People live above us, below us and on both sides of us. Whichever direction we go we see identical box shaped rooms. Our unit consists of two rooms encased by hard cement walls. We spend much time in these rooms. Sometimes we feel our faces becoming square! We put our little aquarium (another small cubic containing five fish – colourful tropical ones!) in the corner of the room. We put our television next to the aquarium. We move them from time to time, not at regular intervals but perhaps suddenly as we feel the walls 'threatening' us. We have no control over the walls but we have control over our aquarium and television set. We want to tell ourselves that we are the masters within the walls. We are free to make changes within the cubic space ... We are not happy. Actually we do not quite know whether we are happy or unhappy. This is a big part of our problem![20]

The best advice I ever received was from a wise woman at my church in Cardiff. When trying to choose what to study at university – I was wrestling with English Literature or French – she advised me to do the thing that I lose myself in. 'In which lesson', she asked, 'does time fly and discussion in your head flow?' She assured me that the path in the future would show itself through the privileged time I could spend doing something that I loved. I had not considered this as a priority until our conversation. This woman is a talented linguist who travelled to Wales to do a liberal arts degree – which was seen by some as a fad at the time. Young people should not be asked to make sacrifices for money before they have been able to even discover what they love yet – or what love is yet.

Alternative Vocations

The constant anxiety to produce more for profit, or for likes – being able to fit in and not be questioned – leaves no room for imagination, for meditation, for self-gratifying exploration:

> Art today is vehemently forced into the straitjacket of the *like* ... The walls between culture and commerce, between art and consumption, between art and advertisement, break down. Artists are forced to become brands. They begin to conform to the market, to be likeable ... Creativity as an economic strategy only permits *variations of the same*. It does not have access to what is wholly other. It lacks the *negativity* of a break which hurts.[21]

Art, theology, history, literature, language-cultural exchange, philosophy are being cheapened to serve the market. But education is not a means to an end. Alexander Solzhenitsyn (1918–2008), Russian writer and Soviet dissident, in his Nobel Prize speech, which reflected upon the abyss into which many Russian artists perished, commented, 'Art re-creates in the flesh all experience lived by other men [sic], so that each man [sic] can make this his own.'[22] The humanities – or just the time at university where students are faced with cultural, class or regional differences – broaden experiences, question presumptions, and allow a time for exploration as a person discovers their place in the world. This exposure also allows young people to question the world. As explored in Dave Korn's chapter, the depths of pain are meant to be explored in the safety, or even disorientation, of literature for us to become fully human – to be restored in community through deeper understanding of the 'other' while having the time and privilege to explore stories of 'others' with others. Solzhenitsyn continued, 'World literature can transmit the concentrated experience of one land to another in such a way that we stop seeing double and being dazzled, the different scales of values coincide, and each nation can learn the true history of other nations in an accurate, condensed form, grasping it fully with that sensation of pain that comes from living an experience oneself, and as a result of that knowledge be protected from eventual error.'[23] As exemplified by Koyama's distressing prayer, our cubic isolation – removing us from our communities, groundedness, our produce and customs – is also removing us from our emotions, we do not know if we are happy or unhappy. We have to be exposed to the pain, injustices and lived stories of the world to belong to it.

We could learn from Adam Randera's chapter how Afro-communitarianism can help us question Western individualism. If reconciliation is to be understood as the restoring of trust and dependency in a community where trust had been broken, and how a re-embracing of a person after pain restores personhood not only for the person who was wrong and the people hurt from the wrong, but for the whole community, then learning is not a removed, personally invested exercise, but an embrace of communal knowledge that can release us to dream dreams through exploring ways of knowing that are different from, or a challenge to, our own.

Eve Parker explains that the aim of decolonization will not be met from adding contextual theologies. It becomes a fetish if Western students read, or Western scholars use, liberation, Black, feminist, queer, womanist, African, etc. theologies without taking their challenge seriously and allowing it to question, or destabilize, the knowledge held by the West. Parker charges that tokenistic usage of global South epistemologies 'enables the continuation of white supremacy because the norm remains unchallenged, whereas decolonizing the curriculum challenges the dominant culture'.[24] A gift of the humanities is their ability to disrupt certainties and to question the ease with which some can live in the world.

The space for deep, interrogative thought in the humanities needs to resist being co-opted by the popular 'public crises' – this is not the purpose of these disciplines. We can cease playing the game of how many successful jobs theology graduates have! Walter Brueggemann explores how the 'task of prophetic ministry is to nurture, nourish and evoke a consciousness and perception alternative to the consciousness and perception of the dominant culture around us'.[25] Instead, these disciplines help us discern what the 'dominant crisis' of the world is, which Brueggemann holds is 'having our alternative vocation co-opted and domesticated'.[26] The alternative vocation of the vicar might be to be with and honour the margins – to spend time with the lonely, the poor, the elderly and the forgotten, not for any kind of gain, but because they belong to the community, are Bodhisattvas, or are made in the image of God, as per Patricia Palazzo Tsai's chapter. It is an act of collective witnessing to know the margins, and from this knowing, new ways of being can arise. Brueggemann holds that a prophetic imaginate straddles the combination of a clear discernment of where we are, and also an alternative view that grounds 'energy' but also hope.[27] The 'god' who is concerned with order and the status quo was shown to be an idol in the story of the Exodus of Moses where 'the gift of freedom was taken over by the yearning for order. The human agenda of justice was utilized for security. The god of freedom and justice was co-opted for an eternal now. And in place of passion comes satiation.'[28]

The Message of the Radical Act of Solidarity

In the book *A Decolonial Feminism,* Françoise Vergès asked the reader to imagine what the redeemed world would look like if viewed through the lens of a female migrant cleaner. Such women clean in early hours of the morning or late at night, their bodies invisible and dirty, taken advantage of, perhaps without citizenship, without rights, or maybe without a safe place to sleep between shifts. Yet their bodies and labour allow the businessmen and women who work for this weird god (called the economy) to go on about their days in their clean and functioning offices and streets.[29] How ridiculous that it took me two years after reading this book to link the eyes of the migrant cleaner with the eyes of Jesus. The incarnation, as the most radical act of solidarity from God to God's world, is a call for humanity to reimagine the world through the incarnated God. George MacLeod, the founder of the Iona Community, summed it up perfectly:

> For what did God essentially do when He chose to appear as a Man? What He did was to take Grace out of the Stained Glass window which Religion had become and put it right back in a Home! By being born in a poor family: Jesus annulled all special families. By being a refugee child in Egypt, Jesus took on Himself, man's [*sic*] political pathos at its most tragic point, for in any refugee camp today the final tragedy is the child.[30]

But why is it that the refugee child does not provoke emotional reaction? Despite the unsettling Kairos Palestine Document being released in 2009, Western churches still turned away from the Kairos moment that followed the tragedy of 7 October 2023, where Hamas members killed and kidnapped Israeli citizens. Kairos – a moment of truth – is a time where we discover the truth 'about the situation with which we are faced, about ourselves and the Other; about the realities of pain and suffering, about the demands of love and justice, and about the God-given possibilities for real and fundamental change'.[31] Palestinian Christians charged the Church of England with prioritizing 'domestic British ecumenical and political considerations' over speaking truth to power.[32] Munther Isaac, the Academic Dean for Bethlehem Bible College and pastor of Christmas Evangelical Lutheran Church in Bethlehem, replaced his church nativity scene with the baby Jesus under the rubble in a keffiyeh. Isaac wrote alongside the image, 'The Child under the rubble. Immanuel God is with us in our pain and suffering. God in solidarity with the oppressed. The child of Bethlehem is our hope.'[33]

Image © Munther Isaac, used with permission.

Chimamanda Ngozi Adichie, sharing her journey with grief after the passing of her father, writes how she was

> filled with disbelieving astonishment that the mailman comes as usual and that people are inviting me to speak somewhere and that regular news alerts appear on my phone screen. How is it that the world keeps on going, breathing in and out unchanged, while in my soul there is permanent scattering?[34]

How can Western societies bear to see (and literally see) 7,700 children killed since 7 October 2023 in Gaza by Israel?[35] Why are we not so overcome by grief for our siblings in this abhorrent moment that anything other than action to prevent further death and destruction is considered? How can it possibly be in the name of justice that people debate whose lives are grievable – or more accurately – whose lives are less costly for the financial endeavours of the capitalist empires. Why can one State defend itself but the other not resist? It is the job of humanity to ask these difficult questions. The Labour Party in the UK, under Keir Starmer, withdrew the whip (meaning his MPs could not be in his Party and vote against him) to deny the call of a ceasefire coming from Humza Yousef, the First Minister for Scotland (whose wife is Palestinian and who had family stuck in Gaza).[36] Some of the reasoning given for staying to support the Labour Party, even after this decision, was that Britain needs a left-wing party voted in in the next election – so the dominant left party needs support. It is true that people are suffering in Britain, children are hungry, but the future prospects for children in Britain should not come at the expense of immediate needs of Palestinian children, adults and the elderly, now. Samuel Murillo Torres explores these questions through thinking about time – Chronos and Kairos – and Michael Morrelli wonders about the effects of technological agitation for our ability to really see.

A worship that forgets the fellowship of the whole world, or oikumene, and is not humble in its approach to the altar is the worship Amos condemned. Matthew 25.40 reminds us, 'Truly, I tell you, just as you did it to one of the least of these who are members of my family, you did it to me'; worship should connect us to God and by extension our neighbours. It should bring items from the news into our emotional, spiritual realm, where death numbers stop being statistics and again become people – beloved children of God. Similarly, if we are to understand the Bible as a 'paradigmatic story' – a story that 'discloses the identity of God outside and inside God's self-revelation in Jesus' – we have not a locked truth accessible in parts, or by some, with a fixed agenda to latch onto, but a story that 'provides paradigms concerning the God-world, God-person and person-person relationships'.[37] The incarnation of Jesus as a refugee child is not a stand-alone historical fact, but a divine act of solidarity. What God are we worshipping if it is not the one under the rubble in Gaza? God taking grace out of the stained-glass window, in MacLeod's terms, is a recognition that grace cannot be held in isolation in the words of scripture, or in a removed, we-have-always-done-it-this-way kind of worship service, but was smashed and scattered by the birth of Christ. To be a disciple of Christ is to stand by God 'in the hour of God's grieving',[38] to use Bonhoeffer's phrase, 'so that creation as a whole may be redeemed'.[39] God's grief is heard when the voice of the voiceless, the poor and oppressed breaks through the dominant culture. 'In those voices we hear the very voice of God.'[40]

These unthinkable moments of destruction, pain and suffering should destabilize us. Kairos time and a Kairos moment is that shattering clarity of where we have been wrong, or ignorant, or misguided. The grace of God in the world reveals these Kairos moments – which often seem to slip through our hands. Crucially, this moment is not a moment of 'gloating, confirming and celebrating our own spiritual superiority ... [it is] not the result of our intelligence and extraordinary cleverness. It is revelation, the gift of the Holy Spirit. We are not the truth: the truth has found, recovered and reclaimed us.'[41] Furthermore, Allan Boesak continues, 'it is the grace of God that calls us from our sinful apathy to commitment and acts of justice, and it is grace that offers the church and the world the opportunity for repentance, conversion and change'.[42] Our following of Christ does not endow special access for discerning Kairos moments, but the community of the church is called to respond when its members (or those outside of the church) have awoken to crises outwith or within the church institution. Christians, therefore, are called to have their eyes open, ready to discern where the 'name of God is falsely claimed to legitimize destructive and oppressive ideologies'.[43]

The outworkings of this, according to José Míguez Bonino, is that a 'necessary' and 'unavoidable' option for Christians may indeed be 'disobedience to the law' of the dominant culture when the Christian community is convinced that the law is not leading to justice. Indeed, a community professing to be on the side of the poor and the marginalized has a 'moral obligation to denounce it, to use all the available instruments of information, appeal, democratic procedures, to abrogate or modify such a law'.[44] There is a confusion about justice and order in society. A lethal combination of 'law and order' is often used which tends to mean instead 'national security'. This national security, as summed up by Boesak, is 'the enforced state of confusion when the law, violence and the abuse of power are used to protect the position of the powerful and privileged and to keep the poor impoverished and the subjugated silent'.[45] Noam Chomsky has discussed how even the term 'peace process' is co-opted and used in the media to refer to whatever the United States happens to be doing at the moment. He found that 'it turns out that the United States is *always* supporting the peace process, by definition. Just try to find a phrase in the US media somewhere, anyway, saying that the United States is opposing the peace process: you can't do it.'[46] Questioning when language such as 'terrorists' or 'national security operations', 'killed' or 'has died' and how it effects the mind of the public is the work of the Christian community, and has to be done in solidarity with Jewish and Muslim friends affected by this language in our own country. In fact, not doing so is idling in privilege, turning our backs to the marginalized and denouncing the sincerity of our prayers. Because our alternative vocation, our hope for the world, is that it will be one where all are welcome, all are treated well, and all can flourish with the life-force of and the Sprit in God's good creation. So, we unequivocally have to affirm that every life is precious, and every life is worth our effort, no matter the risk to our own stature or position, and no matter how geographically or culturally far away – those lives are just as precious as the ones closer to home. The dominant culture wants us to disconnect and to be unsure about our credentials to speak against the injustice of today's world. Chomsky, one of today's best known public intellectuals, when asked about his ability to speak into world affairs, answered,

> I think the idea that you're supposed to have special qualifications to talk about world affairs is just another scam ... it's just another technique for making the population feel that they don't know anything, and they'd better just stay out of it and let some smart guys run it. In order to do that, what you pretend is that there's some esoteric discipline, and you've got some letters after your name before you can say anything about it. The fact is, that is a joke.[47]

David Brandon Smith in his chapter reflects on how Presbyterianism, at its core, depends on the involvement of the whole body – laity and clergy – to map the path of the church in the world. He discusses the quasi-law-making structures of Presbyterianism and how the Reformed ethic necessitates renewed collective wisdom and reaffirmations of accountability within the church community to ensure faithful fellowship in arising circumstances and 'crisis'. His chapter made me wonder about the possibilities of this model being extended into larger society. Also relevant to this conversation is the chapter argued by Nathan Dever, where he poses that being apolitical is a political choice, and Christians would be wise to own their influence in society and mobilize it for teaching, questioning and discernment.

A Prelude to/Continuation from/Challenge to *Young, Woke and Christian* (2022)

Young, Woke and Christian: Words from a Missing Generation[48] is a book concerned with waking up the British Christian public to the activism, faith and grit of young British Christians. Often ignored, or presumed missing, we were tired of being overlooked and gaslit. We were desired, but only in the theoretical sense, for our bodies to sit on hard pews, but not for our minds to re-engage the church in worship and work for/with God.

The book dived straight into discussing our passion for justice. It touched upon ableism, heteronormativity, cisnormativity, the patriarchy, overlooked homeless people, friends from other faiths, the absence of real peace-making, mental health, and food poverty that stemmed from greed. This book touches upon, expands and even argues against some of the arguments made in the previous volume. What is different about this book, however, is that it reflects on *why* young people are so concerned about justice. And, more pertinently, it questions *how* young people today are concerned about justice. In fact, it thinks about how justice should be perceived today, and tries to re-evaluate what justice could look like in our particular time, world and context.

Millennials and Gen Zers have been characterized as individualistic capitalist consumers, as politically unengaged and spiritually selfish, or only interested in identity politics. This edited collection, by bringing together younger generations of theologians, activists, campaigners, creative-thinkers, and those working in politics, academia, the church, or community work, offers a new narrative of justice – one that is globally aware and actively intersectional. A world controlled by the 1% necessitates a collective response from the remaining exploited population. This new generation, who face a burning planet and a politically and religiously right-leaning egotistical Western Empire that is determined to protect its privilege rather than invest in any kind of change, know clearly that the legacies of Empire, which continue white hegemony, patriarchy, heterosexuality, normalize cisgender identities, the class war, colonial debts, Western epistemology, ecological extraction and religious discrimination, must be overcome and replaced by a transnational solidarity of resistance and reimagination. Our generation is often immobilized with climate anxiety, economic fragility and endemic mental health problems. The injustices of the world often seem too great to even begin to contemplate discerning. Rather than a feeble cry for hope in a hopeless situation, this collection instead exposes the fallacy of hopelessness. Our traditions, experiences, histories and relationships reveal rejuvenation, connection and movement. The status quo is not fixed but a successful propaganda campaign that dissipates alternatives and murmurings of transformation or reformation. Societies are being brainwashed to normalize injustice and look back onto the Empire with rose-tinted glasses. This collection aims to smash these glasses and platform revolutionary thinkers and fresh minds to rearticulate the concept of justice for a disconnected and ambivalent world.

Before jumping into each of the chapters I would like to finish with this profound quote from Dietrich Bonhoeffer:

> The meaning of present events is chaos, disorder, and catastrophe; and in resignation or pious escapism they surrender all responsibility for reconstruction and for future generations. It may be that the day of judgment will dawn tomorrow; in that case, we shall gladly stop working for a better future. *But not before*.[49]

The book is split into three major sections: Questioning Western Epistemological Hegemony: Rethinking Approaches to Justice, Insiders and Outsiders: Struggling through History and Context, and Disrupting Theology, Theory and Thinking. The first section deconstructs Western hegemony. Samuel Efrain Murillo Torres started his journey into this chapter by wondering how the mothers in Mexico, whose sons have disappeared, could possibly be met with justice. He concluded that justice is often shackled by Chronos time – in the yet to come. He found an answer in Kairos time, in the being together in community and letting go of what has not been and what is yet to be achieved, that peace will come. Daniel Jara J. questions who gets to set the epistemological agendas. In a critique towards liberation theology, Daniel poses that indigenous ways of knowing often present themselves in worship, and the absence of these alongside real contextual issues is causing the break in communion between scholars and people. Inatoli Aye looks at the colonial legacy in Nagaland and offers a queer indigenous theology of belonging in a context of taboo. Adam Randera, employing well-known terms such as *ubuntu* or *botho*, questions the West's romanticism of them, and directs us to the real challenge of Afro-communitarianism which is concerned with restoring personhood through reconciling communities. Andrew Clark-Howard employs (at an arm's length) Dietrich Bonhoeffer to help him struggle through the injustice of settler-colonialism in New Zealand and Australia. His 'indigenous Christ' incognito challenges white settlers to see how their confessions of Christ are worthless if tied to the continuing colonial project. Finally, Iemaima Vaai ends this section with a creative piece based on the Samoan art of *tatatau/tatau*, where she brings to the fore the crisis of the climate emergency for Pasifika people.

The second section is a deep dive into particular contexts or histories, where responsibility or hidden methods/stories are brought to the fore to expose needed methods and mind-sets to work for justice. Muna Nassar seeks to restore agency to Palestinian women. Often forgotten by male politicians or peacebuilders, or patronized by the West, Muna

INTRODUCTION

gives a raw account of the motivations of and struggles for Palestinian women. William Gibson explores the legacy of trade unions in Britain, their entanglement with Christianity, and the necessity for religion to be a part of the conversation towards equality in work, but also to keep an intersectional lens – understanding that privilege and power work even in the liberationist movements. David Brandon Smith explores the politics of the Presbyterian Church (USA), especially how the denomination overcame racism and sexism, to help us think about the future for LGBTQIA people in churches. David concludes that history is a tool for liberation and could be used to reclaim spaces and bring transformation. Staying in the USA, Nathan Dever questions the non-Trump voting evangelicals who are trying to divorce faith from politics. Despite the threat to the results in the polls, Dever claims this political theology of removal is dangerous, does not allow reflection, and ignores the corporal responsibility of the church. Finally, Ian Rowe discusses the tragedy of homelessness in Britain. Through a conversation with a previously homeless person, Ian questions what kind of progress Britain has made towards justice where the social steps and the economic steps are at odds with each other.

The final section questions how we think and what our priorities are with regards to justice. David Korn, adopting a similar style to the novel *Beloved*[50] takes us on a journey through trauma. Korn feels called to witness in hard places and explores the consequences of the collapse of witnessing through his emotion-invoking art. Shruti Dixit uses Raimon Panikkar to argue for a liberation theology for Hindus. She argues that the Hindu tradition is the religion of evolution and the forgetfulness of the legacy is causing dangerous misinterpretations and collusions for Hinduism where the fullness of the world and sacredness of all is not being affirmed. Arvin Gouw dives into the depths of cultured meat – a scientific phenomenon that might be the answer to climate change. Gouw deconstructs the magic bean and reveals its inherent bias. Patricia Guernelli Palazzo Tsai gifts us a piece of comparative theology where every creature's ability to become a Bodhisattva and the *imago Dei* provide profound critiques against neoliberalism and present a sacred form of human dignity. Amar D. Peterman thinks about belonging in a hegemonic culture of whiteness. He draws from Acts 17 to highlight the lessons that can come from beautiful vulnerability where diversity can draw from but also read into the text. Michael Morelli thinks about visions using the Apostle Peter, Augustine and Paul Virillo to help us think about time, space and possibilities. When so often our gaze only sees ourselves in reflection, what could happen if we (and especially the marginalized) stayed with stillness and silence, could rest and sit with our visions – where might our world go? Iona Curtius transports us to the theory of metamodernism – that place of co-existing deconstruction and hope. Curtius poses that hope is activism, and this necessary grasping of it, although not simple or easy, is an act of justice.

I hope these chapters inspire and challenge you. I also hope you see something differently, or learn something new. The structure of this book is methodologically disobedient. It is a mix of systematic theology, philosophy, gender studies, public and political theology, literary criticism, history, science and biblical studies. The writers come from Scotland, Germany, Ecuador, Palestine, Wales, Mexico, South Africa, Indonesia, India, Nagaland, Brazil, the US, Canada, England, Samoa and New Zealand. I have deliberately not grouped them through methods or locations, but have tried to group them through the heart of their messages.

She who wants the world to remain as it is doesn't want it to remain at all.

These meditations are a gift to strengthen us in a pursuit for a better world.

Notes

1 Otegha Uwagba, *Whites: On Race and Other Falsehoods* (London: 4th Estate, 2020), 37.
2 This is not to belittle Michael Morelli's wonderful and creative use of Augustine in his chapter of this collection!
3 Matthew 21.12–13, NIV.
4 Victoria Turner, 'God's Love as Passion', in Jacci Bulman, ed., *Talking Unity: Because God is the Love that We Are* (2022), https://thelovethatweare.org/resources/ (accessed 20/02/2024).
5 To quote Walter Brueggemann's seminal work – used more later.
6 John Sutherland, *The War on the Young* (London: Biteback Publishing, 2018), 111.
7 See the impact of this on Religious Studies and Theology admissions in the UK here: The British Academy, 'Theology and Religious Studies risk disappearing from our universities, says the British Academy', https://www.thebritishacademy.ac.uk/news/theology-and-religious-studies-risk-disappearing-our-universities-says-british-academy/ (accessed 20/02/2024).
8 The University of Aberdeen, at the time of writing, is latest to this list, with the whole department of Modern Languages coming under risk. University and College Union, 'Anger and Disappointment at Aberdeen modern languages cut proposal', https://www.ucu.org.uk/article/13311/Anger-and-disappointment-at-Aberdeen-modern-languages-cut-proposal (accessed 30/11/2023). The article comments, 'This move by Aberdeen is part of broader pattern that is developing, of deep cuts and closures of whole departments, especially in arts and humanities which can also be seen in places like Oxford Brookes and Staffordshire. UCU stands with all

those threatened, we will not allow members to be picked off, we will fight for them and beat this academic vandalism.' Also see: Royal Historical Society, 'History in UK Higher Education: A Statement from the Royal Historical Society', https://royalhistsoc.org/policy/history-in-uk-higher-education-a-statement-from-the-royal-historical-society/ (accessed 13/06/2023).

9 Kosuke Koyama, *Theology in Contact* (Madras: Christian Literature Society, 1975), 37.

10 Chay Quinn, '"Young people are being sold a false dream": PM vows to crack down on so-called rip-off "Mickey Mouse" degrees', *LBC* (16/07/2023), https://www.lbc.co.uk/news/pm-to-crack-down-on-mickey-mouse-degrees/ (accessed 4/03/2024). Emphasis mine.

11 John Sutherland, *The War on the Young* (London: Biteback Publishing, 2018), 6.

12 Alex Finnis, 'What is Rishi Sunak's net worth? The Prime Minister's family wealth explained', *Inews* (4/10/2023), https://inews.co.uk/news/politics/rishi-sunak-net-worth-prime-minister-family-wealth-explained-1270305 (accessed 21/02/2024).

13 Ha-Joon Chang, *23 Things They Don't Tell You about Capitalism* (London: Penguin Books, 2010), 137.

14 Chang, *23 Things*, 146.

15 Martin McQuillan, 'Never mind the students, tuition fees are a bad deal for the taxpayer', *The Guardian* (3/10/2017), https://www.theguardian.com/education/2017/oct/03/students-tuition-fees-taxpayer-government-borrow (accessed 21/22/2024).

16 Noam Chomsky, *Understanding Power: The Indispensable Chomsky*, ed. Peter R. Mitchell and John Schoeffel (London: Vintage Books, 2003), 62.

17 Mark Fisher, *Capitalist Realism: Is There No Alternative?* (Winchester: Zero Books, 2009), 33.

18 Fisher, *Capitalist Realism*, 34.

19 Mary Grey, 'Living Without Dreams: Is There a Spirituality for Justice in a Globalized World?', in William S. Storrar and Andrew R. Morton eds, *Public Theology for the 21st Century* (Edinburgh: T&T Clark, 2004), 231–53, 233.

20 Koyama, *Theology in Contact*, 5.

21 Byung-Chul-Han, *The Palliative Society: Pain Today*, trans. Daniel Steuer (Cambridge: Polity Press, 2021), 4–5. Emphasis original.

22 Alexander Solzhenitsyn, *One Word of Truth* (London: The Bodley Head, 1972), 14.

23 Solzhenitsyn, *One Word of Truth*, 26.

24 Eve Parker, *Trust in Theological Education: Deconstructing 'Trustworthiness' for a Pedagogy of Liberation* (London: SCM Press, 2022), 152.

25 Waler Brueggemann, *The Prophetic Imagination: 40th Anniversary Edition* (Minneapolis: Fortress Press, 2018), 3.

26 Ibid.

27 Brueggemann, *Prophetic Imagination*, 4.

28 Brueggemann, *Prophetic Imagination*, 35

29 Françoise Vergès, *A Decolonial Feminism*, trans. Ashley J. Bohrer (London: Pluto Press, 2021).

30 George MacLeod, *Four Men and Our Faith: Five Addresses Broadcast from Iona Abbey, August 1953* (Glasgow: The Iona Community Publications, 1953), 6.

31 Allan A. Boesak, *Kairos, Crisis, and Global Apartheid: The Challenge to Prophetic Resistance* (New York: Palgrave Macmillan, 2015), 10.

32 Harriet Sherwood, 'Palestinian Christians call on Justin Welby to "speak truth to power"' *The Guardian* (10/11/2023), https://www.theguardian.com/world/2023/nov/10/palestinian-christians-in-jerusalem-call-on-justin-welby-to-speak-truth-to-power (accessed 21/02/2024).

33 Munther Isaac, 3 December 2023, https://twitter.com/MuntherIsaac/status/1731255993630126121 (accessed 4/12/2023).

34 Chimamanda Ngozi Adichie, *Notes on Grief* (London: 4th Estate, 2021), 12.

35 Accurate as of 12/12/2023. https://www.aljazeera.com/news/longform/2023/12/12/know-their-names-palestinians-killed-by-israel-in-the-occupied-west-bank-2 (accessed 21/02/2024).

36 Sarah Ward, 'Humza Yousaf angry with MPs over "unforgivable" Gaza ceasefire decision', *The Guardian* (16/11/2023); see also https://www.independent.co.uk/news/uk/politics/humza-yousaf-gaza-ceasefire-b2448193.html (accessed 4/03/2024).

37 David Peel, *Sola Scriptura: the Achilles Heel of the Reformed Tradition?* (Colchester: Free to Believe, 2012), 44.

38 Dietrich Bonhoeffer, *Letters and Papers from Prison: Dietrich Bonhoeffer Works,* ed. John de Gruchy (Minneapolis: Fortress Press, 2010), 515–16.

39 Boesak, *Kairos,* 23.

40 Boesak, *Kairos,* 1. Later he quotes: 'the innocent, all cry out, "How long?" And this cry, proceeding as it does from the feeling of nature and the dictates of justice, is at length heard by the Lord … [the oppressed] know that this confusion of order and justice is not to be endured. And this feeling, is it not implanted by the Lord? It is then the same as though God heard Himself, when he hears the cries and groaning of those who cannot bear injustice' (John Calvin, *Commentary on the Twelve Minor Prophets*, Habakkuk 1:2).

41 Boesak, *Kairos,* 11.

42 Boesak, *Kairos,* 18.

43 Boesak, *Kairos,* 23.

44 José Míguez Bonino, 'From Justice to Law and Back: An Argentinian Perspective', in Storrar and Morton, *Public Theology for the 21st Century,* 63–77, 73.

45 Boesak, *Kairos,* 12.

46 Chomksy, *Understanding Power,* 43.

47 Chomsky, *Understanding Power,* 137.

48 Victoria Turner, *Young, Woke and Christian: Words from a Missing Generation* (London: SCM Press, 2022).

49 Geffrey B. Kelly, and Burton F. Nelson, eds, *A Testament to Freedom: The Essential Writings of Dietrich Bonhoeffer* (New York: HarperCollins, 1990), 509.

50 Toni Morrison, *Beloved* (London: Vintage, 2016) (first published 1987).

PART I

Questioning Western Epistemological Hegemony: Rethinking Approaches to Justice

I

Christ's Being Beyond Time: A Theological Emancipation from the Acceleration of Time

SAMUEL EFRAIN MURILLO TORRES[1]

When Christianity passed over souls like a storm that rages all night until morning, the havoc it had invisibly wreaked could be felt, but only after it had passed did the actual damage become clear. Some thought that the damage resulted from Christianity's departure, but this was just what revealed the damage, not what caused it.

And so our world of souls was left with this visible damage, this glaring affliction, without the darkness to cloak it with its false affection. Souls were seen for what they were.[2]

I write these explorations of theology while experiencing the sorrow and darkness of Necropolitics permeating communities. Geographically close and far, Necropolitics is the implementation of a systemic project that holds that the centuries-old domination of the hegemony of Western thought is the only way for societies – including the implementation for what is referred to as law, order, security and governance.[3] Indeed, these structures of thought that unfold historically from St Augustine to our time and the Kantian-Hegelian logic and justification of the way towards social stability has led to a vision of 'peace' that comes through the systemic killing of 'otherness'. Not only epistemology, but we see and hear continuously in our religious spaces (without space to question it) the fallacy, 'war and killing can be a necessity', making it a necessity towards peace is a convolution of justice but a logical necropolitical conclusion.

First, in this chapter, I will explore the Necropolitics of Western theology, questioning the measuring of time *chronologically*, its implementation in Christian dogma, and how this shapes institutional religion – believing it to be arbitrary and subjective. Second, I will explore in contrast the experience of Christian faith from the margins of existence, where there is no privilege of *chronological* time, literally and radically – where there is no time to wait! Third, I will expose the experience of *kairological* time in the public sphere today. This is living beyond measured *chronological* time in community, such as being formed in Christ in the experience of enforced disappearances in Mexico. In conclusion, it will be essential to contrast the evident decay of institutional religion within narratives of progress in *chronological* time, through showing how *kairological* time reveals Christ's being in the present that holds all reality together. Showing us a way to embrace life despite being continuously killed. In other words, it is at the margins of existence and embracing this powerlessness that Christian faith shapes the possibility of life and hope, even when there is no chronological spatio-temporal tomorrow.

Necropolitics and the Problem Measurement of Time as Chronos

Despite assuring the always pronosity (Christ's being *pro nos*, for us and for all) of Christ with and for all in Christian scriptures,[4] trying to logically understand the paradox of Christ's being within and beyond time while being historically present in a moment of time, has always been a question for Christian communities. We can find testimonies from the church in Thessalonica in dialogue with Paul about what it meant for that generation to understand eschatological hope in relation to *chronological* time. This is theologically problematic, interpreting superficially that our Christological hope fits exclusively within spatio-temporal *chronological* time, which is time in a linear way, making time and history just to move from past, to present, and towards future, as a way to wait, to have hope and explain the paradox of Christ's being within us all. Thus, the problem with this spatio-temporal theological limitation and understanding is that the romantic idea of the physical finite coming of Christ was never fulfilled within a lifetime in Paul's generation, as it did also not happen after centuries of waiting. Another problem is that this has severely impacted Western theology with an eschatology of waiting predominantly for a measured *chronological* future, omitting the present's relevance as the only certainty of time.[5] This unfolds in the necessity of a historicity of time (justifying ideologically the acceleration of life from modernity until now), opening the possibility of reducing Christ's pronosity to the demonstrable factual historicity of Christ.

Modern thought instrumentalizes scholastic theology to implement the notion of this measurement of time grounded in the idea of civilization, progress and the promise of an always better *chronological* future. The problem is that we are experiencing an imbalance between the promise of infinite *chronological* time in tension with the intense acceleration that promises progress to individuals who experience a lack of time when facing the possibilities that the present pretends to offer. José A. Zamora unfolds:

> This increase [in the pace of life] and the accompanying feeling of time shortage do not arise because, despite the fact that in almost all areas of social life we can record enormous gains in time thanks to the help of technology, because today tasks can be solved or distances bridged much more quickly ... but in reality there is an over-supply which reproduces the shortage of time. We live with the fear of not being able to take advantage of most of these possibilities or, in any case, the best ones, and with the feeling of finding ourselves in a race against time. The paradox is that the attempt to respond to the increase in possibilities produced by acceleration by appropriating the techniques and tricks offered to increase the pace of life ends up widening the gap between the time of life and the possibilities of the world ... at the same time the events and facts subjected to this speed lack duration and, in a certain sense, lack any lasting consequences.[6]

The myth of infinite and improving time shapes and implements the Necropolitics of the present, with an intertwined system of public policy, governance, capitalism and religion: work, buy and pray with the promise of something better maybe one day.

This imposed acceleration of time relates directly to the sense of emptiness that younger generations experience today. Young people experience life and dying without experiencing the real. They meet the constant dissatisfaction of the present life. This is if you are privileged enough to live. However, for the majority, those on the side of dying daily at the cost of this imposed necropolitical theology, means to exist in a constant state of exception, outside of the possibility of the false promises of civilization and progress. This false promise unfolds in justifying killing some as the necessary cost for a better life of civilization. Those killed totally disappear due to the acceleration of time; they are not allowed to have existence or memory. In this necropolitical implementation for majorities, despite the promise of a chronological future for something new and better,[7] it ends up in an unending accelerating cycle where there is nothing new but just death and annihilation for all. Reyes Mate explains:

If the dead do not matter, then happiness is not a matter for human beings but for the survivor. If the lives of all matter, then we will relate the frustrated lives of the dead to the interests of the living, refusing to pursue a project that would entail disregard for the fallen. When we take the step of forgetting death, we perpetrate a hermeneutic crime that adds to the physical crime ... the happiness of the grandchildren does not repair the suffering of the grandparents, nor is there social progress that will clear up the injustice done to the dead.[8]

The implementation of this necropolitical theological logic, which lacks memory, allows dualistic ideologies regarding otherness in the public sphere. This instrumentalization is grounded in the language of inclusion and development, including the Western Protestant logic of human rights, but that differs from most of its practices in the public sphere by not only excluding but removing the possibility of difference, the possibility of encounter. The acceleration of time affirms our egocentric and individualistic understanding of existence and annihilates alterity. We can see this dualism in the creation of narratives of evil in the public sphere, as applicable to 'cartels' or 'terrorism', thus allowing law and order to have perfect control, this by having acceptable reactionary dosages of violence, creating permanent anaesthetic states for communities and individuals – fearful and unable to question 'authority'. This is what enables the highly blurry oppression of otherness until its extermination, because it is justified logically as legal and necessary. When there is any agency from the oppressed communities and individuals to claim their existence, to make their dignity visible, to claim life over death, and to reveal light in all darkness, the mediatic-political-religious theology preaches out loud: 'Violent terrorists! Kill them all!'[9]

This might help us to explore why Christian pulpits within institutional religion across North America and Western Europe end up without listeners in what have been our spatio-temporal spaces for this indoctrination of superficial hope or justification of death. I consider it to be very superficial to assume that this lack of interest relates to what we ideologically call secularization and atheism. In my experience as a chaplain and priest in those geographical places, society (and specifically an abandoned generation of children and youngsters) is eager to encounter, to dialogue, to belong – with the most relevant questions and sense of life within what reveals as faith in the simplest way. This is what Simon Critchley tries to explore as the faith of the faithless at the margins of existence,[10] or what Reyes Mate insists must be the question to engage with: 'the answer to the demand for justice for the victims of the past is the theological virtue of hope'.[11] This is the question to engage with when considering seriously our spatio-temporal spaces shaped by *chronological* necropolitical and accelerated time, which might promise happiness but, due to its lack of duration, it lacks experience,[12] imposing events as shocks that die at the moment of production.[13]

The Life that Unfolds at the Margins of Existence

To keep the centrality of the question of our understanding of time, how can we live life outside of the acceleration that promises progress but gives only emptiness? In his Christology lectures, Bonhoeffer claims that Christ's being is the centre of all human existence, history and nature.[14] What are the implications of Christ's being – involved in all time, being in radical contrast with that 'wheel of history implemented that rolls over'[15] human beings who have no option for healing, memory, hope and life? In Christ, there is an embracing reality for all, including the forgotten and killed.

Explorations of *kairological* time open up ontological understandings of being in Christ outside of the usual linear understanding of time, history and spatio-temporal experiences.[16] Being in Christ, abiding in Christ, the fulfilment of the promise of 'who Christ is', is the always confirming of eschatological hope that we are always in the limits of time, and it is within that ongoing existential tension that we respond as individuals and communities to the call to discipleship. It is in the irruption of time that individuals listen to become servants in the form of who Christ is, here and now.

In the experience of this irruption of time to become servants in Christ's reality, the individual experiences the frightening tension in the presence of the infinite and total otherness, who Christ is, which unfolds in the *pronosity* of Christ in and within all alterities, demanding our immediate response in that Kierkegaardian *moment* having the temptation in front of our existence: you shall not kill.[17] The temptation as an offence of our own 'I', the 'I' that experiences life with its fallacious promises and its own speed with promise of eternity. When the individual assumes the irruption of time in following Christ, allowing difference and alterity to exist. This formation of the individual, unfolds the paradoxical experience of the politics of love within the margins of existence that permits the experience of community and deep belonging despite differences. The politics of love within this community at the margins is a paradoxical reality beyond the usual moral and ethical programmes that try to keep humanity within the Western understanding of original sin as a constant debt in relation to waiting in chronological time until death.

In the experience of this irruption of time to become servants as good news in Christ, the doctrine of eschatological hope is not in the future as measurement of *chronological* time, but Christ's being is embracing all reality beyond limitations of what is to come in *chronological* future. Christ is always just being here and now, irrupting in history, revealing his fulfilment in the embracing of otherness. Reyes Mate explores this other understanding of apocalyptic consciousness in Paul's theology: 'The apocalyptic consciousness of the expiry of time translates into understanding life as "love your neighbour". The other is not someone who needs us, but "the door through which the Messiah passes", that is, the access to an attained humanity.'[18] In embracing the other we are fulfilling who Christ *is* as an existential reality to whom all shall respond; this is the constant recognition in the present, as the limit of time, of a transcending openness,[19] and this is our Christian hope.

In contrast with the acceleration of eternal finitude as negation of life and the false necessity of continuity within the acceleration of time that allows barbarism in our societies, emerges the relevance of the irruption of messianic hope in the understanding of Walter Benjamin, presented by Gabriel Amengual

> to reveal its cracks [in time], for it is only through them that salvation can come to us. The category of interruption is fundamentally exposed in the field of history and as a critique of the idea of progress, which is nothing other than change so that everything remains the same ... interruption supposes the understanding of time not as *kronos*, as continuous flow, always the same, equally insignificant and indefinite, but as *Kairos*, as instant and as opportunity. The reason for this is none other than that the historical phenomena 'are saved by showing in them the leap ... There is a tradition that is catastrophe'. The same reason expressed in the terms of Jewish theology is that 'every second was in it [in time] the small door through which the Messiah can enter'. Barbarism can be this moment in which the cultural and social, historical concatenation is interrupted, and can bring about the re-emergence of experience, the new beginning.[20]

Amengual, unfolding Benjamin, insists that from the complexity of the lack of human experience after barbarism (from Auschwitz to the present), it is in that limit of time, in fragility and vulnerability that salvation comes through. Considering the previous description of acceleration in time, the question is, is it possible to unfold experience and belonging in a community as a collective response towards life?[21] Amengual insists that it is in the centrality of the symbol within the cultic and liturgy that in *kairological* time, memory unfolds in experience, that unifies in renewing and actualizing in the disposition of the community that has found hope in a time of barbarism and death.[22] This contrasts with the market liturgy of today in Western institutional religion, that departs in the imposition of speed, focusing in emotional entertainment with continuous stimulation of sound and lights, lacking duration and experience. How do we describe or experience duration of time within liturgical symbol in community? This is the conclusive and last part of this chapter.

The Community that Emerges within the Crucified Humanity

Ignacio Ellacuría, one of the Jesuits killed by the dictatorship in El Salvador, insists that it is in the limit of time as *Kairos* that emerges our constant responsibility for discipleship – to take crucified humanity down from the cross[23] – while at the same time being where we experience both suffering and a paradoxical hope. The hope translates in communal resistance, moving towards life despite systemic death within this suffering reality that always forgets.[24]

Something paradoxical beyond any logical understanding happens within majorities in community who are resisting the constant state of exception; this is constantly ignored by the necropolitical western theology that exterminates. For example, how do we explain and understand that in the biggest open prison in the world, in the Gaza strip, (which has become today a concentration camp under genocide with the justification of institutional religion aligned to necropolitical geopolitical interests) we find that 50% of the population are children? I think this exposes the depths of Western barbarism.[25] How is it possible that within the cruelty of the crucified humanity, there is hope for life, family, community and belonging to have the joy of so many children? And how is it that in the centre of the narrative of progress and the myth of the first world, people not only lack a sense of belonging to hope to have children, but the existing small percentage of children in these societies experience such loneliness and lack of community – a struggle that is often communally abandoned and 'solved' with psychiatric medication – showing the priorities of *chronological* time where it is more important to have someone functional than the possibility of a different measure of time to abide together in community.[26] This reveals not only the omission of institutional religion but the total collapse of all possible language of hope and experience towards societies within the implementation of Necropolitics.

Gustavo Petro, the current Colombian president, similarly insists on the possibility of a shared humanity beyond the barbarism of governance grounded in law, security and order. He questions the logic of 'the war against drugs' that understands the solution with public policy as providing armament to exterminate the public enemy, ending up with millions of killings and millions of mourning families. Petro confronts: has capitalism not shown us that we cannot eliminate the market while there is demand? Why do we gather Ministries of Defence instead of Public Health in this public discussion? How do we eradicate the market despite the demand of consumption subsisting? He answers that it is this extreme loneliness that children and youngsters experience, the same that government and churches leave to psychiatric treatment, loneliness that comes from trying to fulfil sense while experiencing total annihilation, barbarism and Necropolitics as the only option to exist. This enunciation as an answer, he concludes, to be totally contrasting with the impositions from the north. He insists on how we eradicate the demand – with love! Less money and more love, less technology and more love, less acceleration of time and more love in community.[27] Theologian Jon Sobrino asks for another way:

> Together with the crucified people, now in other ways, the Church will find light and salvation. It will find its place of conversion, it will cease to be worldly and can become earthly and salvadorian. It will find its fundamental task, that of 'bringing the crucified people down from the cross'. It will receive the forgiveness – which we all need – from that same suffering people. It will learn the most difficult of lessons: 'how to tell the poor that God loves them', as Gustavo Gutiérrez asks. And, against all worldly calculations, it will regain hope and be able to communicate it to others and do so with credibility.[28]

Ignacio Ellacuría correctly insisted that it is better to have no answers from our suffering and pain within crucified humanity than to have wrong answers, such as the answers provided by the northern hemisphere that would continue to justify Necropolitics as a way forward.

In Mexico, we have experienced more than 250,000 killings, having more than 100,000 disappeared people, with more than 60 people killed every day, of which 10 are femicides. One person disappears every hour in some states.[29] In 2006, the public policy from the government was imposed with the same logic of extermination and death, taking the army to the streets and justifying killing of civilians as collateral damage.

Today in Mexico, after so much pain, confusion and darkness, despite superficial options of response from the state and NGOs, the only sense of hope in the public sphere has come from individuals and families. Despite their mourning and pain they have shown in collectivity that there is another possible way. This way involves realizing that the only hope is here and now, in the uncertainty of any possible future, just as Ricardo Forster unfolds:

> If indeed the catastrophe has already happened, if the anguished wait for the apocalypse has given way to its realization beyond the fact that most people do not want or do not know how to see it, and if the time we live in lacks, in that sense, salvation, because we have submerged ourselves in the mire of history, then, what a paradox. Another opportunity arises but without any guarantee, an opportunity born from the lack of any opportunity that has been devoured by the radical evil that crossed from side to side the 20th century and that continues to expand ...[30]

He continues the relevance of Benjamin's messianic irruption linked with Kafka's statement that 'salvation is in the most radical despair, in the certainty that the only saved are those that have lost all possible hope, only in loving those in despair we can preserve hope, wrote Benjamin'.[31]

Critchley could complement that this statement in relation to faith is that sanction that corresponds to the witnessing in each of our lives, and this proclamation becomes certain for all, Christians or not. In fact,

> even more certain for non-Christians, as their faith is not grounded in any dogmatic creed, institutional religion as church, or any metaphysical belief in affairs such as the immortality of the soul or life after death, paradoxically ... the faith of the faithless reveals the true nature of faith: the rigorous activity of the subject that proclaims in every moment their own existence without any type of guarantee or security, and that focuses in its strength to fulfil the infinite demand of love. Faith is the proclamation of the I in relation to an infinite demand that exceeds all my faculties but simultaneously requires it all.[32]

The previous description links with the experience of a religionless Christianity described by Bonhoeffer in a world that has come of age. Bonhoeffer asked:

How do we talk about God – without religion, that is, without the temporally conditioned presuppositions of metaphysics, the inner life, and so on? How do we speak (or perhaps we can no longer even 'speak' the way we used to) in a 'worldly' way about 'God'? How do we go about being 'religionless-worldly' Christians, how can we be ἐκ-κλησία, those who are called out, without understanding ourselves religiously as privileged, but instead seeing ourselves as belonging wholly to the world? Christ would then no longer be the object of religion, but something else entirely, truly lord of the world. But what does that mean? In a religionless situation, what do ritual [Kultus] and prayer mean? Is this where the 'arcane discipline' [Arkandisziplin], or the difference (which you've heard about from me before) between the penultimate and the ultimate, have new significance?[33]

Which brings the relevant question today, how do we identify ourselves as religious Christians after the total exposure of necropolitical institutional religion? As even Bonhoeffer in his time, facing the nationalistic church, discerned,

> we are approaching a completely religionless age; people as they are now simply cannot be religious anymore. Even those who honestly describe themselves as 'religious' aren't really practicing that at all; they presumably mean something quite different by 'religious'. But our entire nineteen hundred years of Christian preaching and theology are built on the 'religious a priori' in human beings. 'Christianity' has always been a form (perhaps the true form) of 'religion'. Yet if it becomes obvious one day that this 'a priori' doesn't exist, that it has been a historically conditioned and transitory form of human expression, then people really will become radically religionless – and I believe that this is already more or less the case (why, for example, doesn't this war provoke a 'religious' reaction like all the previous ones?) – what does that then mean for 'Christianity'?[34]

This is the possibility of hope in the public sphere in a necropolitical time, which in shaping time and theology reveals who Christ is and allows discernment of where the church is. More and more, we can see that Christ's existing as community might not be inside the spatio-temporal boundaries of institutional religion, which in the best of cases has become an entertaining social club without the transcendental grounding of hope for its members. Due to the acceleration of time that lacks symbol, experience and duration, communities have forgotten the centrality of abiding together beyond time; this means that the witnessing of the body of Christ to the world today would be the community that 'waste' time together, not consuming or gaining anything from each other; that is what being gathered in one faith despite differences looks like. But, how can we see that witnessing today?

Going back to the irruption of the community that emerges in the Mexican context, it is in that collectivity of despair and suffering, while searching for mass graves, when Mexican mothers embrace all young people in the public sphere as their own children, even if that individual might be the killer of their own children – this collective embracing unfolds the sacramental experience of community beyond the static cultic liturgies and resonates with Amengual's reference to the symbol that reveals its transcendence in tension with the real. The possibility of Christ experience is recovered when the Eucharist is celebrated in the garbage, before or after collective lamenting from a finding of a human body in small pieces, or with a public fasting in the streets – all with its ontological, theological and political dimension.

It is in the power of the word as proclamation, when mothers scream from the depth of their breath 'les buscamos porque les amamos' or 'buscando nos encontramos'.[35] The aesthetics of this sacramental public collective process irrupts the anaesthetic sleeping and indifference that results from the acceleration of time.[36] This resonates with the indigenous collectivity of the indigenous communities of Chiapas Mexico, 'por un mundo donde quepan muchos mundos' and 'hasta morir si es preciso'.[37] Or beyond Mexican borders, the proclamation of dignity and life in the oppressed Palestinian territory.[38] These previous examples irrupt and interrupt *chronological* time, which I have described as an infinite ongoing movement within the finite at high speed, and that is why, theologically, these declarations from Mexican mothers and Palestinians united across borders and the world provoke an uncomfortable reaction due to the offence that they are to the necropolitical ways of the state and institutional religion. Noticing and dwelling with these moments of *kairological* time is in line with the incarnated Christ, Bonhoeffer says: 'Even the church, as the presence of Jesus Christ – God who became human, was humiliated, resurrected, and exalted – must receive the will of God every day anew from Christ. For the church, too, Christ becomes, every day anew, an offence to its own desires and hopes.'[39]

Christ being as community in a religionless time explores a theology of emancipation from acceleration as a liturgical way forward. Not as a theology that promises in the *chronological* future something eternal but that allows to stop for encounter in the everyday, and most of the time embraces in silence the reality of human beings.

In conclusion, we must be confronted, as individuals and community, daily, with the limit of time, which is the given life here and now. To understand that the only possible experience of theological language that fulfils the encounter of hearts and souls unfolds from the experience of discomfort, suffering and pain. Hope is not in the palliative society that avoids pain,[40] pretending eternal finite life in death, but in the radical community that allows intentional encounters with otherness,[41] where we embrace the pain of our fragility as individuals, which in *kairological* time means to embrace our own despair, fragility and death to be able to be human beings. This is embracing of living, not as the repetitive cycle of *Chronos* with nothing new, but as the only possible way for the real, the experience of belonging and community that last with duration as a pain of birth for human life in which all can live and 'souls are seen for what they are'.[42]

Notes

1 This chapter tries to be a simple effort in recognition of all those who are light in this world, especially all the mothers in Palestine and Mexico searching for a beloved disappeared.

2 Fernando Pessoa, *The Book of Disquiet* (London: Penguin Books, 2002), 53.

3 See Achille Mbembe, *Necropolitics* (Durham, NC: Duke University Press, 2021).

4 See Dietrich Bonhoeffer, *Christology Lectures*, in *Dietrich Bonhoeffer Works in English* (DBWE), Vol. 12 (Minneapolis, MN: Fortress Press, 2009), 300–27.

5 'As the Crucified and Risen One, Jesus is at the same time the Christ who is present now. This is the first statement: that Christ is the Christ who is present in history. He is to be understood as present in time and space. *Nunc et hic*, the two flow together in the concept of the church. Christ in his person is indeed present in the church as person. Thus the presence of Christ is there in the church.' In DBWE 12:310.

6 José A. Zamora, 'Dialéctica Mesiánica: tiempo e Interrupción en Walter Benjamin' in *Ruptura de la Tradición: Estudios sobre Walter Benjamin y Martin Heidegger* (Madrid: Trotta, 2008), 90. This quotation is my own translation to English from Spanish.

7 '[Walter Benjamin] surprises saying that progress as fashion "is the new always old and the old always new" (the usual that dresses as new [das Immergleiche am Neuen])', in Reyes Mate, *El Tiempo: Tribunal de la Historia* (Madrid: Trotta, 2018), 57. This quote is my own translation from English to Spanish.

8 Reyes Mate, *Medianoche en la Historia: Comentarios a las Tesis de Walter Benjamin 'Sobre el Concepto de Historia'* (Madrid: Trotta, 2006), 27.

9 Reyes Mate concludes that to explore options outside of nihilism and destruction in the logic of progress, to be able to allow humanity to exist we must change our understanding of time. Ibid., 62.

10 See Simon Critchley. *The Faith of the Faithless: Experiments in Political Theology*. (London: Verso, 2012), Chapter 5.

11 Reyes Mate, *Medianoche*, 28.

12 For more on the lack of experience with lack of duration and its relation to trauma and violence, see Gabriel Amengual, 'Pérdida de la experiencia y ruptura de la tradición: La experiencia en el pensamiento de Walter Benjamin', in *Ruptura de la Tradición: Estudios sobre Walter Benjamin y Martin Heidegger* (Madrid: Trotta, 2008), 39–41.

13 Reyes Mate, *La Piedra Desechada* (Madrid: Trotta, 2013), 27. For more on acceleration and time, see Paul Virilio, *War and Cinema: The Logistics of Perception* (London: Verso, 1989), and Paul Virilio, *Speed and Politics* (Pasadena, CA: Semiotexte, 2006).

14 Dietrich Bonhoeffer, *Christology* in DBWE 12:324–7.

15 Dietrich Bonhoeffer, *Ethics* in DBWE 6:144.

16 See the diagrams in John Behr, 'Reading from the End, Looking Forward', in *The Oxford Handbook of the Bible in Orthodox Christianity*, ed. Eugen J. Pentiuc (Oxford: Oxford University Press, 2022), 519–38.

17 'Levinas's work is marked by utter fragility, and most profoundly in the experience of the commandment "You shall not commit murder" ... For Levinas, the commandment is expressed in the face of the other, indeed as the face of the other. It is not expressed in a situation of peace, but in a life-and-death struggle where I am about to put the other to death, when "the sword or the bullet has touched the ventricles or auricles of his heart," as Levinas writes. For Levinas, crucially, "the other is the sole being I can wish to kill"', in Simon Critchley, *The Faith of the Faithless: Experiments in Political Theology* (London: Verso, 2012), 224.

18 In Reyes Mate, *El Tiempo: Tribunal de la Historia* (Madrid: Trotta, 2018), 40. This quote is my own translation to English from Spanish. This unfolds John Behr's insisting theological understanding of the link beyond linear time, that it is at the cross that we can see the real human being.

19 Mate, *El Tiempo*, 32–3.

20 Gabriel Amengual, 'Pérdida de la experiencia y ruptura de la tradición: La experiencia en el pensamiento de Walter Benjamin', in *Ruptura de la Tradición: Estudios sobre Walter Benjamin y Martin Heidegger* (Madrid: Trotta, 2008), 44–5. This is my own translation to English from Spanish.

21 The market of liturgies within institutional religion does not respond to and fulfil the sense of emptiness from individuals and communities because it is part of the problem of entertainment and acceleration that lacks experience: 'a dictate, which ends up imposing a unification of procedures, a levelling out of differences, despite the variety of objects, events, happenings and choices on which they are applied. Under the imperative of acceleration, a true experience of the diverse and different is destroyed and disappears behind the appearance of an immense diversity subjected to accelerated consumption schemes' ('Dialéctica Mesiánica: tiempo e Interrupción en Walter Benjamin', in *Ruptura de la Tradición*, 91. This is my own translation to English from Spanish.

22 Amengual, 'Pérdida', 58–9.

23 See Jon Sobrino, *Fuera de los pobres no hay salvación: Pequeños ensayos utópico-proféticos* (Madrid: Trotta, 2007), 18.

24 'Where life is threatened, where death seems omnipresent, in the same place

life vibrates in a density like in few other spaces', in Benjamin J. Schwab, *Violencia y Redención: Una Reconciliación a partir de las Víctimas* (El Salvador: UCA Editores, 2022), 14. This is my own translation to English from Spanish.

25 For the population of children in Gaza and the Necropolitics that implement the genocide, read: https://www.unicef.org/gaza-israel-cost-of-war-counted-children-lives (accessed 21/02/2024).

26 I do not mean at all to omit mental health awareness and care, but for theological interest I point out pastoral and community needs in contrast to increasing medication of children in recent years in Europe. This is a report from the EU on mental health and children: https://ec.europa.eu/health/ph_determinants/life_style/mental/docs/camhee_infrastructures.pdf (accessed 04/12/2023).

27 See Gustavo Petro's speech given at the Latin American and Caribbean Conference on Drugs and Future Perspectives: https://www.youtube.com/watch?v=piMqGvrGIwQ&t=2153s (accessed 4/12/2023).

28 In Jon Sobrino, *Cartas a Ellacuría* (Madrid: Trotta, 2004), 71–2. This is my own translation to English from Spanish.

29 See the recent report from the United Nations on Enforced Disappearances in Mexico: https://www.ohchr.org/en/statements/2022/05/mexico-dark-landmark-100000-disappearances-reflects-pattern-impunity-un-experts (accessed 21/02/2024).

30 Ricardo Forster, *Los Hermeneutas de la Noche: de Walter Benjamin a Paul Celan* (Madrid: Trotta, 2009), 165. This is my own translation to English from Spanish.

31 Ibid., 165. This is my own translation to English from Spanish.

32 Simon Critchley, *La Fe de los que no tienen Fe: Experimentos de Teología Política* (Madrid: Trotta, 2017), 27. This is my own translation to English from Spanish.

33 Bonhoeffer, DBWE 8:364–5.

34 Bonhoeffer, DBWE 8:362–3.

35 'We search for them all because we love them' or 'while searching we find each other'.

36 For a theological account of the formation of the theologian in this aesthetic-ontological-dynamic in contrast with the anaesthetics of society, see Samuel E. Murillo Torres, 'Going Ahead as Real Human Beings in the Gemeinde: Bonhoeffer's Christological Form and Formation in Suffering and Dying', in *Bonhoeffer and Christology: Revisiting Chalcedon*, ed. Matthias Grebe, Nadine Hamilton and Christian Schlenker (London: T&T Clark, 2023), 210–11.

37 We resist with violence that is non-violent 'for a world that fits many different worlds' until 'physical death if it is precise'. This is the EZLN (National Zapatista Army of Liberation) that have organized their communities to respond to the implemented Necropolitics since the 1990s. To read more on violence that is non-violent see Critchley, *The Faith of the Faithless*, Chapter 5.

38 The famous slogan 'from the river to the sea' points to the oppression of Palestinians in Israel, the West Bank and Gaza and the desire for Palestine to control its own land. It does not, by hoping for the freedom of Palestine, threaten the existence of Israel, but points to Palestine's oppression. See https://www.aljazeera.com/news/2023/11/2/from-the-river-to-the-sea-what-does-the-palestinian-slogan-really-mean (accessed 20/05/2024).

39 Bonhoeffer in DBWE 12:360.

40 For more on an account of the palliative society see Byung-Chul Han, *The Palliative Society* (Cambridge: Polity Press, 2021).

41 I consider the only possible way of hope for the education of children is to be intentionally intercultural and interreligious in all imaginable creative ways. It is in that cultic collaborative aesthetic way that the community as body in Christ reveals and will continue to be despite the inevitable disappearance of organic institutions that monopolized institutional religion for centuries.

42 Fernando Pessoa, *The Book of Disquiet* (London: Penguin Books, 2002), 53.

2

Against Western Cognitive Hegemony in Academic Theology: The Quest for Epistemological Justice in Liberation and Intercultural Theology(ies)

DANIEL JARA J.

While the humanist right to free thinking lies at the centre of the Western liberal-democratic project, after centuries of tight control of people's consciences from royalties, noble elites and clergymen, the dissimilar status of these 'free ways of thinking', and the unjust conditions that this dissimilarity replicates, is a phenomenon of relatively new consideration and analysis in humanistic and social studies. From the nineteenth century, the efforts from postcolonial and posterior decolonial studies to explain how certain hegemonic epistemologies and logics have eclipsed other ones, both in the academic sphere and in common speech, did unveil some of the social mechanisms that are responsible for such an imbalance. In this way, while the formal decolonization of continents and regions such as Africa, Latin America or South East Asia was a sometimes bloody and traumatic experience that lasted about 150 years, the colonization 'of the mind', as Franz Fanon called it, proved itself much more resilient than the political one on both sides of the equator. In the West, the effervescence of this hegemonic illuminist and rational thought, with the fantastic technical and scientific innovations that aided Modernity, expanded its shadows broadly from the reign of the natural to the social, the humanistic, and even the religious and theological, creating an asymmetrical monopoly of the rational, the historic and the scientific over the spiritual, the mythological or the corporeal.

Theology and the study of the religious, as Western projects, promoted and were at the same time shaken to their grounds by the modern impulse. On the one hand, clergymen and missioners saw in the 'savage' souls a fruitful soil for the word of God, regardless of already existing religious beliefs and practices, which had to be simply uprooted to allow the *good seed of the gospel* to flourish. For most of the conquerors and their elites back at home, mission constituted the intrinsic pious face of colonization. In the early phases of this enterprise especially, they reinforced, legitimated and mimicked each other. As Hegel affirmed: 'British are the missionaries of civilization in the entire world (*Missionare der Zivilisation in der ganzen Welt*).'[1] On the other hand, Western academics openly defied the privileged position of theology to study and understand the diversity of the religious phenomenon. They adopted an objectivistic-positivistic approach, opting to replicate the principles of scientific and positivistic practice, such as its objectivity, the preference for what is quantifiable and measured, and an approach that prioritized 'religious fact' over the opinion, interpretation or speculation of the scholar. In the words of Durkheim: 'The first and fundamental rule [of social and religious research] is to consider social facts as things.'[2]

Similarly, theology was not immune to the influence of Modernity. For example, decades before Durkheim, the German Lutheran pastor, theologian and Berlin professor Friedrich Schleiermacher conjugated elements of Moravian conservatism and Romantic mysticism with modern rationalism when reinterpreting theology as a 'positive science, the parts of which join into a cohesive whole only through their common relation to a distinct mode of faith, that is, a distinct formulation of God-consciousness.'[3] From his perspective, 'church statistics' had to combine elements of philosophical, historical and practical theology. In his *Brief Abstract of Theological Studies* (*Kurze Darstellung des theologischen Studiums*[4]), Schleiermacher applies Kantian critical method to theology, including 'church statistics' as a part of dogmatic theology and thus of historical sciences. This theological enterprise included 'knowing the condition of society regarding all parts of the Christian church' (§195), studying 'all the single church bodies' (§233), their organization of leadership (§236), their relations to society and other groups in general (§238), their relation to the state (§241), among other similar aims. As an obvious consequence, the author notices that church statistics 'can be stretched to the infinite' (§242) and that the discipline is not to be practised with a narrow scope while still being developed (§243, §245). Due to his impact on subsequent Christian thought, Schleiermacher went down in history as the 'Father of Modern Liberal Theology'.

A current example of the influence of Modernity on Western theology is the hermeneutical method of Rudolph Bultmann, the gifted heir of Schleiermacher's tradition. Under the clear influence of Heidegger's existentialism, Bultmann managed to reconnect 'theology again with the movement of philosophical hermeneutics which Schleiermacher had initiated more than a hundred years before'.[5] His famous, and often misunderstood, 'demythologization' project engaged with the modern underlying worldview of the first half of twentieth-century Europe and the need for a critical Bible interpretation that 'tries to recover the deeper meaning behind the methodological conceptions [aiming] not to eliminate the mythological statements but to interpret them'.[6] Truth be told, the German scholar did not intend to eliminate the mythical and fantastic language of the Gospels, but he argued for a serious hermeneutical effort to consider both the hermeneutical conditions of the specific (modern European) interpreter and the mythological language adopted by the text. Unfortunately, this attempt spread throughout the world in a wave of pretended intellectual superiority, by which a herd of intellectually lazy theology lecturers, pastors and missionaries showed disdain for 'outdated' worldviews and cosmovisions of people from the entire globe. This occurred although 'Bultmann never claimed that the scientific world-view was good or preferable to any other, but he defended both the duty of the theologian to translate the Christian faith into our *modern* [Western] world-view (Bultmann's context) and the actual possibility of such a translation.'[7] The consequences of the colonial and hermeneutically negligent approach of these 'lazy lecturers' echoes until today, often manifest in incomprehension, suspicion and mistrust among non-Western Christians regarding Western theology scholars.

Liberation Theology: A new contextual way of thinking God?

All the previous examples share a common historical feature: regardless of their prior intention, or non-intention, to establish a unique globally valid religious or theological paradigm, diverse academic and social logics ended up instituting them as universally conclusive reference frameworks among theologians and religious scholars, perpetuating a 'spirit of pure imitation or repetition in the periphery of the [knowledge] prevailing in the imperialist center'.[8] Theological seminaries and faculties around the world dedicated themselves for centuries to the *modernization* of young and adult minds to the detriment of local 'expressions and reflections of the Christian faith and the *ways of knowing* that embody them'.[9] For this reason, when during the second half of the past century a group of Latin American theologians and priests formulated and put into practice a novel theological doctrine/praxis at the intersection of the life of the believers of local parishes and slums and biblical reflection, it constituted a truly theological and academic revolution. Liberation Theology was formulated by authors such as Gustavo Gutiérrez, Leonardo Boff, Carlos Mesters, John Sobrino and several others, and inspired by the life or even martyrdom of pioneers such as Carlos Mugica, Hélder Câmara, Óscar Romero or Ignacio Ellacuría. It presented itself as one of the few projects to theoretically and practically establish an autonomous and 'third-worldly made' agenda in the so-called 'global South'.

The consequences in terms of human dignity and social empowerment of this new theological and pastoral agenda were enormous. For example, in terms of the promotion of human rights and accountability of their violations by military and authoritarian regimes, the martyrdoms of Monsignor Óscar Romero due to his public sermons against the oppression of the Salvadorian government and army, and of Bishop Juan José Gerardi two days after the publication of his 'Nunca más' ('Never again' – a human rights violations report for the recovery of the historic memory in Guatemala), constituted truly blood baptisms of this theology in one of the most glorious and terrible chapters of the Latin American Church's history.[10] The contextualization of the gospel message that began in the 'continent of hope', as Pope Paul VI and Pope Benedict XVI respectively referred to it in 1968 and 2007, produced powerful shock waves far from their coasts. In this way, despite being conceived in the historical context of Latin America during the 1960s and 70s regimes, the epistemological and programmatic principles embedded in Liberation Theology reached the far regions of postcolonial Africa and Asia inspiring the emergence of all kinds of indigenous and dissenting theologies, such as the Ubuntu, Black, Filipino, Minjung, Sangsaeng, Dalit, and dozens more.

Revolutionary and 'third-worldly made' as the preferential option for the poor made enormous advances in areas such as theological production, pastoral care, human rights promotion, communitarian empowerment or popular biblical appropriation. Liberation Theology was not alien to many of the vices of Modernity's epistemological matrix. Lots has been written about the use of Marxist categories and its materialist method for social analysis in Liberation Theology. Nevertheless, even its most fierce critics recognize that Liberation 'ortho-praxis', despite being clearly influenced by the Marxist imperative of transforming society instead of just studying it, legitimately addresses several of the social and political imperatives of the Judaeo-Christian tradition. The use of Marxist theory in this 'autochthonous' theology is not an academic coincidence, especially as most of the fathers of this school of thought studied in European universities. As their Marxist colleagues did in the old continent, most of their work was on social and political vindications of the 'forgotten ones', while keeping in second place the legitimate spiritual necessities and mystical aspirations of these people. As was commonly heard, partly as a joke and partly as a complaint in theological conferences decades later: 'The church became poor but the poor ones became Pentecostals!'

The apparent neglect of this theological approach regarding the spiritual demands and mystical eagerness of the believers is far from the only trace of modern logics in Liberation Theology. Feminist theologians rightly pointed to the almost non-existent denouncing of gender subjugation among all social strata in Latin America; it was perhaps even more accentuated among 'popular' classes, who were less influenced by liberal Western values. Likewise Liberation Theology broadly exposed the oppressive relations among social strata in the region, it almost totally ignored the unfair conditions that women had to bear in the public sphere, at home and at religious institutions such as seminaries, monasteries, parsonages and the ecclesial hierarchies. These oppressive conditions, though experienced differently, were a common feature of both Catholic and Protestant congregations. It was no coincidence that Liberation Theology could openly brag about the prolific work of its 'founding fathers' while nothing was mentioned about its 'mothers', because there was no space at the table. Only in the following decades did female figures such as Elsa Támez, Ivonne Gebara, or Mercedes Navarro appear with feminist proposals largely inspired by the main principles of Liberation Theology.

Many of the initial critics of this model referred to the place this theology kept for the 'poor ones'. These critics denounced the alleged indistinguishable nature of 'the church of the poor' and a church of 'social strata',[11] which over-emphasized the social class of the believer. Likewise, Cardinal Ratzinger as Prefect of the Congregation for the Doctrine of the Faith explicitly condemned what he considered was the 'disastrous confusion between the "poor" of the Scripture and the "proletariat" of Marx'.[12] If we ignore for a moment how accurate or just these critiques are, considering Jesus' declarations in the Gospels regarding those he called 'you the rich' (Luke 6.24, Matthew 19.21, Mark 10.24) and 'you the poor' (Matthew 5.3, Luke 4.18 and 6.20), it is fair to point to an idealization of the 'poor ones' in Liberation Theology. This occurs, for example, when considering them as 'the ultimate and most scandalous prophetic and apocalyptic presence of the Christian God, and therefore, the privileged place of the Christian praxis and reflection'.[13] This conception of the poor of Liberation Theology reserves for them a 'decisive importance ... not only as an epistemological place – context from and for which theology must be done – but also as a properly theological place because in them God is making himself present'.[14] Criticism of this approach was harsh and came not only from Europe but also from Latin America. For example, Clodovis Boff, brother of the Franciscan monk censured by Ratzinger at a personal consultation in the Vatican, suggested: 'Liberation theology inadvertently arrives at this perversion: God became poor, therefore the poor is God. Aberrant operation, by which the poor-god relationship is ontologized, which, from free and loving ends up petrified into a miserable metaphysics. Thus perpetuating poverty itself, consummating the extreme ideologization of the poor.'[15] This 'ideologization' occurred while apparently ignoring the poor's need for repentance from their own sins, such as the prevalent sexist culture, the generalized homo/transphobia it generates, or the almost general prevalence of corrupt practices among all social strata in the continent.

By over-emphasizing the intellectual reflection of the surrounding historic and socio-political conditions, Liberation Theology increased the existing tendency among priests, theologians and missionaries to neglect the legitimate space of mystical and transcendental experiences and practices in popular religiosity. These experiences and practices, which were present for hundreds of years in the continent, 'because of their performative nature ... were both technically and culturally embodied' and constituted *ways of knowing* [embedded in social and individual practices such as] rituals, celebrations, prayers, dances, physical ecstasy, visions, or dreams'.[16] The corporeal dimension in religious practice was sidelined, when not openly censured, by a theological tradition which aspired to transform the minds and consciences of the people but ended up alienating their 'religious souls'. The fact that Liberation Theology is nowadays much more alive in seminaries and faculties rather than in the streets of the global South, where new Charismatic, Pentecostal or Evangelical churches multiply endlessly, is a powerful testimony to the limited relevance of this theological project among less theological/academically trained believers.

A final pitfall of Liberation Theology refers to its weak cultural and epistemological embeddedness. It claimed to articulate the speech of the forgotten ones, but most of the categories used by Liberation Theology referred more to the Western intellectual background of their authors rather than to local cosmovisions and logics. For example, concepts and categories such as oppression, exodus, class struggle, liberation, emancipation, structural injustice etc., or social practices like communitarian Bible reading or democratic governmental style structures used to interpret the religious, were completely strange to the impoverished communities, so the missionaries and clerics had to 'teach' about them.

This intercultural negligence represented a total alienation of ancient indigenous logics, mythologies, cosmovisions, rituals and spiritual duties, which ended up planting a foreign seed in Latin American soil, it grew up and produced fruit, but in the long term, competing 'local flora' proved itself much more deeply rooted and fit to adapt and spread during the profound social, economic and political changes of the coming decades.

Intercultural Theology: A Call for Epistemological Reflexivity Against Western Epistemological Hegemony

Rome ne fu pas faite toute en un jour,[17] neither was Western cognitive hegemony in theology. On the contrary, the hegemonic status of the cognitive and rational epistemological system was a long, and sometimes brutal, process that arose from a complex confluence of political, economic, religious, missionary, scientific and colonial dynamics; and which, through different strategies, managed to infiltrate almost every knowledge and *way of knowing*[18] in the Western church. As the previous critical approach to Liberation Theology exemplified, every effort to develop theologically contextual answers to the various circumstances that the global church faces must be accompanied by a continuous exercise of epistemological reflexivity aimed to recognize, expose and deconstruct the unveiled modern logics that tend to impregnate theological reflections, especially in its academic tradition. This nevertheless is not a call for a counterproductive and impossible return to a precolonial thought, which naively pretends to restore a 'pure' epistemological matrix of the past, as if hundreds of years of trans-cultural exchanges could be suddenly erased, and ignoring that epistemological logics are always in flow informing and transforming each other. Besides, due to current globalization, there are almost no 'intact' or precolonially minded populations in the world who could identify with these 'pseudo-uncontaminated' theologies any more.

To fulfil this duty, intercultural theology must avoid exoticism and self-reference in all its forms and dedicate itself to the study of religious interests and developments as they actually occur in global Christendom. For example, theology faculties must once and for all analyse the actual interests and issues of the Christian communities studied, rather than the legitimate but ultimately irrelevant (for these communities) intellectual trends that so persistently position themselves as academic monologues and aim to fill their curricula. Western academic fixation on topics such as colonialism, sexual diversity, or social deconstruction, even though important and legitimate topics, are frequently far behind in the list of priorities of non-Western communities, while poverty, corruption, lack of employment for young people, constant stress, evil spiritual entities, or honour issues appear again and again as the top priorities of some of these groups. To illustrate this point, I quote some examples of the field data of some of my previous research.

Example 1: Discussion extracts from a project of intercultural Bible reading between students from the United Kingdom and Kenya

Jennifer[19] **from the United Kingdom:** I think [the colonial past topic] definitely plays a role and I think that churches in the UK still have a lot of reflecting and learning and apologies and reparations and so many things to do from colonialism and all the history with that. And I think ... that tension earlier you're talking about between culture and religion that we didn't have to grapple with that and that's a place of privilege and that kind of refers to the colonial past, so we had this imperialist notion that we are perfect as white people and ... we still kind of have that idea a lot of the time in mainstream churches.

Rorie from Kenya: Okay, I'll give you my take, my reflection concerning [the colonial past topic]. On a personal level, it might not affect me as much and I was reflecting back to then when we were starting this discussion, I didn't really think about 'Ah we are meeting guys from the UK we're from Kenya we have a past and all that' and it's not even come up until that time we had to discuss about racism and all that, so for me on a personal level it might not affect me because history is just history ... because, as they say, we cannot rewrite history definitely, but on a personal level it's something that I had not thought about.

Velkin from Kenya: I'm trying to think that [the colonial past topic] doesn't play a huge role because I tend to feel that we have our own culture which actually plays a bigger role when it comes to interpretation of the Bible, and I would love to quote a specific example: like when we talk about theologies of health and healing, there's the doctrine that we have, about Jesus Christ and, you know, healing. But then we have our own African traditionalists who believe that as much as they will pray for you they will recommend that you need to take some brews or traditional medicines that should actually be the ones that help you. I know that medics would actually don't recommend people to take the brews but these are some of the things that I would feel like ... play a key role when it comes to us interpreting the Bible and that's why we have a lot of controversies that are coming around and you know, people are working every day to try and see if they can resolve them, but the whole thing about colonialism and all that, I think it's moved history.

Sara from Kenya: I think we had a little privilege because most of us do not experience the colonization personally ... so for us like when in the discussion we don't directly think [about] the colonizers. For us, it doesn't really come to our mind until we are forced to try and remember ... We didn't speak much of this because it's not something we see or think or need on our day-to-day basis.

Marc from Kenya: From a personal level, [the colonial past topic] did not actually play a role ... Especially coming from Kenya and they are British, there's no connection ... for most guys our age it doesn't really play a role, you find that for most of us, what we tried to relate to is the current realities that we are living ... because the colonialism was with our forefathers and stuff, I think maybe that's why we find that for most of us it doesn't really play a big role.

Example 2: Extract of testimonies and dialogues between evangelical 'prophets' and church members in rural Ethiopia

Dialogue in Church No 1

Prophet: In your dream, a wild beast was following you, you were stressed out, now you are going to come out of the evil!

Woman: Amen!

Prophet: Evil is not going to devour you!

Woman: Amen!

The woman cries out raising her hands, with closed eyes she cries.

Prophet: You are created for honour!

Woman: Amen!

Prophet: You will receive it!

Woman: Amen!

Prophet: When the enemy wants to devour you, God is going to save you!

Woman: Amen!

Dialogue in Church No 2

Prophet: You have always been like this, your whole life is full of problems, now it is going to be full of honour for you. God says so!

The woman cries with her arms raised and eyes closed.

Prophet: I hear when you ask: What I am going to eat? God is going to interfere! The spirit that has followed you all your life is going to be destroyed! I remove the spirit of worry!

He places his hands on her head and pushes her back, she moves but does not fall.

Testimony in Church No 3

Woman: Jesus is Lord!

Community: Amen! Amen! Amen! Amen!

Woman: I have one hectare of land on which I plant potatoes. Last year the harvest was bad, but this year we produced a lot. God helped us! There is an orthodox person next to me who invited me to give an offer in that church. But the product from his land was taken by the monkeys. Here I took the blessed water [which the prophet sells] and watered the land with that, and by the power of Jesus Christ the animals did not touch the land and we produced a lot! Even when the animals come, they stop and go away and do not touch my land. Blessed are you prophet! May your enemies be destroyed! The Holy Spirit in this prophet is very strong! There is too much to thank God for! Next time I will bring an offering from my land! When I first came here my stomach and kidney were sick. The prophet prayed and I am healed!

As these examples reveal, the priorities of non-Western church attendants are on most occasions radically different from those of Western academic elites (even when they deal with postcolonial topics). Fixation on the previously described 'Western' issues, even though important ones, seems to refer much more to Western assumed colonial filial responsibility or to its fetish to explain 'the good and the bad in this world' solely in terms of Western actions. In a colonial paradox, this tends to neglect the agency of non-Westerners in the construction of their own societies. In this sense, is there something more colonial than explaining the achievements or failures of non-Westerners solely on the basis of Westerners' actions? What right do Western academics have to impose the 'actually important' topics or hermeneutical keys to the communities in the South?

Conclusion

Throughout this chapter, I have worked on two general complementary principles (of certainly many others) to impulse the development of epistemological justice in religious and theological reflection. First, the necessity to dedicate an active effort to identify, analyse and deconstruct the theological and religious knowledge of Christian communities. This is not a call for a pre-modern Christianity, but a call for constant epistemological reflexivity, which avoids general rules and has much more to do with a craftsperson's work, based on the experience with the material, and together with the community that produces it, knowing to which extent it can be moulded, transformed, debugged and refined. And second, the necessity to avoid exoticism and the imposition of alien topics and categories on local Christian communities. Intercultural theology is based foremost on the right and capacity of each believer and congregation to speak by themselves and autonomously choose what is important to them, what topics resonate in their daily practice, and how to reflect theologically in a way that makes sense to them. Any other attempt to impose Western interests, agendas or categories on the study of these groups and their spiritualities will prove itself colonial and end up in a total divorce between the reality of the field and the well-intended researcher.

Notes

1 G. W. F. Hegel, *The Philosophy of History* (New York: Colonial Press, 1900), 455.

2 Emile Durkheim, *The Rules of Sociological Method* (New York: The Free Press, 1982), 62.

3 Friedrich Schleiermacher, *Brief Outline of Theology as a Field of Study* (Louisville, KY: Westminster John Knox Press, 2011), 1.

4 Friedrich Schleiermacher, *Kurze Darstellung des Theologischen Studiums* (Berlin, 1811).

5 Werner Jeanrond, *Theological Hermeneutics: Development and Significance* (London: SCM Press, 2022), 14.1.

6 Rudolf Bultmann, *Jesus Christ and Mythology* (New York: Charles Scribner's Sons, 1958), 18.

7 Jeanrond, *Theological Hermeneutics*, 143.

8 Enrique Dussel, *Philosophy of Liberation* (New York: Orbis Books, 1985), 10.

9 Daniel Jara J., 'Christian knowings from the Global South: A theological approximation to De Sousa Santos' "Epistemologies of the South"', in *Interkulturelle Theologie. Zeitschrift für Missionswissenschaft* (Vol. 47, 1, 2021), 150–69, at p. 158.

10 Irregardless of the personal affinity of these figures to Liberation Theology, their life, ministry and martyrdom became cornerstones in the foundation and/or further propagation of this theology.

11 Phillip Berryman, *Teología de la liberación: Los hechos esenciales en torno al movimiento revolucionario en América Latina y otros lugares* (Madrid: Siglo XXI de España Editores, 2003), §12.

12 Congregation for the Doctrine of the Faith, *Instructions on Certain Aspects of the 'Theology of Liberation'* (Vatican City, 1984), §9.10.

13 Ignacio Ellacuría, 'Los pobres: lugar teológico en América Latina', *Misión abierta* 4–5 (1981), 225–40, at p. 231.

14 Sergio Silva, 'La Teología de la Liberación', *Teología y Vida* 50 (2009), 93–116, at p. 98.

15 Clodovis Boff, 'Volta ao Fundamento: Réplica', *Revista Eclesiástica Brasileira*, 272 (2008), 907–20, at p. 912.

16 Daniel Jara J., 'Christian knowings', 160.

17 'Rome was not built in one day', in Adolf Tobler, *Li Proverbe au Vilain*, 1895.

18 '*Saberes* in Spanish or *savoirs* in French ... These ways of knowing are characterized by their collective authorship because they are not developed by an academic "elite" of theologians and exegetes but by common non-theologically trained believers. Unlike scientific, theological, and philosophical knowledge, the ways of knowing openly claim for their contextual and culturally embedded character.' Daniel Jara J., 'Christian knowings', 157.

19 All names have been changed for anonymity.

3

Indigenous Queer Subjugation and Lessons from Nagaland

INATOLI AYE

The white colonists have a long history of characterizing communities of Black, Indigenous and People of Colour (BIPOC) as sexually perverse, savage, gender non-conforming, cross-dressers, and blaming them for homosexuality. They believed that the white civilization was defined by a framework that only acknowledged two genders, male and female, that corresponded to anatomical sex. The white colonists and Christian missionaries propagated this false, yet deep-seated, racist narrative of heterosexual gender binary into their conquests. They executed violent laws, perpetrated genocide and ensured the erasure of indigenous wisdom and practices. Western gender myths saw indigenous peoples as 'morally perverted', lacking comprehension of the Western manufactured gender binary. Non-Western cultures were observed to engage in a blending of behaviours and attire associated with both male and female genders.[1]

In light of this, the British imperial conquests enshrined 'sodomy laws' criminalizing 'homosexuality' in various regions of Asia, Africa and the Pacific islands. These laws continue to be in effect in many of the nations formerly subjected to colonial rule. The sodomy law, modelled on the English Parliament's Buggery Act of 1533, was first codified in 1860 under Section 377 of the Indian Penal Code, which was subsequently exported to a series of British colonies and countries.[2] The imposed legal prohibitions were consequently borne by queer folx, considering their 'relationship and behaviour' as constituting 'carnal intercourse against the order of nature'.[3] Queer folx are often perceived as unnatural or anomalies in the context of evolution, consequently leading to their categorization as taboo or forbidden. This colonial gender and sex narrative continues to endure in formerly colonized spaces, including indigenous peoples' worldviews.

Many of the indigenous queer folx find themselves dehumanized by their own communities due to the legacies of colonialism and the influence of Christianity. This phenomenon is notably observable among indigenous queer folx in Nagaland. They are under further scrutiny from the prevailing negative global discussions on LGBTQIA+ matters, both on social platforms and church institutions. LGBTQIA+ individuals are considered a modern phenomenon, the 'predilections' or 'disorders' of which, they believe, can be overcome through guidance, counselling and prayer. Moreover, a prevailing sentiment contends that queer folx do not exist within the Naga community, effectively invisibilizing them.

In examining the experiences of indigenous queer folx in Nagaland, this chapter explores the potential of the cross, to challenge and subvert oppressive taboos and heteronormative theologies, thereby contributing to the empowerment and visibility of marginalized communities. This exploration holds significance for discussions on the discourse of the theology of justice. I will be specifically examining the idea of taboo and the cross of Christ, which entails unspeakable, offensive rejection and prohibition and exclusion – leading to Christ harbouring an untouchable body. Out of this arises the potential, given to us, to challenge the prevailing dominant narrative.

Challenges of Taboos in Indigenous Communities

James George Frazer, a Scottish social anthropologist and folklorist, describes the word 'taboo' as derived from a general Polynesian word *tapu* or *tabu* from Tongan and *kapu* from the Hawaiian word, which means 'marked thoroughly' or 'off-limits' or 'holy'. The word 'taboo' was then repositioned in colonized preliterate societies to those ideas and things that were beyond the colonizer's comprehension.[4]

Frazer understood taboos as a system of superstition in which 'savages' could not make a distinction between 'holiness' and 'pollution', unlike civilized societies.[5] Expanding and challenging this, Mary Douglas, a British anthropologist, illustrates the commonalities of taboos across different societies. Douglas points out that taboos surrounding the concept of dirt and pollution are similar both in Western and non-Western societies and both serve to order society. Dirt is considered a disorder or an anomaly and is therefore dangerous, but one that can also be controlled. Douglas explains, 'Where there is dirt, there is system. Dirt is the by-product of a systematic ordering and classification of matter, in so far as ordering involves rejecting inappropriate elements.'[6] Therefore, those who transgress social ordering are considered a threat to social institutions. Similarly, Heidi Kosonen, a visual cultural researcher on taboos, says, 'we can define the taboo as both the object and the structure wielding control: the system of taboo forbids something, and the object of this forbiddance becomes a taboo'.[7] The shared understanding that dirt signifies disorder and the necessity to control forbiddance underscores the intricate relationship between taboos and societal organization.

Closer to home, Longchar, a Naga theologian, explains that taboos in indigenous communities are sets of prohibitions aimed to limit, control, preserve order, or regulate one's activities to protect the entire indigenous community.[8] It is a way of sustaining indigenous peoples' life. Taboos are further regulated by giving religious meaning through the creation of myths. Taboos relating to social, religious, sexual, ethical, warfare and legal taboos help regulate the way of life of Nagas and many indigenous communities. Any act that transgresses the boundaries and enters into the realm of taboo has dire consequences. Among the Nagas, transgressing taboos incurs a 'supernatural penalty' upon the individual and to the community.[9] Many indigenous communities believe that taboos help maintain a healthy relationship with creation and the community, especially when their sustenance hinges on nature. Nature is protected from overexploitation by maintaining a balance with the natural world. For example, in a Naga community, adhering to the taboo against hunting and slaughtering animals during breeding seasons reflects an understanding of the interconnectedness that extends to human well-being. Other taboos include prohibitions like men refraining from killing animals while wives are pregnant, and women avoiding the consumption of fish lacking scales.

Sometimes, social taboos can be patronizing and can potentially demean the younger generation's autonomy. Young people among the Naga communities are prohibited from cutting trees or stripping their bark. It is believed that spirits dwell in these trees and any act of cutting down and hurting the trees would only disturb or frighten the spirits, and shorten young people's lifespan or bring about their sudden death. Young people are prohibited from propagating certain sacred trees, for if the trees were to surpass them in size and age, they could 'outgrow the fortune of the planter'. These taboos are considered to have ecological significance and demonstrate the centrality of creation in the lives of indigenous communities.[10] However, Vibha Joshi, an Indian anthropologist who conducted research among the Angami Nagas, remarked that taboos that have ecological significance are now rationalized as modern justifications among educated Nagas. Joshi said: 'As a 'modern' rationalization of an old taboo, an educated Christian Angami remarked that these prohibitions were meant to put a stop to hunting during the mating season of different animals and added that because nowadays nobody follows these old rules very few animals are left in the jungle.'[11] This perspective may reflect a colonial influence on the Nagas' worldview.[12]

Furthermore, taboos can be patriarchal; hence, they are destructive to women, children and young people.[13] Often, older men in the community hold a higher authoritative status not only within their families but also within the broader societal framework. The elderly and the ancestors are granted a higher social standing in most Asian and indigenous cultures. They are to be respected and revered. In this social context, taboos often dictate the relationship between the young and their elders. One such taboo among the Sümi Naga tribe, one of the tribes in Nagaland, is called *tüghapu chini*: 'Timi hami no apuh amu züu no kichimi ghilishi eno pi ishi aye tüghapu chini,'[14] translated as 'It is taboo upon those who act and speak before fathers or brothers.' In other words, do not act or speak before the elders. The consequence of this is short lifespan accompanied by community disgrace.[15] This prohibition reinforces male supremacy within the community.

The particular *tüghapu chini*, a social taboo, can be interpreted in the context of a balanced order of life. Young people are considered to have much rigour and strength; hence, they are able to offer assistance to older people. For example, it is taboo for young people to walk past the elderly without lending their hands to their load. However, one must critically examine the social hierarchy reinforced by taboos. We must question the concept of balance, and whose order it serves. Those who transgress social order are penalized – it can be aimed at taming them, even to the extent where some are kicked out of their homes.

In exploring the multifaceted roles of taboos in indigenous communities, from preserving the indigenous worldview to upholding societal order to perpetuating gender constructs, we will explore how taboos intertwine with queer identities within indigenous communities.

Taboos Surrounding Queer Identity

Taboos have functioned as a tool to uphold homogeneity in communities, serving as mechanisms to suppress those who deviate from societal norms. Notably, queer folx have often been regarded as deviants, and therefore their person can be considered a taboo as their existence threatens the 'natural' order of society. Heidi Kosonen illuminates the conceptualization of queer as 'one of the anomalies of the reproduction-centred patriarchy'.[16] Kosonen underscores how the concept of queer challenges the way society focusses on reproduction and, consequently, forming taboos helps society control sexual marginals such as queer folx and children. These taboos serve as regulatory mechanisms that do not fit normal categories, especially related to reproduction and gender roles. Queer folx in Western societies were known to exist but their presence has been limited to isolated cases of intolerance such as police raids or criminal sex offence in the urban settings in historical records. However, Chauncey's work reveals that queer individuals not only existed in such instances but they flourished, occupying diverse spaces from British monarchs to urban scenes.[17] Meanwhile, British colonizers targeted and criminalized indigenous and queer folx for deviating from the norms of a civilized heterosexual behaviour.

It is evident through criminalizing and inciting violence to those who behave outside of gender binary normativity that indigenous peoples lived outside of the euro-white-heteronormative gender binary. They have been dehumanized and misunderstood. In the book *Asegi Stories: Cherokee Queer and Two-Spirit Memory*, Driskill, an indigenous scholar, emphasizes the experiences and resilience of indigenous queer and Two-Spirit individuals in the face of European colonization and the subsequent difficulties they encountered. These individuals have faced misconceptions and misunderstandings, which were used as a pretext for invading and attempting to impose civilization upon the indigenous people, often labelling their sexuality as 'unregulated'. The stories resonate with the broader struggles encountered by indigenous queer folx worldwide, illustrating the shared impact of colonialism and the resilience exhibited in preserving their identities.

The practical aspects of reproduction have deeply influenced the fabric of Naga society. The Naga society is mainly sustained through agriculture. The greater the number of individuals in a family, the more their labour contributes to agricultural production. Concerning marriage, when a woman is wed, she moves to her husband's household, adding value to their family through labour and reproduction. Thus, agriculture and reproduction are intrinsically tied to marriage arrangements. Within this framework of reproduction-centred patriarchal community dynamics, the labour of queer folx becomes challenging to commodify. Kosonen underscores the challenge posed by queer folx who do not perform traditional reproductive roles in a society that prioritizes labour and production. This lens highlights the challenges faced by indigenous queer folx in Nagaland who do not adhere to reproductive norms. Taboos rooted with these reproductive norms may hinder the ability to commodify their labour within the conventional social structure. The commodification of labour may not differ so much in precolonial times, as the mode of production in indigenous communities may differ from market economies; the ownership of labour and production are predominantly owned by men, unlike in matrilineal communities. Nonetheless, direct evidence of same-sex relations or their existence in the precolonial era remains elusive. The experiences of queer folx in Nagaland, as influenced by reproduction-centric norms, offer a microcosm of the global landscape, where indigenous queer folx face similar hurdles in reconciling their identities with established societal norms.

Erasure and Invisibility

The enforced gendered norms systematically erased and invisibilized the presence of indigenous queer folx. Driskill highlights well the invisibilizing of queer folx through a heteropatriarchal lens despite the indigenous collective memory of the Cherokee people:

> As Cherokee TwoSpirit people tactically remember these kinds of moments in historical records, we recognize that, even if people we would now recognize as TwoSpirit people were present, they also become rendered invisible through colonial heteropatriarchy's 'reading' of all Cherokee bodies, genders, and sexualities as outside of proper gender and sexual norms.[18]

Driskill's reflection of how the white heteronormative lens refutes and contaminates indigenous memory brings a further layer of invisibility or dehumanization to indigenous queer people. The complexity of erasure and invisibility of queer folx is expounded in Reddy's *With Respect to Sex: Negotiating Hijra identity in South India*. Gayatri Reddy, an Indian anthropologist who has made an impressive contribution to gender studies, expounds the tensions that arose in the postcolonial era when *hijra* men who sleep with men were exposed in print and visual media. Hijras in India are usually known as third gender, *kinnar*, eunuchs, cross-dressers among others, and most broadly and commonly known as transgender. The hijras have their distinct beliefs and practices, often involving joining under the guidance of a guru, who acts as a leader and caregiver. Their livelihood involves begging, singing and dancing at auspicious events to confer blessings or a curse. Indian law recognizes transgender as a third gender; however, they continue to face discrimination.[19] They are revered because they hold religious significance; paradoxically they are considered a nuisance because they beg at traffic points and in running trains. They hold both holy and polluted connotations in post-independence India. Despite their revered status, most confront rejection when looking for employment, compelling them to beg and engage in sex work. In precolonial times there was a potentially tolerant attitude to diverse sexuality and the presence of hijras was ambivalent and perhaps they made themselves visible on their own terms such as at auspicious events or to seek sexual pleasure. However, colonization vilified them as taboo. Regardless of having their presence in the past, Reddy's work illustrates how recent study by foreign scholars of alternative genders in non-Western societies and in mainstream films has heightened scrutiny of hijra lives, jeopardizing their safety. The constant unwanted visibility has resulted in adverse effects on the hijra community. Also, subsuming hijras under the global umbrella term of 'transgender' despite their distinct cultural and traditional presence, contributes to the ideological systemic erasure of traditional diverse sexualities in academic works and in real-world contexts. However, Reddy's work among the hijras indicates their willingness to share their stories knowing full well the further scrutiny they might endure. Reddy shows how colonial legacies impact on cultural norms and gender and sexuality across cultures.[20] Reddy's analysis aligns with Driskill's observations, highlighting the systemic erasure faced by queer folx.

As Driskill highlights, the colonial presence invisibilized queer lives and this erasure of queer folx can be seen in the Naga community as well. Queer folx are considered a taboo in Naga society, especially within Naga churches.[21] The intricate nexus between the Naga community and Christianity arises from historical interactions with American Baptist missionaries during British colonial rule, establishing Nagaland as a predominantly Christian state. This translated homophobia in Christianity into society. Many church leaders attribute the prevalence of 'homosexuality' to changing trends such as drug abuse, adultery and the consumption of pornography. The unanimous repudiation by Naga church leaders of the Indian Supreme Court's Section 377 decriminalization of homosexuality subjects queer folx to heightened scrutiny in Nagaland. The Nagaland Baptist Church Council (NBCC), the top Baptist institution in Nagaland, alongside other Naga pastors, labelled homosexuality as a sin, biblically unfounded, and unnatural. The trope of 'love the sinner, hate the sin' is invoked frequently within church youth gatherings.[22]

Nagaland's Christian identity clashes with India, which projects itself as a masculine Hindu nation and subdues all other religions by assimilation and genocide. When the British Empire withdrew, Nagas refused to be under British Overseas Territories as well as under Indian rule but found themselves under Indian governance. In response, Nagas retaliated against the occupation of Naga territories and projected themselves as a heteronormative masculine Christian state that inadvertently invisibilizes queer presence in Naga history and society. The Indian government imposed the Armed Forces Special Power Act 1958 (AFSPA) in Nagaland and a few other states in the northeast part of India who refused to be under Indian rule after the British colonial rule left India. Under the guise of controlling revolutionary activities, the AFSPA was employed to exert dominance over the Naga region, leading to brutal violence as the Nagas resisted assimilation. Operating under the AFSPA, the Indian military violated human rights with impunity, punishing Nagas at large who deviated from India's heteronormative assimilative rule. This often resulted in disappearances, torture, executions and sexual assaults, creating an enduring void in Naga history. The AFSPA's impact persisted through generations, leaving a legacy of unresolved cases and missing individuals – symbolizing the missing generations in Nagas' history.[23]

Furthermore, many mainstream Indians possess limited knowledge of northeast Indians.[24] Tourism has become a pivotal tool for showcasing the diversity of Indian culture, driven by a surge in Indian tourists and vloggers who explore the northeastern region. Unfortunately, this exposure often oversimplifies and stereotypes northeast indigenous peoples as nature enthusiasts, consumers of insects and dog meat, and adherents of traditional practices. This presentation reinforces their depiction as ancient and unsophisticated. Naga young people, meanwhile, are portrayed as bridging the gap between tradition and modernity, but this portrayal inadvertently exoticizes their lives, deepening the sense of otherness.[25] This narrative enforces the perception that deviation from mainstream Indian culture is taboo, fostering an environment where indigenous traditions are both sacred and polluted. This complicated Indo-Naga relationship obscures the challenges faced by queer folx within Naga society.

In indigenous contexts, the challenges of erasure and invisibility of queer identity are intricately intertwined with various dimensions of identity-race, ethnicity, class and religion. Driskill and Reddy's mechanisms of erasure can be understood in the context of these intersecting aspects of identity, which both amplify and complicate the challenges faced by indigenous folx.

INATOLI AYE

Lessons from Nagaland's Queer Folk

The documentary film *Oh My Soul!* by Naga filmmaker Ms Kivini Shohe effectively captures the presence and plight of many young indigenous queer folx in Nagaland. Within Nagaland, most queer folx are often classified as Men Sleeping with Men (MSM) or transgender. The classification may arise from the practicality of NGOs connecting with the queer community, allowing them to provide essential medical assistance without explicitly using labels such as lesbian and gays. One story describes the life of Toshi, who was kicked out of her home because of her sexuality. She narrates her journey to embracing hijrahood.[26]

In the docufilm, Toshi recounts her sister's public expulsion, calling her a 'hijra',[27] which prompts Toshi to embrace this identity. This is evident as Toshi adorns a saree, a distinctive Indian garment, and seeks alms from train passengers. Shohe aptly remarks that, 'Being a hijra is horrifyingly unthinkable in Naga society.'[28] This transformation challenges both heteronormative and religious norms, as Naga identity is intertwined with Christianity. Toshi's status as a Naga and Christian complicated her adoption of hijrahood, disrupting the conventional order of Naga Christian society. Her subsequent refuge among fellow hijras to escape familial harm exemplifies the systematic efforts to erase queer folx.

The act of rendering queer folx invisible in Nagaland is normalized, further solidifying the surrounding taboo. The invisibilizing was evident when the docufilm *Oh My Soul!* was screen in 2015. It shocked many in the audience with its portrayal of multiple gender and sexual identities in Nagaland.[29] Toshi's story illustrates how economically and socially disadvantaged queer Naga young people are. They are swiftly marginalized, confined to society's fringes, and depicted as symbols of dirt and chaos. They are compelled to engage in sex work, making them susceptible to exploitation. They are quickly forgotten by society and become an object and subject of a taboo.

When queer folx transgress heteronormative borders, it pollutes sacred hierarchical spaces. Yet it also creates an emancipatory space of solidarity. In the context of Naga food and primitive exotification, Naga anthropologist Dolly Kikon describes how:

> Moralities, transgressions and boundaries can be traced to everyday practices of production and consumption within and across human societies ... While smell is local, it is also invisible. It crosses borders. There is something unnerving and subversive about the way it manages to pollute and infringe the most intimate and sacred spaces. It enters

the nostrils and, in some, produces feelings of revulsion. For others, the same smell invokes feelings of comfort or remembrance of home. To invoke and remember home is to start by exploring the ways in which relationships, obligations and ways of belonging are established or threatened, especially in unfamiliar surrounds.[30]

The practice of taboos disrupts sacred and dominant spaces. However, out of dirt and pollution, there arises the potential to challenge the dominant narrative. There is a potential to create liberating spaces.

Naga queer folx challenge the boundaries of the patriarchal order, resisting established systems of order and showing new ways of building and sustaining relationships and belongingness. Toshi's narrative exemplifies boundary-crossing as she both embodies a transwoman identity and embraces hijra, a concept distinct from her own religious and cultural background. She does not subscribe to her given circumstances. Her belongingness was, rather, made expansive. Moa, a gay person who is in his thirties, shares in the docufilm that his family disowned him due to his gender and sexuality, erasing him from his family and community. He dropped out of school because of persistent teasing from his peers. He is now working with Guardian Angel, a non-government organization that works with Men Sleeping with Men (MSM), to help build a support system for queer folx.[31]

While Driskill and Reddy make explicit the erasure of queer folx by colonialism, cultural shifts and media, Kikon complements the discussion that the everyday practices of purity and pollution can be used to marginalize and control certain groups, including indigenous queer folx. However, liberating spaces are created through the everyday practice of transgression and solidarity. The stories of Toshi and Moa show their transgression from normative Christian gender roles and underscore their resilience in overcoming social stigma and adversity. The formation of support networks and NGOs demonstrates the significance of community empowerment and collaboration in challenging systemic erasure. It can inspire similarly marginalized communities globally to amplify their voices through cultural expression and build networks of deep solidarity across sexuality, religion, race, culture, nationality and so on for greater visibility and recognition in the context of systemic erasure.

The Transformation of Taboos: The Cross as a Symbol

Jesus as the Rooster is an indigenous theologizing of Christian theology and can be considered a decolonial process. Yangkahao Vashum, a pioneer Naga theologian, drawing from Naga-indigenous socio-political and cultural values, explains that among other animals, the rooster is sacred and plays an important role in ceremonial rituals, especially in purification and restoration rites required for individuals as well for the community. In these rituals, the rooster is released into the jungle. Its failure to return signifies a positive outcome, such as healing from illness or the reversal of impending calamities. However, if the rooster returns, it means the person will never recover from the sickness. Vashum identifies parallels between a rooster sacrificed for communal well-being and the sacrificial death of Jesus Christ. Vashum explains that the rooster is not without its limitations, as it is limited to its immediate community, but it nonetheless offers indirect well-being to the larger world. Vashum argues that 'What is of real importance here is that both Jesus and the rooster died so that the people might live!'[32]

The rooster, used as a metaphor for Jesus, symbolizes resistance against dominant theology. It 'absorbs and reworks' oppressive atonement theology and serves as an act of adversarial justice by offering an indigenous perspective. When indigenous peoples' cultures, practices and wisdom were deemed as savage, taboo and satanic, the embrace of indigenous theology became a transformative act of justice. Further, Jesus portrayed as the Rooster challenges the heteronormative economic theology of indebtedness. This metaphor is not a profit-based contractual relationship but one that seeks out those like Toshi and Moa who have been excluded by the community. However, its transformative potential seems limited.

Traditionally, in the context of Naga indigenous theology, the rooster was identified as the Christ figure. While this connection may be understandable when the rooster is sacrificed, a unique scenario arises where the rooster is not sacrificed but is instead set free into the forest. This imagery of setting free invokes a sense of liberation, of slaves escaping Egypt to go into the wilderness – Egypt being a place of unjust laws and slavery and the wilderness being a place of freedom and liberation. In this sense, the rooster not only symbolizes the sacrificed victims of history but also those who escape injustice, those who are set free into the forest to live as they should, fulfil their life's desires and live the life that they were created and destined for. Consequently, the rooster here can also symbolize Toshi and Moa, who live in the possibility of being set free from heteronormative patriarchy to live their life and live it in its fullness.

It is significant that the ritual indicates that if the rooster continues to live in the forest prosperity will come to the community and if it returns then sickness comes. This interpretation suggests that if folx like Toshi and Moa are set free to live their lives, there is the possibility of freedom and a dismantling of heteronormative patriarchy for all. However, there is disaster awaiting the community if they are to return to normal and normative society, reinforcing homophobic and transphobic values and denying any possibility of liberation.

Returning to the idea of the rooster as the Christ figure who was sacrificed also compels us to consider the cross. Contrary to traditional theology, in which the cross was a symbol of personal sin, salvation and imperial power and triumph, German theologian Jürgen Moltmann signifies the meaning of the cross and points to its potential to challenge the dominant narrative and create emancipatory space. In *The Crucified God*, Moltmann explains that 'The symbol of the cross invites rethinking'.[33] He connects it as being significant in understanding justice. He argues that the 'paradox of the cross' is that the crucifixion of Jesus, which was a symbol of shame, violence, abandonment and death, is a symbol of an act of solidarity with human suffering and that liberates from suffering. Moltmann contends that 'God allows himself to be humiliated and crucified in the Son, in order to free the oppressors and the oppressed from oppression and to open up to them the situation of free, sympathetic humanity.'[34] Adding to this discourse, Mark Lewis Taylor, a liberation theologian, in his *The Executed God: The Way of the Cross in Lockdown America*, says that the cross, which was a symbol of terror and control, is also able to signify adversarial resistance against unjust systems of oppressions. Taylor explains it 'is not that Jesus' death makes life, but that the kind of life Jesus lived for, radical love and justice' cannot be quashed by systemic structures.[35] Taylor emphasizes that Jesus' crucifixion exemplifies solidarity with the oppressed. To follow Jesus is to do adversarial politics, that is, to be among the crucified. God's solidarity with the oppressed calls us not just to show solidarity, but to be among the terrorized and fight for justice and peace. The transformative aspect of the cross then is to take action for justice.

Both Moltmann and Taylor symbolize the meaning of the cross, suggesting that just as Jesus' crucifixion signifies solidarity with the oppressed, it also now calls on society to stand with and advocate for marginalized communities, including queer folx. It means not only acknowledging struggles, but actively working towards dismantling discriminatory systems and advancing equal rights. Just as Jesus' crucifixion was a demonstration of love and solidarity, it calls on us to engage in adversarial politics against oppression, and to work tirelessly for justice.

Queer folx are dehumanized and left outside the borders of Naga society and theology. This prompts the question: is God not on the side of Toshi and Moa? Does God transgress boundaries imposed by heterosexual theology or offer feelings of sorrows and prayers from across fixed borders? Marcella Althaus-Reid's *The Queer God* offers insight. She suggests that God's presence is qualified by '"Vulgarity", where what qualifies the location of God is outside the non-civilized sites of theology, and in the space of the dirty.'[36] This shows the transformative role of a queer God who can be found among and in obscene spaces of taboo. God being on the side of the oppressed and marginalized reshapes the significance of taboo and dominant theological narratives.

Despite Vashum's effort, his framework maintains the traditional notion of the cross as a site for repaying debts, perpetuating the existing understanding. He attempts to bridge Naga indigenous theology and Western theology through inculturation, to preserve Naga indigenous rituals. However, it is still constrained by the lens of colonial theology. One replaces the other. The conventional interpretation of the cross as a symbol both of triumph and of suffering persists in Vashum's perspective. He does not fully embrace the notion of the cross as a site of transgression. This reinterpretation holds the promise of radically reshaping taboos and rituals, moving beyond mere transference to genuine transformation, but falls short and continues the traditional exchange metaphor present in Christology.

Translating the aims of heteronormative political theology into uncomfortable solidarity, Marcella Althaus-Reid, a queer liberation theologian from Argentina, queered the traditional interpretation of the cross, which is rooted in a hierarchical, patriarchal economic order. Althaus-Reid critiques the notion of using debt as a metaphor for salvation in Christian theology: the idea of God sacrificing divine life to reconcile human lives reflects a theology of indebtedness. She observed that while Christian theology claims divine salvation, people continue to struggle with external debts. She connected oppressive heteronormative theology to oppressive economic systems and posited that the genuine essence of redemption is not contractual but is instead a gift of unmerited grace. The cross can become a symbol of resistance only when we embrace alternative practices that are outside of Western paradigms, and instead are based on an economy of loving relationships, reciprocity and grace.

The gift of unmerited grace holds profound implications for Naga queer youths who navigate the complexities of their tribal heritage and non-conforming identities. The idea of redemption as a gift can empower them to reframe their self-worth and embrace their identities without feeling obliged to conform to established norms. Further, the prevalent practice of engaging in transactional relationships, such as 'I love gay people', or 'I have many gay friends, but it does not mean I agree with what they do', commonly found in evangelical circles, requires scrutiny. It is essential to interrogate these interactions and emphasize the concept of unmerited grace. Unmerited grace transgresses. It disrupts the present and offers a vision of an alternative future.

Conclusion

This chapter has explored the transformation of taboos and the cross, highlighting the resilience of indigenous queer folx in Nagaland. Religious symbols, such as the cross of Christ, were laden with taboos. Yet, symbols are given meaning by those in power. Despite the attempts by heteronormative theology to erase the lives of queer folx, their persistence symbolizes taboos. Perhaps seeking empowerment within religious frameworks is contentious, but it highlights the tensions and the need to engage in a critical way to seek liberation from within established systems. The insights drawn from Naga queer folx showed their resilience, strategies for community solidarity, and empowerment. The power of religious symbols, such as the cross and the metaphor of the rooster, emerge as potent forces that challenge heteronormative theology, dismantle taboos and empower marginalized communities. These insights resonate with indigenous communities worldwide. The transformative potential of taboos and the cross can inspire inclusivity, agency and resistance in the face of erasure. It also has the potential to enable indigenous communities to reclaim their identities and dismantle unjust systems and theologies. The solidarity of God among the marginalized calls us towards lived, disruptive solidarity among the marginalized, shaking dominant narratives and working towards a more inclusive and just future.

Notes

1 Peter Boag, *Re-Dressing America's Frontier Past* (London: University of California Press, 2011), 5, 249–50; Quo-Li Driskill, *Asegi Stories: Cherokee Queer and Two-Spirit Memory* (Tucson: University of Arizona Press, 2016), 83; Greg Thomas, *The Sexual Demon of Colonial Power: Pan-African Embodiment and Erotic Schemes of Empire* (Bloomington: Indiana University Press, 2007), 24; Mary

Mead Clark, *A Corner in India* (Philadelphia: American Baptist Publication Society, 1907), 54.

2 The Indian Penal Code Section 377 states that, '377. Unnatural offences. – Whoever voluntarily has carnal intercourse against the order of nature with any man, woman or animal, shall be punished with 1[imprisonment for life], or with imprisonment of either description for a term which may extend to ten years, and shall also be liable to fine. Explanation. – Penetration is sufficient to constitute the carnal intercourse necessary to the offence described in this section', https://indiankanoon.org/doc/1836974/ (accessed 21/02/2024). In 2018, the Supreme Court of India struck down parts of the archaic Victorian law, thereby decriminalizing consensual same-sex relationship and intercourse.

3 Section 377 in The Indian Penal Code.

4 *Encyclopaedia Britannica: A Dictionary of Arts, Sciences, and General Literature*', 9th ed. (Edinburgh: Adam and Charles Black, 1888), 15, https://digital.nls.uk/encyclopaedia-britannica/archive/193592633#?c=0&m=0&s=0&cv=0&xywh=-1441%2C-244%2C5904%2C4861 (accessed 7/03/2024); Lynn Holden, *Encyclopedia of Taboos* (Oxford: ABC-CLIO Ltd, 2000), ix. While Frazer's perspective acknowledges that taboos are part of the complex fabric of society, it is important to recognize that the notion of taboo, entwined with the concept of the unknown, aligns more closely with Western perspectives. To Frazer, 'Taboo is only one of a number of similar systems of superstition which among many, perhaps among all races of men [sic] have contributed in large measure, under many different names and with many variations of detail, to build up the complex fabric of society in all the various sides or elements of it which we describe as religious, social, political, moral and economic', J. G. Frazer, *Taboo and the Perils of the Soul* (London: Macmillan, 1911), v–vii.

5 Frazer, *Taboo and the Perils of the Soul*, 224.

6 Mary Douglas, *Purity and Danger. An Analysis of the Concepts of Pollution and Taboo* (London: Routledge, 1984), 36.

7 Heidi Kosonen, 'Behind the Scenes of Queer: The Post-Modern Taboo', in *Queer Sexualities: Diversifying Queer, Queering Diversity* (Leiden: Brill, 2013), 62, https://doi.org/10.1163/9781848882188_007.

8 A. Wati Longchar, *The Traditional Tribal Worldview and Modernity* (Jorhat: Eastern Theological College, 1995), 53–8.

9 Longchar, *Traditional Tribal Worldview*, 53–4.

10 Longchar, *Traditional Tribal Worldview*, 54–5; Lovely Awomi James, *Tribal Theology: Reviewing the Naga Traditional Worldview* (New Delhi: Christian World Imprints, 2017), 99.

11 Vibha Joshi, *A Matter of Belief: Christian Conversion and Healing in North-East India* (New York: Berghahn Books, 2012), 78.

12 The role of taboos in preserving the environment through indigenous knowledge systems is also reflected in Emmanuel Abeku Essel's, 'The Role of Taboos in Solving Contemporary Environmental Degradation in Ghana: The Case of Cape Coast Metro', *Social Sciences* (Vol. 9, 4, 2020), 89, https://www.academia.edu/97926834/The_Role_of_Taboos_in_Solving_Contemporary_Environmental_Degradation_in_Ghana_The_Case_of_Cape_Coast_Metro (accessed 21/02/2024).

13 James, *Tribal Theology*, 77–80.

14 Hekhevi Achumi, *Sütsah Kuthoh* (Dimapur: Dimapur Sümi Baptist Church, 2005), 170.

15 A British anthropologist who studied the Nagas documented the death of a medicine man as he violated a taboo by revealing his powers: J. P. Mills, *The Lhota Nagas* (London: Macmillan, 1922), 164.

16 Kosonen, 'Behind the Scenes of Queer', 63.

17 George Chauncey, *Gay New York: Gender, Urban Culture, and the Making of the Gay Male World, 1890–1940* (New York: Basic Books, 1994).

18 Driskill, *Asegi Stories: Cherokee Queer and Two-Spirit Memory*, 89.

19 Devdutt Pattanaik, *The Man Who Was a Woman and Other Queer Tales from Hindu Lore* (New York: Routledge, 2012), 11–12.

20 Gayatri Reddy, *With Respect to Sex: Negotiating Hijra Identity in South India*, Worlds of Desire: The Chicago Series on Sexuality, Gender, and Culture (Chicago: University of Chicago Press, 2005), 2–5.

21 Moasashi Ao, 'A Preparatory Reorientation for the Dimapur Ao Pastors in Addressing the Issue of LGBTQIA in the Church: An Ethical Reflection' (Dimapur, Oriental Theological Seminary, 2019), 22.

22 'Churches Protest against Homosexuality', *Nagaland Post* (blog), 23 October 2018, https://nagalandpost.com/index.php/churches-protest-against-homosexuality/; 'Homosexuality, Adultery Unacceptable: NBCC', *Nagaland Post* (blog), 2 November 2018, https://nagalandpost.com/index.php/homosexuality-adultery-unacceptable-nbcc/; John Malhotra, 'Nagaland Pastors Blow Whistle on Gay Judgment', *Christian Today*, 2009, http://www.christiantoday.co.in/article/nagaland.pastors.blow.whistle.on.gay.judgment/4209.htm (accessed 7/03/2024).

23 Kaka. D. Iralu, *Nagaland and India. The Blood and the Tears: A Historical Account of the Fifty-Two Year Indo-Naga War and the Story of Those Who Were Never Allowed to Tell It* (India: Kaka D. Iralu, 2003); Akum Longchari, *Self-Determination: A Resource for JustPeace* (Dimapur: Heritage Publishing House, 2016); Charles Chasie, *The Naga Memorandum to the Simon Commission, 1929* (Kohima: Standard Printers and Publishers, 2017).

24 Mainland Indians often consider people of northeastern states as outsiders due to caste discrimination prevailing in India. The discrimination is so severe it leads to the perception of indigenous peoples from northeastern states as foreigners or outsiders. During the onset of the Covid-19 pandemic in India, numerous cases emerged from Indian citizens returning from international travel, but this narrative shifted as cases escalated. Instead, it was blamed on the northeastern indigenous people. Mainstream Indians called the indigenous peoples 'Chinese' and 'corona', resulting in physical assaults. Despite the recognition that the northeastern indigenous peoples were not Chinese, the landlords still evicted them from their apartments. The prejudiced targeting of northeasterners was exacerbated during the pandemic, especially affecting young people in universities, grocery stores, public transport and footpaths. Soumitra Das, 'Harassed, Abused, Spat at: Stop This Racism, It's Not Ok to Taunt Northeast Indians with "Corona" Slurs', *The Times of India*, 2020, https://timesofindia.indiatimes.com/life-style/spotlight/harassed-abused-spat-at-stop-this-racism-its-not-ok-to-taunt-northeast-indians-with-corona-slurs/articleshow/74896715.cms (accessed 21/05/2024).

25 *Tried Insects for the First Time! My Reaction* 😋, 2021, https://www.youtube.com/watch?v=ePfP7_02AjQ (accessed 7/03/2024); *Nagaland: Hornbill*

Festival | The Land Of Festivals | I Love My India Ep 64 | Curly Tales, 2022, https://www.youtube.com/watch?v=K9oI1iQJv1o (accessed 7/03/2024); *Take Me to Nagaland | The Fashion Revolution | Dimapur Edition | Ep1 Part1 | North East India Travel*, 2019, https://www.youtube.com/watch?v=XMyfNnFLtOU (accessed 7/03/2024).

26 The hijra community has a long historical and cultural legacy in India. Reddy, *With Respect to Sex: Negotiating Hijra Identity in South India*. They served as soldiers in the Mughal court, some held religious authority, and as catamites and royal servants in Hindu courts. However, colonization stigmatized traditional gender and sexuality as taboo.

27 Here, it means transgender or a man who behaves like a woman.

28 *Oh My Soul!*, 2015.

29 'Transgender Struggle in Nagaland', *The Morung Express* (blog), 17 August 2015, http://morungexpress.com/transgender-struggle-in-nagaland/ (no longer accessible 2024).

30 Dolly Kikon, 'Fermenting Modernity: Putting Akhuni on the Nation's Table in India', *South Asia: Journal of South Asian Studies* (Vol. 38, 2, 2015), 324, https://doi.org/10.1080/00856401.2015.1031936.

31 Atono Tsükrü Kense, 'Nagaland's MSM Community Looks to Future with Hope', *The Morung Express* (blog), November 2019.

32 Yangkahao Vashum, *Christology in Context: A Tribal-Indigenous Appraisal of NorthEast India*, Christian Heritage Rediscovered 49 (New Delhi: Christian World Imprints, 2017), 137.

33 Jürgen Moltmann, *The Crucified God: The Cross of Christ as the Foundation and Criticism of Christian Theology*, 2nd ed. (London: SCM Press, 1974), 6.

34 Moltmann, *The Crucified God*, 307.

35 Mark Lewis Taylor, *The Executed God: The Way of the Cross in Lockdown America*, 2nd ed. (1517 Media, 2015), 282, https://doi.org/10.2307/j.ctt155j3fk.

36 Marcella Althaus-Reid, *The Queer God* (London: Routledge, 2004), 36.

4

African Approaches to Transitional Justice

ADAM RANDERA

This chapter attempts to describe an approach to justice based on a particular sub-Saharan African worldview. To do this I explore how African philosophers have understood concepts such as *ubuntu*, the community, and the self, and how this understanding has led to the worldview and ethic I term 'Afro-communitarianism', which values communal identity, solidarity and the harmonization of individual and communal interests. Proponents of this approach, either implicitly or explicitly, contend that establishing a strong sense of community should be a primary aim of societies and reconciliation should therefore be prioritized in societies looking to move from conflict to peace. This is because an understanding of *ubuntu* as a moral theory seems to entail that establishing or re-establishing 'community' should be seen as a necessary aim of justice and, following on from this, that reconciliation should be seen as necessary in resolving conflict. Examples of this in practice are given from South Africa's post-apartheid Truth and Reconciliation Commission (CRC). While the Afro-communitarian approach to post-conflict justice I articulate here may align closely with contemporary 'transformative' approaches to post-conflict justice popular in other parts of the world, it is nevertheless distinct and may offer valuable insights into peacebuilding efforts globally.

While terms like '*botho*' and '*ubuntu*' are often associated with South Africa's transition to democracy, both these terms and the concepts they encapsulate pre-date the colonial period and have been the subject of significant academic and public discussion in areas unrelated to democratization. Afro-communitarianism discourses are concerned with broad social, political, spiritual and personal topics; however, this chapter focusses on the ethical, and to a lesser extent the political, dimensions of these debates, and in particular how an Afro-communitarian worldview impacts the question of what is just after a conflict. The primary reasons for this are to assess how an indigenous African approach can address peacebuilding challenges and to identify entry points for a dialogue between African approaches to addressing the consequences of conflict and similar, more commonly understood approaches.

Explaining Afro-communitarianism

Before beginning in earnest it is worth clarifying what is meant by 'post-conflict justice' here. The phrase refers to the processes by which societies address the grievances caused by, or which lead to, a conflict. The use of the prefix 'post-' here may imply that this process occurs after a conflict has ended; however, it is more accurate to say that this is a process that occurs as a society transitions from conflict to peace. For this reason, post-conflict justice is often referred to as 'transitional' or 'transformative' justice. This is distinct from other forms of justice in several ways, but primarily post-conflict justice processes have a broader moral scope than some other justice processes in more stable societies.[1] Such processes must recognize and address not only the individual crimes that have been committed and the specific harms that particular victims have sustained, but also collective wrongdoings and harms, as well as the institutional and systemic factors that made such harms possible, permissible or even normalized.[2]

The term 'Afro-communitarianism' also bears some unpacking. While this is the term that will be used most commonly in this chapter, the term most commonly associated with the concepts discussed here is '*ubuntu*'.[3] '*Ubuntu*' came into popular discourse towards the end of Apartheid and with South Africa's transition to democracy. '*Ubuntu*' is regularly associated with transitional justice and nation-building. However, the term both pre-dates this period and has come to be associated with a variety of different ideas since.[4] '*Ubuntu*' is traditionally used to refer either to a human quality or to a phenomenon, ethic or worldview.[5] However, the term has, in recent years, been subject to a fair degree of semantic drift, being used not only as a philosophical term, but also as a catch-all term for charity and a name for a variety of private companies.[6] To avoid confusion, and so as to capture an understanding of *ubuntu* both as a worldview and as a human quality, the term 'Afro-communitarianism' is used here. The term 'Afro-communitarianism' has the added bonus of being inclusive of the wide variety of African cultures in which the concepts being discussed are prevalent, and not just those in South Africa. Afro-communitarianism, it must be noted, is not communitarian in the Western sense, where morals are defined as relative to the social norms embraced by any particular community.[7] Rather, Afro-communitarianism prescribes particular ethical values, but these are values that relate to the valuing of community.

While the view being proposed here is based on the various cultural institutions and practices present in pre- and postcolonial African societies, it is important to address the risk of romanticization. While some generalizations may be appropriate (indeed, the variety of African authors from different cultures who all feel there is some commonality in the worldviews of sub-Saharan Africans is testament to this), one must also acknowledge that sub-Saharan Africa is incredibly diverse in languages and cultures, and there is a great diversity of political institutions and practices in the region. Moreover, there are certain cultural traditions that are obviously inappropriate to the modern day. For example, many precolonial political institutions in Africa were unjustly chauvinistic by modern standards. Of course, this was not a problem unique to African cultures at the time, but just as it would be inappropriate to impose seventeenth-century British patriarchy onto modern states, it would be unjust to insist that modern African courts be exclusively made up of men. As Murithi argues, we can combine modern understandings of gender and equality with 'progressive indigenous norms and principles to create something that is uniquely African'.[8] With this in mind, the account of post-conflict justice articulated here can be described as Afro-communitarian because it is derived from the worldview and values of many sub-Saharan Africans. However, this account should not be understood as an anthropological description of specific practices, nor an *in toto* account of the justice practices of African societies.

It is also important to note that not all thought traditions and discourses from sub-Saharan Africa relate specifically to Afro-communitarianism – even the broadest generalizations acknowledge metaphysical themes that are more concerned with causation, the nature of substance, or God than they are with communal relations.[9] This being said, however, one particularly important motif in African metaphysics is harmony, which in turn has a profound impact on how the relationship between individuals and the community is understood. These notions can also be seen as vital to how one understands the individual as a person, which can be understood both in terms of harmonization with, or in relation to, the community, and as undergoing a process of ontological progression.

What is the African Approach to Community and Society?

While Afro-communitarianism is often associated with post-conflict transitions, transitions such as those in South Africa, Rwanda and Uganda, as stated above, this general worldview is far broader than just a political or legal philosophy. As such, one cannot take it as given that Afro-communitarianism provides a ready-made theory of post-conflict justice. Indeed, while Afro-communitarianism is often seen as politically relevant, this is usually as an appeal to a broader worldview or ethical theory. It is therefore necessary to articulate how Afro-communitarianism is understood in this broader range of values, norms and concepts. It must be noted that there is significant debate and disagreement as to how exactly Afro-communitarianism should best be understood but there is also broad agreement among philosophers, theorists and the public, at least with regard to the kinds of values that are most central to an Afro-communitarian worldview, namely those relating to 'harmony' and 'community', and what these entail for individuals in relation to society.

For some, rather than providing a theory of justice or ethics, Afro-communitarianism is best understood, at least initially, as an ontology or metaphysics. One such view is articulated by Mogebe Ramose, who argues that individuals are in a constant state of flux, and actively shaping both themselves and their communal environments. For Ramose, an entity cannot be separated from the actions it performs or undergoes and individuals actively participate in the world by way of metaphysical necessity.[10] Harmony becomes an ontological necessity in this worldview as there is a need for individuals to harmonize their actions with other active be-ings.[11] As a result, the need to harmonize with others also becomes ontologically necessary, as it is only through harmonizing with others that one is actively be-ing.[12] This in turn leads to the sense in which an individual can be said to be more or less a person (*umuntu*) as they can be said to be actively demonstrating their humanness (*ubuntu*) to a greater or lesser degree depending on the extent to which their be-ing is conducted in harmony with others. It is important to note here that the imperative to harmonize applies to all people (*abantu*) and not just any one particular individual in relation to a monolithic community. That is, there is not necessarily a transcendental entity with which one needs to harmonize, as there is in certain Chinese traditions, with the *dao*, or Western traditions, with God.

Given that actively be-ing is a metaphysical necessity, and that this can only be done in harmony with other entities, it is often argued that the ontological identity of the individual is determined by the way in which they are embedded in and harmonize with their community. As such the harmony of the community members may be seen as coming prior to at least some, if not all, of the individual's moral value.[13] To this end, the dignity of the individual person, which in the West is generally seen as inherent in all people, can, in this Afro-communitarian perspective, be seen as a value created, at least in part, by the necessary harmonization between individual community members.[14] This is exemplified in the isiXhosa proverb *umuntu ngumuntu ngabantu*, 'a person is a person through other people'.[15] Both strong[16] and weak[17] forms of this argument have been put forward, with scholars disagreeing on the extent to which an individual's moral worth is determined by social relations. However, there is broad agreement among scholars that, in an Afro-communitarian worldview, an individual's personhood, or moral relevance, is scalable, and to some degree dependent on the extent to which an individual participates in, and contributes positively to, their community.

It is worth noting that this is not just a descriptive, but also a normative framework. That is to say, it is not merely the case that those with stronger communal links have greater moral worth, but that individuals should aim to build and maintain harmonious relationships so as to attain fuller personhood, and, as a corollary, the purpose of communities should be to foster harmonious relationships with and between individuals. Such a framing resembles the beginnings of an Aristotelian virtue ethic; however, insofar as it does, this virtue is not held by the individual alone but by the community as a whole. In this way ontological and metaphysical discourses in the Afro-communitarian tradition often overlap with ethical considerations, but this overlap falls short of providing an overarching ethical theory as such. What we do have is an idea of moral values tied to the communal relationships that individuals have. To this end, more developed Afro-communitarian theories of ethics emphasize a need for a shared *communal identity*, *solidarity* and *harmony* between members. This reflects the privileged position which communal relationships are given in moral considerations. The manner in which these values arise is worth making explicit, as well as how philosophers have attempted to work these values into more codified ethical theories.

While individuals' (*qua* individuals) moral value is seen as less weighty in African views than in many Western views, this does not mean that persons are not the primary focus of Afro-communitarian moral values. As Wiredu argues, the Afro-communitarian moral tradition tends to be deeply humanistic, holding both that human interests are the primary source of most, if not all, value, and that human fellowship is the most basic of human needs.[18] At this point it becomes necessary to elaborate on what has thus far been referred to as 'communal relationships'. The term is often used to refer to the *voluntary* relationships one forms with either individuals in one's immediate geographical surrounds or, increasingly with the use of social media and the internet, those with whom one shares particular interests or social identities. This is not a trivial sense of the word 'community', but it does not capture the full sense with which the term is used in Afro-communitarian discourses. Rather, in the Afro-communitarian view, individuals are seen as born into communities already possessing complex social identities, made up of their kinship relationships and broader social positioning.[19] These relationships are further characterized by the various obligations owed to them as helpless infants in need of care from their immediate carers and their broader community, as well as the reciprocal obligations they owe to others.[20] These relationships, as well as an acute sense of the ultimate dependency of the human condition, lead to *communal belonging* being seen as of paramount importance.[21] From this arises the idea that human beings have, at the most basic level, common interests as a communal unit, and that the aim of moral or justice systems are to *harmonize* individual interests, that arise in the face of everyday problems, with this common interest, through constant adaptation and adjustment.[22] As such, Afro-communitarian moral theories can be characterized by *communal identity* and a nexus of obligations between community members, compelling members to act in one another's interest and giving rise to a necessary alignment of these interests, or *solidarity* with other members of the community, which together must be *harmonized* with one's own and others' individual interests.[23]

African Values in Practice

What is most clear from the above discussion is that community relations form the centrepiece of Afro-communitarian ethical concerns. As such, when individuals and communities who adopt this worldview respond to wrongdoings, they do so mainly in an attempt to safeguard, and even promote, positive communal relations between conflicting parties. This has led to an emphasis on restorative justice processes and, in particular, forgiveness,[24] albeit often a qualified forgiveness, as responses to harms inflicted upon individuals and communities. In addition, justice processes are seen as involving entire communities.

From the Afro-communitarian perspective, one of the primary ways in which crimes cause harm is through threatening the harmony of the community generally.²⁵ In light of this, Bongani Finca, a former TRC commissioner, has argued that, in the wake of a crime, it is more important to restore relationships than it is to punish the perpetrators. In an interview with Gade (2012) he states:

> Instead of pursuing punishment, you are more interested in restoring relationships. That is fundamental to *ubuntu* because *ubuntu* does not focus on what has been done to you, *ubuntu* focuses on how we can be restored together as a community, so that we can heal together. *Ubuntu* does not only concentrate on the pain that has been caused to me, but also recognizes the damage that has been done to you. In the course of what you are doing to me, you are also hurting yourself.²⁶

This implies both that the harm of a wrongdoing is not just the pain felt by the victim, but the harm this has caused to the social fabric or humanity of the wrongdoer, and that wrongdoings should be responded to in a way that restores the values they jeopardized. Pursuing punishment for such an action only serves to entrench the damage done. This motif was recurrent during the TRC, espoused by both commissioners and those testifying. One particularly striking example comes from the inquiry into the killing of the 'Gugulethu Seven'. This case involved seven young men who, thinking they were going to be receiving training to join *Umkhonto we Sizwe* (the armed wing of the African National Congress), were lured by agents of the Apartheid government into an ambush and killed.²⁷ Eyewitness reports from the event recount police executing the men at close range, including killing a man who was attempting to give himself up and shooting a man in the head while he was lying on the ground.²⁸ After giving testimony, one of the perpetrators of this event, a man of African descent, requested a private meeting with the family of those who had been killed. After confronting the man complicit in the killing of her son, Cynthia Ngweyu, one of the mothers of the victims, is quoted as having said:

> This thing called reconciliation ... if I am understanding it correctly ... if it means this perpetrator, this man who has killed Christopher Piet, if it means he becomes human again, this man, so that I, so that all of us, get our humanity back ... then I agree, then I support it all.²⁹

Ngweyu explicitly draws the connection between the crime and the damage this has done to the personhood of everyone involved. What is more, she demonstrates that, according to her understanding, reconciling with the individual who caused the disharmony allows for them all to regain their personhood.

Other accounts of this event draw attention to the importance of forgiveness in this process. In an interview with Gade, Dumisa Ntsebeza, a TRC commissioner, recounts one of the mother's responses, quoting her as saying:

> Look, there is nothing we can do now about the people who died. But one thing that causes us to feel released and liberated is the fact that you are sitting here. You are somebody and some other woman's child. You are sitting here, and you are telling how you slaughtered our children, and the mere fact that you have now found the courage to come and talk to us ... Whatever happens to your amnesty application, we have forgiven you.[30]

Here, the victim's mother, a victim in her own right, explicitly acknowledges the perpetrator's humanity in terms of his social relations, being someone's child, as well as his attempt to repair the communal relations with the victims of his crime, which she sees as making him worthy of forgiveness. These accounts together tell us that reconciliation, more than punishment, is seen as an ontological and moral necessity when one responds to crimes in the Afro-communitarian worldview.

More specifically, one can say that a corollary of the notion that humans are socially embedded, and that communal dependence is necessary for personhood, is that ostracism becomes existentially threatening. If one is isolated from one's community, one loses one's very personhood and the mechanism through which one derives meaning in life.[31] However, this loss is not borne solely by the individual. It is also an existential threat to the community. As such, reconciliation is seen as an inherent part of justice processes. Furthermore, forgiveness, and the re-establishing of interpersonal relationships between parties, is seen as necessary for this process to begin.[32] Note however that forgiveness is not sufficient to begin this process in and of itself – the perpetrators of wrongdoing need to actively denounce their actions and aim to repair the relationships that they have damaged.[33] Through this restorative process, victims and perpetrators play an active role in redeveloping their own personhood.

The above indicates that the Afro-communitarian worldview does indeed form the bases for how some traditional sub-Saharan African societies make sense of practical moral problems. Reconciliation, therefore, can form the basis of justice processes, particularly those aimed at restoration; however, it may be worth hashing out some of the semantics of the term 'reconciliation' itself, as well as some of the more universally accepted concepts associated with it. The term is often used to refer to the process or action by which an individual or group comes to terms with an aspect of their life or history, as in, 'She reconciled herself to her fate.'[34] This is not the sense in which 'reconciliation' is being used here. Rather, 'reconciliation' as I am using it refers to relationships between people or groups who were formally in a state of discord or enmity with one another.[35] A second, but important point is that reconciliation does not constitute a final aim for the society as a whole.[36] Rather, this is merely the aim of a post-conflict justice process. The aims of post-conflict justice are distinct from ordinary justice processes insomuch as they are concerned with mass wrongdoings, systemic or institutionalized violence and oppression, and breakdowns of social order, and this is also applicable to an Afro-communitarian approach. Specifically, while the aim of an Afro-communitarian post-conflict justice process is national reconciliation, the aim of more ordinary justice processes in the Afro-communitarian view would be something akin to maintaining harmony, unity or cohesion.[37] These aims can be seen as distinct in two related but differing ways. First, national reconciliation, as articulated here, is a process that takes place after a period of conflict, while cohesion does not require a prior state of conflict.[38] Second, and perhaps more importantly, national reconciliation is a process undertaken after a systematic breakdown in relationships has occurred and not merely individual disruptions to an otherwise harmonious system. To this end, while the morpheme {re-} indicates that there must exist a prior friendly relation, this is generally not considered necessary when discussing national reconciliation. That is, one can still speak of reconciliation if the parties concerned have never had a shared communal identity, provided they have been in a state of conflict that can be transformed.

Conclusion

The Afro-communitarian approach to post-conflict justice I have laid out provides the basis for post-conflict justice processes. This approach holds that a central aim of both individuals and communities is, and should be, to harmonize with one another, and that such harmony is a necessary aspect of one's personhood. A corollary of this is that one can be seen to be more or less of a person, depending on how they are able to harmonize with their community, but also that a community can fail in its functions as a community if it fails to harmonize and grant personhood to its members. Such a worldview and ontology create the ethical imperatives for individuals to create a sense of communal identity, to align their wants and interests in solidarity with one another, and to act in harmony to achieve these. It is because of this need for harmony, shared identity and developing joint interests that ostracizing individuals from society as a response to wrongdoings becomes unsatisfactory. Such an approach undermines the purpose and function of a community as a harmonious coordination of individuals. For the Afro-communitarian, responses to wrongdoings must address the pain and suffering caused by a wrongdoing in such a way that restores the relationships between the conflicting parties, and if necessary, repairs the damage done to the social fabric. In post-conflict societies, which are characterized by collective and institutionalized wrongdoings, which have damaged or jeopardized social relations to the extent that they have resulted in direct violence, the Afro-communitarian therefore prioritizes reconciliation as a crucial outcome of any justice process. This is not, of course, a complete picture of the post-conflict justice process, not least because even from a theoretical perspective one must acknowledge the nuances provided by specific local contexts. However, this conceptualization can form a basis for an understanding of transitional justice processes in Africa, and grounds to promote a reconciliatory approach to peacebuilding globally.

Notes

1 John Paul Lederach, *The Journey Toward Reconciliation* (Scottsdale: Herald Press, 1999), 36; Ruti G. Teitel, *Transitional Justice* (Oxford: Oxford University Press, 2000), 65–6; Pablo de Greiff, 'Theorizing Transitional Justice', in Rosemary Nagy, Melissa S. Williams and Jon Elster, eds, *Transitional Justice* (New York: New York University Press, 2012), 63; Colleen Murphy, *The Conceptual Foundations of Transitional Justice* (Cambridge: Cambridge University Press, 2017), 26.

2 For a fuller exploration of post-conflict, or transitional, justice, including the distinctions between this and other forms of justice, such as retributive, corrective and distributive justice, see Murphy, *The Conceptual Foundations of Transitional Justice*, 27; David C. Gray, 'A No-Excuse Approach to Transitional Justice: Reparations as Tools of Extraordinary Justice', *Washington University Law Review* (Vol. 87, 1043, 2010), 75; John Paul Lederach, *Building Peace: Sustainable Reconciliation in Divided Societies* (Washington: United States Institute of Peace Press, 1997), 28–31.

3 The term *'ubuntu'* has cognates in most Niger-Congo languages. In South Africa's nine official languages from Niger-Congo family: *'ubuntu'* is used in isiXhosa and isiZulu; *'botho'* is used in Setswana, Sesotho and Sepedi; *'uvhutu'* is used in Tshivenda; *'uvunhu'* is used in Xitsonga; *'ubundu'* is used in Ndebele; and *'ubunftu'* is used in siSwati.

4 Christian Gade, 'The Historical Development of the Written Discourses on Ubuntu', *South African Journal of Philosophy* (Vol. 30, 3, 2011), 303–29, at p. 304.

5 Christian Gade, 'What is Ubuntu? Different Interpretations among South Africans of African Descent', *South African Journal of Philosophy* (Vol. 31, 3, 2012), 484–503, at pp. 487–8.

6 For some perspective on the scale of this phenomenon, I have in the past seen the word '*ubuntu*' used in the names of an investment fund, a construction company, a window blinds supplier, a furniture store, a type of software and a paper supplier.

7 I do not discuss this type of communitarianism here, but for an example and a more illustrative account, one can look at Michael Walzer, *Spheres of Justice: A Defense of Pluralism and Equality* (New York: Basics Books, 1983).

8 Tim Murithi, 'African Approaches to Building Peace and Social Solidarity', *African Journal on Conflict Resolution* (Vol. 6, 2, 2006), 9–34, at p. 14.

9 For a more detailed discussion on these other themes, see L. J. Teffo and A. P. J. Roux, 'Themes in African Metaphysics', in P. H. Coetzee and A. P. J. Roux, eds, *The African Philosophy Reader*, 2nd ed. (New York: Routledge, 2003), 192–208.

10 Mogebe B. Ramose, 'The Philosophy of Ubuntu and Ubuntu as a Philosophy', in Coetzee and Roux, *The African Philosophy Reader*, 270–80, at pp. 272, 275.

11 Ibid., 273–3. Ramose uses the term 'be-ing' to emphasize the gerundive nature of this concept, in which one actively exists, or is both existing and 'doing' existence.

12 Ibid.

13 Ifeanyi A. Menkiti, 'Person and Community in African Traditional Thought', in Richard A. Wright, ed., *African Philosophy: An Introduction* (Lanham: University Press of America, 1984), 171–81, at p. 171.

14 Kwasi Wiredu, *Cultural Universals and Particulars: An African Perspective* (Bloomington: Indiana University Press, 1996), 159–60.

15 In Sepedi this would be written as '*motho ke motho ka batho*'. These translations are my own. These phrases are often rendered in English as, 'a person is a person *because* of other people'. I prefer the word 'through', however, as it emphasizes the processual nature of this relationship.

16 See Menkiti, 'Person and Community', 171–81.

17 See Kwame Gyekye, 'Person and Community in African Thought', in Heinz Kimmerle, ed., *I, We, and Body: First Joint Symposium of Philosophers from Africa and from the Netherlands at Rotterdam on March 10, 1989* (Amsterdam: John Benjamins Publishing, 1989), 47–60. See also Michael Onyebuchi Eze, 'What is African Communitarianism? Against consensus as a regulative ideal', *South African Journal of Philosophy* (Vol. 27, 4, 2008), 386–99.

18 Kwasi Wiredu, 'The Moral Foundations of an African Culture', in Coetzee and Roux, *The African Philosophy Reader*, 338–9.

19 Wiredu, *Cultural Universals and Particulars*, 158.

20 Wiredu, *Cultural Universals and Particulars*, 158–9.

21 Wiredu, 'The Moral Foundations', 340.

22 Ibid., 341.

23 Thaddeus Metz, 'South Africa's Truth and Reconciliation Commission in the Light of Ubuntu: A comprehensive appraisal', in M. Swart and K. van Marle, eds,

The Limits of Transition: The South African Truth and Reconciliation Commission 20 Years on (Leiden: Brill Nijhoff, 2017), 221–52, at p. 225.

24 It may be tempting to ascribe any emphasis on forgiveness to the influence of Christianity in sub-Saharan Africa and not the Afro-communitarian worldview. However, I feel that the discussions in this and previous sections make it sufficiently clear that an emphasis on forgiveness can arise out of an Afro-communitarian understanding of positive relationships as paramount to human well-being. Comparing Christian and Afro-communitarian conceptualizations of forgiveness is beyond the scope of this essay, but for a more detailed discussion, see Antjie Krog, '"This thing called reconciliation …" forgiveness as part of an interconnectedness-towards-wholeness', *South African Journal of Philosophy* (Vol. 27, 4, 2008), 353–66.

25 Egbeke Aja, 'Crime and Punishment: An indigenous African experience', *The Journal of Value Inquiry* (Vol. 31, 1997), 353–68, at pp. 355–6.

26 Gade, 'What is Ubuntu?', 494.

27 *TRC Final Report*, Vol. 3 (Cape Town: CTP Book Printers, 1998), 451.

28 Ibid.

29 Krog, '"This thing called reconciliation"', 356.

30 Gade, 'What is Ubuntu?', 491–2.

31 Aja, 'Crime and Punishment', 355.

32 Krog, '"This thing called reconciliation"', 359.

33 Krog, '"This thing called reconciliation"', 357–8.

34 It is rare for this sense of 'reconciliation' to be used in post-conflict justice discourses, but it is used by some. See, for example, Susan Dwyer, 'Reconciliation for Realists', *Ethics & International Affairs* (Vol. 13, 1, 1999), 81–98. Dwyer argues that this too is an important aspect of post-conflict peacebuilding, but I do not feel this sense is captured by an Afro-communitarian understanding and is thus beyond the scope of this paper.

35 De Greiff, 'Theorizing Transitional Justice', 51–2.

36 Metz, 'South Africa's Truth and Reconciliation Commission', 227.

37 Ibid., 226–7.

38 Thaddeus Metz, 'A Theory of National Reconciliation: Some insights from Africa', in C. Corradetti, N. Eisikovits and J. V. Rotondi, eds, *Theorizing Transitional Justice* (Farnham: Ashgate, 2015), 120–2.

5

The 'View from Below' from Above: A Critical Genealogy of Settler Christianity in Oceania[1]

ANDREW CLARK-HOWARD

The lands now called Australia and New Zealand were among the last significant landmasses to be colonized and settled by Europeans. Inspired by Portuguese and Spanish empires before them, Britain set sail into lands previously unknown to Europe in search of wealth, global influence and *Lebensraum*, 'living space', in which both an overpopulated industrializing nation (and a significant number of its social derelicts) could be resettled. Within such a project came Christianity – missionaries following the 'webs of empire' that developed under this age of expansionism in order to convert and Christianize indigenous communities under colonial rule.[2] Yet the distinct project of settler colonialism is a type of colonialism in which colonizers 'came to stay', developing forms of national and religious identity premised on the displacement and eventual eradication of indigenous peoples.[3] Alongside missionaries, then, British settlers brought with them forms of Christianity that they entrenched into the social fabric of their new colonial societies from which the modern nations Australia and New Zealand directly descend. Any account of justice within the wide region of Oceania, including Australia and New Zealand, requires rigorous interrogation of the project of settler colonialism and its ongoing affects within Oceania today.[4] Furthermore, any *theological* account of justice in these lands requires an unflinching appraisal of the way in which Christian beliefs aided and abetted the settler colonial project.

In his famous reflection 'After Ten Years', written to fellow conspirators in 1942, German theologian and political dissident Dietrich Bonhoeffer wrote: 'It remains an experience of incomparable value that we have for once learned to see the great events of world history from below, from the perspective of the outcasts, the suspects, the maltreated, the powerless, the oppressed and reviled, in short from the perspective of the suffering.'[5] Writing as an upper-middle-class elite in early twentieth-century Germany, Bonhoeffer's reflections here on the *Kirchenkampf* and resistance to Nazism speak of the ways in which his experiences have placed him in a completely different social and political positionality and so taught him valuable lessons about how to 'do justice to life in all its dimensions and in this way affirm it'.[6] From prison, Bonhoeffer would later write of the 'world come of age' – attending to the conditions of European modernity in which humanity came to believe they could live without God and instead identify God in the suffering and desolation of modern life.[7] Speaking at the far end of Europe's ravaging of the New World before Europe turned the tools of colonialism onto itself in the Holocaust, Bonhoeffer sought to imagine a post-war German Christianity that could honestly and openly face its complicity in the violence of the modern world.[8]

Within his wide reception, Bonhoeffer is generally understood as a theologian who spoke poignantly to issues of justice within his own life and work. Due to his ideological and political resistance to National Socialism – a resistance accentuated by his remarkable biography, imprisonment and execution – Bonhoeffer is often appealed to in addressing contemporary issues of justice as varied as race and racism, anthropogenic climate change, or politics and globalization.[9] Despite this important work, Bonhoeffer's theological legacy is not without its limitations, particularly as it relates to his positionality as a theologian of power and privilege. Gustavo Gutiérrez, for example, argues that Bonhoeffer's new-found 'view from below' only took him so far in that he correctly identifies the various exploitations of modernity without being able to truly move beyond them.[10] In this way, Bonhoeffer's theological vision alone cannot speak to the array of causes for justice that face our contemporary world.

This chapter therefore seeks to take Bonhoeffer's theological legacy as paradigmatic for those of us who participate in the conversation of theology as settler peoples in Oceania, especially within Australia and New Zealand. Bonhoeffer was a theologian of privilege who at various points within his own life and work grappled with his privileged position in the world. Yet, as I shall argue with and beyond Bonhoeffer: divorced from concrete attention to the varieties of colonial, racial and economic injustices that characterize modern settler states in Oceania, one's entanglements with power and privilege upend seemingly straightforward Christian confessions and ideas about justice. I therefore argue, with attention to my own context as a settler person in Oceania, that Bonhoeffer's 'view from below' is most useful as a diagnosis for theologians who, like Bonhoeffer, inhabit positions of power and privilege. Drawing from Gutiérrez's analysis of the limitations of Bonhoeffer's legacy, I seek to reread Bonhoeffer's theology as a wrestling with power from within the context of power. Such attention to the 'view from below' as a person who recognizes their social location 'from *above*', so to speak, draws settler Christians away from their assumptions and therefore demonstrates important lessons about the limits colonial history places on our categories of knowing. Speaking as a settler Christian in Oceania requires the willingness to be disrupted and disturbed by indigenous counter-testimonies that upend ready assumptions about what the work of decolonial justice requires.

The Limitations of Bonhoeffer's Theological Legacy

In his 1979 essay, 'The Limitations of Modern Theology: On a Letter of Dietrich Bonhoeffer', Gutiérrez argues that while Bonhoeffer's famous prison writings on the 'world come of age' rightly attempt to register the consequences of modernity for Christianity, his insights are limited by their lack of concrete analysis into the wider structural violence that attends to modernity itself.[11] This is because the Enlightenment, Gutiérrez avers, cannot be understood divorced from the 'bourgeois revolutions' of modern capitalism which 'opened up an age of important changes in the concrete life conditions of the Christian churches in the West'.[12] Though Bonhoeffer squarely challenged his contemporaries to account for the transformation of a religionless age, he failed to concretize his 'view from below' via specific political, social and economic analysis. Devoid of such analysis, Bonhoeffer's prison theology therefore risks falling short of achieving its own ends, and so requires further contextualization into the various conditions of structural power that characterize the modern age. Though he made a start, and despite his acts of resistance to Nazism, such experiences 'did not lead Bonhoeffer to a deeper analysis of the "crisis in today's society"'.[13]

The limitations of Bonhoeffer's theological legacy, identified by Gutiérrez, resonates with criticisms of dominant forms of theological practice and discourse within Oceania. Upulo Lumā Vaai, for example, criticizes theological education within Pasifika contexts for their unwillingness to engage in the radical political implications of the gospel: 'The result is that theology has become an upper-class product that weaponizes the powerful while at the same time endorsing a culture of conformity' amid the settled arrangements of Pacific Christianity and its colonial past.[14] Similarly, John Flett has identified the ways in which a significant portion of published theological research across Oceania fails to meaningfully engage in local issues. In a longitudinal study on three major Australasian theology journals across the last 50 years, Flett found that a mere 1.89% of published articles mention or engage with material related to settler colonialism or indigenous theology in any way.[15] The absence of sustained attention to the ongoing histories of colonization speaks of the profound limitations of a white settler Christianity that is unable to reckon with its past nor speak with integrity in the present.

Such resonances between Gutiérrez's critique of Bonhoeffer and settler colonial theology in Oceania help identify what is required for a theology of justice from the perspective of being a settler person today. Gutiérrez, Vaai and Flett all speak to the need for modern theology to engage deeply with the deformed conditions of colonial and capitalistic modernity in which Western Christianity has played a fundamental part. This brings us back to Bonhoeffer's understanding of the 'view from below'. Unlike Gutiérrez, I do not speak from the perspective of dispossessed people. Instead, as a settler person living in Oceania, my ancestry, or *whakapapa*, lies with the various British subjects that arrived on indigenous land under the conditions of British colonization and conquest.[16] 'Whakapapa' is a Māori word that loosely refers to genealogy or ancestry but might best be understood as the 'process' in which a person comes to be, recognizing the various lineages, locations and geographies that place a person in the world today.[17] Reflecting on this whakapapa in both Bonhoeffer's life and in my own reveals important insights for a contemporary theology of justice in Oceania.

Doing Theology as a Settler Person in Oceania

When British explorers and surveyors arrived in the lands now called Australia and New Zealand, the project of European colonialism and empire was centuries old, as part of Europe's wider social, racial and theological imaginary since at least the Age of Discovery and Europe's ravaging of Africa and the New World in America.[18] While the stories and histories of these empires are vast and complex,[19] I want to offer a brief reflection on some of the Christian colonial histories that relate to the lands I currently live and work upon.

I live and work on Burramattagal land in Parramatta, the so-called second city centre of Sydney, Australia, after moving here from New

Zealand to pursue doctoral studies in theology. Before more recent urban sprawl brought Parramatta and Sydney together into one metropolitan area, Parramatta was a critical early British settlement in the colony of New South Wales, particularly as it related to the Church of England mission launched in New Zealand. From London, the Church Missionary Society (CMS) appointed Samuel Marsden – Senior Chaplain to the New South Wales government and the founding Rector at St John's Paramatta (the oldest Anglican parish in Australia) – as the Society's Agent to New Zealand. Leaving Parramatta in 1814, Marsden preached his famous Christmas sermon at Rangihoua, often recognized and celebrated among churches as the 'arrival of the gospel in New Zealand', and visited the new colony seven more times to help establish the CMS mission.

According to the journals and records of Marsden and his companions, the events that took place in the lead-up to the service included 'entertainment' from local Māori in the form of a 'mock battle'.[20] The Christmas service itself was preceded by a bewildering 'sham fight' which the British travellers found perplexing; then, following the sermon, there was a similar response in honour of 'the solemn spectacle [local Māori] had witnessed'.[21] Yet as Alison Jones and Kuni Kaa Jenkins point out, what was far more likely occurring were processes of Māori welcome and custom – processes of *haka pōwhiri* (ceremonial welcome) and *whaikōrero* (oratory) which Marsden did not have access to, least of all due to his lack of te reo Māori (Māori language).[22] Marsden, however, as assumed 'master' of the scene unfolding before him, is confident to 'know' and name what he believes is a form of entertainment for his arrival rather than a complex exchange on the basis of *tikanga Māori* (Māori protocol). Marsden assumes that he has come to preach a Christmas sermon and conduct an Anglican service, whereas his hosts far more likely understood their gathering as a *hui* (meeting) with a foreign *rangatira* (leader).[23]

Within this event – and countless others like it across Christian colonial history – one can observe the ways in which settler peoples centre their own understandings of the world and, conversely, denigrate and patronize indigenous ways of knowing. As Willie Jennings writes, 'it is as though Christianity, wherever it went in the modern colonies, inverted its sense of hospitality.'[24] Instead of seeing themselves as guests in a different land – needing to therefore acknowledge their ignorance in submission to their hosts – British missionaries and settlers centred their own understandings of the world and so refused to see what truly lay before them. It was precisely this process of centring one's own assumed knowledge that so often resulted in the dehumanizing of the indigenous other and therefore offered justification for their subjugation and oppression.

Indeed, to live and work as a settler person in Oceania is to live amid the ongoing dynamics of settler colonialism which continue to shape cultural values, ecclesiastical and educational life, and the manifest inequalities which make up our current social orders.[25] Across the lands in which I live and work, the entanglements of settler colonialism and Christianity continue to profoundly shape theology and theological education. The various institutions I have studied at bear the names of British colonizers and missionaries. My current institution was named after Charles Napier Sturt, the famed British officer and explorer whose expeditions of Australia were fundamental in opening the continent to land confiscation and exploitation under British rule.[26] My previous institution is named after William Carey, a British Baptist minister and the so-called 'father of the modern mission movements', whose own understandings of indigenous people lay trapped within primitivist and racist notions of indigeneity and the supposed superiority of European civilization.[27] Examining the social, racial and political positionality in both Bonhoeffer's life and my own is fundamental in imagining a contemporary theology of justice within an Oceanic context.

Reflecting on these legacies, I can locate myself in relation to the 'great events of world history' which Bonhoeffer speaks of. This means that when I turn towards colonial history today, I do not find myself amid 'the outcasts, the suspects, the maltreated, the powerless, the oppressed and reviled'.[28] Instead, my own whakapapa lies elsewhere. In this way, Bonhoeffer is a theological ancestor, someone who, like me, can only ever speak of the 'view from below' from *above*. Like Bonhoeffer, my own life and theological formation is entangled with the various exploitations of the modern colonial world in which I live and so, as Gutiérrez points out, must be openly and radically faced for a theological account of justice.

Bonhoeffer's 1933 Christology Lectures and the 'Proletarian Christ'

While Bonhoeffer's prison writings have long been looked to for their radical political insights, less attention has been given to his earlier academic writings. Of these, his 1933 Christology lectures are fundamental in understanding how the person of Jesus Christ functions for Bonhoeffer in determining theological and political questions.[29] For Bonhoeffer, the person of Jesus Christ is determinative of fundamental questions about the character of God, humanity and human community, right ethical action, and the nature of the world. And if Christ reveals anything about such matters, it is a revelation of God's own suffering and weakness in the world, taking form not in glory, to repeat Luther's insight, but rather, 'the God-human of history is always, already, the God-human who is humiliated, from the manger to the cross ... He comes among us humans not in μορΦὴ θεοῦ but rather incognito, as a beggar among beggars, an outcast among outcasts.'[30]

Within the Christology lectures, Bonhoeffer develops his understanding of Christ incognito in a brief, enigmatic framing of Christ as the one who 'stands beside members of the proletariat'.[31] The full excerpt reads:

> But what does all this mean in concrete terms? Human beings today still cannot get around the figure of Jesus Christ. They have to deal with him ... For example, in the world of the proletariat Christ may appear to be as finished off as the church and bourgeois society as a whole. There seems to be no occasion for giving Jesus a qualified place. The church is the stultifying institution that sanctions the capitalist system. But this is not the case. The proletariat actually disassociates Jesus from his church and its religion. When the proletariat says that Jesus is a good human being, it means more than the bourgeoisie means when it says that Jesus is God. Jesus is present in factory halls as a worker among workers, in politics as the perfect idealist, in the life of the proletariat as a good human being. He stands beside members of the proletariat as a fighter in their ranks against the capitalist enemy.[32]

This passage is rich and provocative, and, in typical Bonhoeffer fashion, fragmentary in a way that opens itself to a diversity of interpretation. On the surface, the confession that 'Jesus is God' is fundamental to historic Christianity. This means that Christ's being a 'good human being', while also true, risks seeing Christ as merely another religious teacher and not the very incarnate Son of God. Yet Bonhoeffer argues that such assumptions only go so far when one considers the positionality of those making them. In fact, when the proletariat, in their struggle against the exploitation and alienation of capitalism, recognize Christ among themselves as 'worker among workers', they name something more important than mere lip-service to Christian orthodoxy: Christ is the one hidden among the suffering and the dispossessed. Conversely, the bourgeois class, those benefiting from the very same system of exploitation, misidentify Christ's activity in the world. The bourgeoisie are therefore deluded, assuming they recognize Christ as God yet do not see him in the life of the worker.

The moral implications are startling: because of their participation in the capitalist system and its exploitation of the proletariat, the confessions of bourgeois Christianity are worthless. In other words, true knowledge of God's workings in the world is not to be found within the confessions of the powerful, even in a seemingly straightforward confession like 'Jesus is God'. Christ's risen presence, then, is experienced by those entangled with class power as judgement and condemnation, as a 'fighter' against the exploitations of the rich, even those who identify themselves among the faithful fold of God in the church.

This is also not the only time within Bonhoeffer's personal experiences and wider theological corpus where the dynamics of class struggle are brought to the fore. Bonhoeffer offers a longer treatment, for example, of the relationship between the 'church and proletariat' in the thesis version of his doctoral dissertation *Sanctorum Communio*, proposing that the alienation of capitalism and its commodification of the worker ought to be met by the church-community in Christ who overcomes isolation.[33] In a 1931 report on his studies in New York, Bonhoeffer connects the class struggles of the labour movement with the experiences of the Black church, arguing that they may be understood as 'proletarian churches, perhaps the only ones in all America', and holds white, bourgeois Christianity accountable for the disillusionment of the younger Black generation 'who see how Christian preaching made their fathers so meek in the face of their incomparably harsh fate'.[34] Later in life, Bonhoeffer also returns to the question of class in his unfinished fiction writings in prison.[35] His fiction writings display poignant and unresolved tensions in his own theological and political imagination at the time, reflecting various stories in which characters encounter each other across the lines of class and struggle to connect.

Yet tensions remain. While it is true that Bonhoeffer spent time among working-class communities – particularly within his youth work in New York and Berlin in the early 1930s – it is also true that, as Gutiérrez writes, the 'protest movements of the poor, from the late Middle Ages on, find no place in Bonhoeffer's historical focus, nor does the contemporaneous labor movement'.[36] Even in reflecting about his experiences among dispossessed communities, Bonhoeffer's Christology continues to contain a certain abstraction.[37] While he offers a provocative explication of Christ incognito in terms of class struggle, Bonhoeffer does not actually engage in voices from the labour movement or speak from the positionality of his proletarian students or peers. He remains still at some distance from the communities in which he speaks, as Gutiérrez maintains, never drawing these experiences into the material centre of his theological discourse.[38]

Connecting Bonhoeffer's context to my own, similar parallels can be drawn. The long legacy of settler Christian beliefs are premised on the idea that white settlers can know and access forms of indigenous knowledges without learning from indigenous people themselves or taking seriously the structural violence that now attends all settler-indigenous encounters. By failing to draw such attention to the entanglements of power and violence within theological knowing itself, there is a limit to how much those who benefit from power can actually speak to the concrete work of justice. Neither Bonhoeffer nor Marsden nor myself will ever truly know what it means to speak 'from below' given that our own location within history will always be 'from above'. As Bonhoeffer suggests within the Christology lectures, Christ's disruptive voice therefore must be heard in the real, material voices of dispossessed communities in ways that move beyond Bonhoeffer himself. This task often upsets one's settled assumptions about God's presence in the world, even within beliefs that appear self-evident.

Speaking of Christ in the Modern (Colonial) World

In his analysis of Kaytetye filmmaker and artist Warwick Thornton, trawloolway theologian Garry Worete Deverell offers a reflection on dominant forms of settler Christologies and white images of Jesus. In his exposition 'Stranded 2011', Thornton depicts himself as a Christ-like figure hanging on a lightbox cross suspended over various desert landscapes, the bright artificiality of the cross standing in contrast to the more muted, natural surroundings.[39] Reflecting on these images and their reference to Christ's crucifixion, Deverell recalls Thornton's comments:

> Well, look, the poor bloke's been stuck up there for, what, 2000 odd years. And those Christians won't let him down, poor bugger; they're the mob keeping him up there. Can't you just bring him down and he can sit on the chair with us, rather than him being up there? Time to pull him down and he can sit in the pews with us.[40]

Thornton's comments expose how settler Christologies that emphasize the suffering of God on the cross can imagine Christ alienated and detached from the concrete lives of Aboriginal communities and, specifically, from the land that has cared for such communities. That Christians themselves are 'the mob keeping him up there' might even reveal a troublesome valorization of suffering and an acceptance of oppressive circumstances.[41] Referencing Bonhoeffer's famous prison adage that 'only the suffering God can help' – often used to uphold such a theology of suffering that does not account for varied racial and gendered experiences – Deverell writes:

> Thornton's wry observation potentially inverts the popular wisdom of those who endlessly trot out Bonhoeffer's aphorism ... Perhaps colonizers need the crucified Christ because, as Moltmann famously argued, the cross is God's critique of colonial empires. Indigenous people, however, need the resurrected Christ more urgently, because only a living and powerful Christ can ally with us in the struggle for a better world.[42]

Deverell here speaks to the ways in which one's view 'from below' or 'from above' reveals different insights on common theological loci. As Deverell identifies, perhaps the powerful need the cross precisely because Christ's crucifixion means death to human distortions of power and oppression. Yet speaking from the perspective of an indigenous person in Australia, other forms of Christology are required 'in the struggle for a better world'.

The above analysis demonstrates how settler peoples, in centring their own experience of the world, often refuse to submit and learn from indigenous peoples and land. As Deverell identifies, even the 'theology of crisis', which emerges out of the shock of twentieth-century European history, often employed as a response to issues of justice and oppression, can centre one particular type of (privileged, European) experience over and against other perspectives and positionalities.[43] Such perspectives within the confines of settler colonialism in Oceania therefore need to be continually unsettled by the counter-testimony of indigenous theologies and responses. To move beyond Bonhoeffer by reworking his understanding of Christ incognito within my own context, then, 'When an *indigenous* person says that Jesus is a good human being, it means more than when a *colonizer* says that Jesus is God.' This provocative modification of Bonhoeffer's understanding of Christ incognito could easily repeat the very dangers of abstraction that I earlier identified. However, by listening to indigenous perspectives such as Thornton and Deverell, I seek to attend to indigenous Christologies on their own terms. Such attention follows the logic of Bonhoeffer's understanding of Christ incognito by concrete investigation into the conditions of settler colonialism and its violent performances within settler-indigenous encounters.

This modification of Bonhoeffer's understanding of the 'proletarian Christ' incognito as an 'indigenous Christ' incognito is taken as a specific diagnosis to white settler Christians and offers a contextual theology of justice *for* settler persons, just as Deverell's insights, among others, offer a contextual theology of justice for indigenous Australians. As Michael Mawson has recently demonstrated, 'at least two different Christologies or understandings of Christ are needed in the aftermath of colonization, reflecting two standpoints or experiences'.[44] Indigenous theologians, for example, might seek to understand Christ in light of their own traditions and knowledges, reinterpreting or relating to Christian theology in light of indigenous worldviews and the cultural sovereignty ignored and suppressed by the colonial state.[45] Settler Christians inhabit a different positionality in which 'we need images and understandings of Christ that can interrupt strategies of avoidance', resisting the temptation to smooth over one's entanglements in colonial violence and history.[46] That Christ appears among the life of indigenous peoples disrupts the assumptions about Jesus that settlers often make, identifying Christ and Christianity within the confines of settler colonialism and its abject violence to indigenous peoples, land and tradition.[47]

With such qualifications, encountering the 'indigenous Christ' incognito from the perspective of a white settler person in Oceania has radical implications. Most fundamentally, the indigenous Christ reveals to white settlers the ways in which we are profoundly blinded to God's presence in history by our own collusions with the structural violence and exploitation of the settler colonial project. The implication here must be taken in its full force: when settler churches and theologians refuse to divest from the ongoing benefits of settler colonialism, even their most basic confessions of Christ's being God are worthless. Settler colonialism needs to be actively dismantled because of its heinous effects on indigenous peoples, but *also* because of the ways it blinds settlers to Christ's presence in the world and so misidentifies Christ with the status quo.

Settler encounters with the indigenous Christ therefore limit and restrict easy recourse to ideas about justice itself, lest such strategies become yet another way to assert settler control. For even those notable witnesses such as Bonhoeffer, the danger consistently remains that without detailed attention to the structures of social, class and racial exploitation that make up our world today, we continue to risk blaspheming Christ's name even in our proclamation of his being God. In this way, the work of justice for settler Christians in Oceania and beyond first requires an honest and uncomfortable interrogation into how one's faith, and its ready assumptions about the nature of reality, came to be within the modern, colonial world. Tracing this whakapapa reveals just how blind settler Christianity remains to Christ incognito among indigenous communities.

In their reading of Marsden's arrival to Rangihoua, Jones and Kaa Jenkins assert that, contrary to popular settler understandings of the events that occurred, 'there was no sermon' just as there was no 'sham fight', because Marsden's words only make sense as a sermon within contexts in which they would be understood as such.[48] Two accounts, therefore, arise regarding what happened that day in 1814 when Christianity 'arrived' in Aotearoa. One account views Marsden as the active and powerful agent, arriving to a foreign land to preach the gospel and conduct a Christmas service. This is the story of the 'sermon' and the 'fight'. The other foregrounds the indigenous hosts of this encounter – Māori – who conducted a *pōwhiri* and *hui* in order to welcome and relate to this newcomer. Might it be the case, Jones questions, that 'two hundred years later' Māori are *'still waiting for a positive response from [settlers] to that first powhiri'*?[49] Or, is it the case that we are 'still largely *unable* to see or understand the *powhiri*, or to participate in it properly or positively?'[50] In much the same way, we might here ask: does the indigenous Christ demand a response still not recognized by settler Christians in their collusions with violence? Jones concludes: 'The sham fight and the sermon, of course, can be found in our written stories about ourselves; the powhiri and the hui can not ... yet.'[51]

Notes

1 I want to acknowledge all those who read draft versions of this chapter and whose feedback improved it dramatically, especially that of Christopher Whyte, Stephanie Chan and Jaimee van Gemerden.

2 See Tony Ballantyne, *Webs of Empire: Locating New Zealand's Colonial Past* (Wellington: Bridget Williams Books, 2012).

3 Jane Carey and Ben Silverstein, 'Thinking With and Beyond Settler Colonial Studies: New Histories After the Postcolonial', *Postcolonial Studies* (Vol. 23, 1, 2020), 1. 'The basic precepts of "settler" colonialism as a distinct form of European empire are famously defined by Australian historian and theorist Patrick Wolfe as such: colonial invasion as a "structure not an event," premised on a "logic of elimination" of Indigenous peoples; invasion followed by settlement with the intent that settlers "destroy to replace".' See Patrick Wolfe, 'Settler Colonialism and the Elimination of the Native', *Journal of Genocide Research* (Vol. 8, 4, 2006), 387–409.

4 Oceania at its widest definition refers to the regions of Australasia, Polynesia and Melanesia. Australia and New Zealand, the two contexts in which I live and work, are unique within this region in their status as British colonies with white settler majorities.

5 Dietrich Bonhoeffer, 'After Ten Years', in *Letters and Papers from Prison*, ed. John W. de Gruchy, trans. Isabel Best et al., *DBWE* 8 (Minneapolis: Fortress, 2010), 52.

6 Bonhoeffer, 'After Ten Years', 52.

7 See, for example, his letter to Eberhard Bethge on 8 June 1944, in Bonhoeffer, *Letters and Papers*, 428.

8 Though Bonhoeffer's precise knowledge of extermination camps during the War may be uncertain, the basic colonial and genocidal structure of Nazism can be observed within the movement's earliest writings. See, for example, the connection between Hitler's articulation of *Lebensraum* and manifest destiny in North America: Timothy Snyder, *Black Earth: The Holocaust as History and Warning* (London: Vintage, 2016), 12–21.

9 Recent examples include: Ross E. Halbach, *Bonhoeffer and the Racialized Church* (Waco: Baylor University Press, 2020); Dianne P. Rayson, *Bonhoeffer and Climate Change: Theology and Ethics for the Anthropocene* (Lanham: Lexington Books/Fortress Academic, 2021); Esther D. Reed, *The Limit of Responsibility: Dietrich Bonhoeffer's Ethics for a Globalizing Era* (London: Bloomsbury T&T Clark, 2018).

10 Gustavo Gutiérrez, 'The Limitations of Modern Theology: On a Letter of Dietrich Bonhoeffer', in *The Power of the Poor in History: Selected Writings*, trans. Robert R. Barr (Maryknoll: Orbis Books, 1983), 222–34.

11 The essay first appeared as: Gustavo Gutiérrez, 'Los límites de la teología moderna: Un texto de Bonhoeffer', *Concilium* (No. 145, 1979), 222–36.

12 Gutiérrez, 'The Limitations of Modern Theology', 222.

13 Gutiérrez, 'The Limitations of Modern Theology', 229. See also Chung Hyun Kyung's incisive critique of the limitations of Bonhoeffer's legacy in her paper from the VII International Bonhoeffer Congress: 'Dear Dietrich Bonhoeffer: A Letter', in *Bonhoeffer for a New Day: Theology in a Time of Transition*, ed. John W. De Gruchy (Grand Rapids: Eerdmans, 1997), 9–19.

14 Upolu Lumā Vaai, 'From *Atutasi* to *Atulasi*: Relational Theologizing and Why Pacific Islanders Think and Theologize Differently', in *Theologies from the Pacific*, ed. Jione Havea (Cham: Palgrave Macmillan, 2021), 238.

15 John G. Flett, 'Plotting an Oceanic Voice: A Longitudinal Review and Analysis of Regional Theologising', *Colloquium* (Vol. 54, 1, 2022), 5–60. Flett specifically identifies the outsized reflection on Bonhoeffer's theology within Australasian theology, reflecting that German theology and theologians receive far greater attention than any indigenous traditions. For a rich reflection on this dynamic, see also Peter Kline, 'Dietrich Bonhoeffer: Faith as Sovereign Attention', *Anglican Focus*, 5 April 2019, https://anglicanfocus.org.au/2019/04/05/dietrich-bonhoeffer-faith-as-unsovereign-attention/ (accessed 7/03/2024).

16 For a reflection on the entanglements of settler colonialism and Christianity written from within the whakapapa of two white settlers in New Zealand, see Andrew Picard and Andrew Clark-Howard, 'The Christian Settler Imaginary: Repentant Remembrances of Christianity's Entanglement with Settler Colonialism in Aotearoa New Zealand', *Practical Theology* (Vol. 15, 1–2, 2022), 78–91.

17 For a more extensive definition of whakapapa, see: Rāwiri Taonui, 'Whakapapa – genealogy', *Te Ara – the Encyclopedia of New Zealand* (5 May 2011), http://www.TeAra.govt.nz/en/whakapapa-genealogy (accessed 21/02/2024). See also Picard and Clark-Howard, 'Christian Settler Imaginary', 79.

18 Willie Jennings identifies the earliest development of modern racial imaginaries within the fifteenth-century Portuguese slave trade in West Africa and sixteenth-century Spanish exploration and conquest of the Americas. Jennings then

links the development of Spanish and Portuguese empires to the later rise of the British Empire, particularly within Anglican missions in, for example, southern Africa. See Willie James Jennings, *The Christian Imagination: Theology and the Origins of Race* (New Haven: Yale University Press, 2010).

19 Two classic general histories from indigenous scholars in Australia and New Zealand respectively can be found in: Anne Pattel-Grey, *The Great White Flood: Racism in Australia* (Atlanta: Scholars Press, 1998); Ranginui Walker, *Ka Whawhai Tonu Matou: Struggle Without End*, rev. ed. (Auckland: Penguin, 2004).

20 Samuel Marsden, *The Letters and Journals of Samuel Marsden 1765–1838*, ed. John Rawson Elder (Dunedin: Coulls Somerville Wilkie and A. H. Reed, 1932), 92.

21 John Liddiard Nicholas, *Narrative of a Voyage to New Zealand, Performed in the Years 1814 and 1815, in Company with the Rev. Samuel Marsden, Principal Chaplain of New South Wales*, Vol. 1 (London: James Black and Son, 1817), 203–6.

22 Alison Jones and Kuni Kaa Jenkins, *He Kōrero – Words Between Us: First Māori-Pākehā Conversations on Paper* (Wellington: Huia, 2011), 79–88. That Marsden could not understand *te reo Māori* at the Christmas service in Rangihoua is of some historical debate. For an alternative, more defensive interpretation of these events see: David Pettett, 'Samuel Marsden – Christmas Day 1814: What Did He Say? The Content of New Zealand's Christmas Sermon', in *Te Rongopai 1814 'Takoto Te Pai!': Bicentenary Reflections on Christian Beginnings and Developments in Aotearoa New Zealand*, ed. Allan Davidson et al. (Auckland: General Synod Office of the Anglican Church in Aotearoa New Zealand and Polynesia, 2014), 73–85.

23 Each of these bracketed translations of Māori words are simplified approximations of their meaning in English.

24 Jennings, *The Christian Imagination*, 8.

25 See Avril Bell, *Relating Indigenous and Settler Identities: Beyond Domination* (New York: Palgrave Macmillan, 2014) for a detailed account of how settler and indigenous identities are formed and continue to shape contemporary public life in North America, Australia and New Zealand.

26 Sturt's various writings detailing his 'explorations' were instrumental, for example, in decisions made by colonists such as Edward Gibbon Wakefield in expanding settlements into South Australia. Wakefield's theories of settlement were fundamental in the British colonizations of both Australia and New Zealand, theories which were put into practice within institutions such as the New Zealand Company and his own political career as a Member of Parliament within the first New Zealand Parliament.

27 See, for example, Carey's comments about Māori as 'in general poor, barbarous, naked pagans, as destitute of civilization, as they are of true religion', despite having never visited New Zealand, in *An Enquiry into the Obligations of Christians to Use Means for the Conversion of the Heathens* (Leicester: Ann Ireland, 1792), 63.

28 Bonhoeffer, 'After Ten Years', 52.

29 Despite its relative neglect for political theology, there have been some recent treatments of Bonhoeffer's 1933 Christology lectures that examine how the lectures might interact with contemporary arrangements of race and white supremacy

in North America. See Koert Verhagen, 'Justification Against White Supremacy: Retrieval as Critical Corrective', in *Being and Action* Corem Deo: *Bonhoeffer and the Retrieval of Justification's Social Import* (London: T&T Clark, 2021), 139–53; Michael Mawson, 'The Stumbling Block and the Lynching Tree: Reading Bonhoeffer's "Lectures on Christology" with James Cone', in *Standing Under the Cross: Essays on Bonhoeffer's Theology and Ethics* (London: T&T Clark, 2023), 172–81.

30 Dietrich Bonhoeffer, 'Lectures on Christology', in *Berlin: 1932–1933*, ed. Larry Rasmussen, trans. Isabel Best and David Higgins, *DBWE* 12 (Minneapolis: Fortress, 2009), 356.

31 Bonhoeffer, 'Lectures on Christology', 306.

32 Ibid.

33 Dietrich Bonhoeffer, *Sanctorum Communio: A Theological Exploration of the Sociology of the Church*, ed. Clifford Green, trans. Reinhard Krauss and Nancy Lukens, *DBWE* 1 (Minneapolis: Fortress, 2009), 271–4.

34 Dietrich Bonhoeffer, *Barcelona, Berlin, New York: 1928–1931*, ed. Clifford J. Green, trans. Douglas W. Stott, *DBWE* 10 (Minneapolis: Fortress Press, 2008), 315.

35 Dietrich Bonhoeffer, *Fiction from Tegel Prison*, ed. Clifford Green, trans. Nancy Lukens, *DBWE* 7 (Minneapolis: Fortress, 2000).

36 Gutiérrez, 'The Limitations of Modern Theology', 229.

37 See Mawson, 'The Stumbling Block and the Lynching Tree'.

38 See, for example, Michael DeJonge's claim that the category of race ultimately has no theological significance for Bonhoeffer: 'Race is an Adiaphoron: The Place of Race in Bonhoeffer's 1933 Writings', *Evangelische Theologie* (Vol. 80, 4, 2020), 267–77.

39 The exposition is currently housed within the Queensland Art Gallery | Gallery of Modern Art. See https://collection.qagoma.qld.gov.au/objects/17331 (accessed 21/05/2024).

40 Quoted in Garry Worete Deverell, '"The Poor Bugger has Suffered Enough": Vernon Ah Kee, Warwick Thornton and the Unmaking of a White Jesus', in *Unsettling Theologies: Memory, Identity, and Place*, ed. Michael Mawson and Brian Kolia (New York: Palgrave Macmillan, 2024), 31.

41 Such a valorization of suffering, especially as it intersects with the unequal sufferings of women, has long been an important insight of feminist and womanist theology. See Chung, 'Dear Dietrich Bonhoeffer'.

42 Deverell, 'The Poor Bugger has Suffered Enough', 32–3.

43 Moltmann, for example, sets up his Christology explicitly as an attempt to reckon with the horrors of World War Two and the mass devastation brought on by European genocidal and nuclear powers. See Jürgen Moltmann, *The Crucified God: The Cross of Christ as the Foundation and Criticism of Christian Theology*, trans. Margaret Kohl (London: SCM Press, 1974).

44 Michael Mawson, 'Unsettling Jesus Christ: Indigenous and Settler Christologies in the Aftermath of Colonisation', in *Unsettling Theologies*, ed. Mawson and Kolia, 39.

45 For a selection of recent indigenous understandings of Christ in Oceania that make such moves, see Te Aroha Rountree, 'Jesus Does a Haka Boogie: *Tangata Whenua* Theology', in *Theologies from the Pacific*, ed. Havea, 47–62; Anne Pattel-Gray, 'Jesus and Australian First Nations Identity and Context' and Seforosa

Carroll, 'Jesus through Pacific Eyes', in *Cultural Afterlives of Jesus: Jesus in Global Perspectives* 3, ed. Gregory C. Jenks (Eugene: Cascade, 2023), 22–36, 67–82.

46 In this task, Mawson turns to Luther's *theologia crucis* which, as mentioned above, is a significant source within Bonhoeffer's own Christology. Mawson, 'Unsettling Jesus Christ', 52. For a selection of recent indigenous understandings of Christ in the region of Oceania that explore Christ as a 'native', see Te Aroha Rountree, 'Once Was Colonized: Jesus Christ', in *Theology as Threshold: Invitations from Aotearoa New Zealand*, ed. Jione Havea, Emily Colgan and Nāsili Vaka'uta (Lanham: Lexington/Fortress, 2022), 161–76; Anne Pattel-Gray, 'Jesus and Australian First Nations Identity and Context', and Seforosa Carroll, 'Jesus through Pacific Eyes', in *Cultural Afterlives of Jesus: Jesus in Global Perspectives*, ed. Gregory C. Jenks (Eugene: Cascade, 2023), 22–36, 67–82.

47 As Te Aroha Rountree reflects, though Jesus has often been made into the image of the 'white man' to oppress and subjugate indigenous peoples, '*What if Jesus was not the colonizer, but rather among the colonized? … What if Jesus was a forced immigrant stowed away in the baggage of Pākehā [white settler] Missionaries?*', 'Once Was Colonized: Jesus Christ', in *Theology as Threshold*, ed. Havea, Colgan and Vaka'uta, 161. Emphasis original.

48 Jones and Kaa Jenkins, *He Kōrero*, 87.

49 Alison Jones, '*Ka Whawhai Tonu Mātou*: The Interminable Problem of Knowing Others' (Inaugural Professorial Lecture, University of Auckland, 24 October 2007), 13. The original text does not use macrons for Māori terms such as 'pōwhiri'. Emphasis original.

50 Jones, '*Ka Whawhai Tonu Mātou*', 14. Emphasis original.

51 Jones, '*Ka Whawhai Tonu Mātou*', 15.

6

Restoring Wholeness in Creation: A Samoan Indigenous Spiritual Perspective on Climate Justice

IEMAIMA VAAI

The spirituality of the indigenous Pacific people recognizes a deep relationship woven between humankind and the environment as part of God's creation. Our Pacific spirituality shares interlinkages with our culture and our identity. It is what underpins the well-being of our Pacific people. It is 'holistic'. This worldview often shapes the Pacific perspective of doing things. It shows that our personhood is not a stand-alone, rather we are believed to be relational beings. We are raised and grounded in the concept of 'community', where our identity is framed around service and love to others even in times of personal troubles and uncertainties. Our community does not limit itself to our people but is inclusive of our environment and spiritual surroundings. It is believed that as we are given the responsibility to give and care for others, we too are also provided with blessings, shelter and life from our community. It is what creates our consciousness – to not exploit, to use only whatever is needed, and to base our decision-making on whether our actions will either benefit or affect our community.

Our journey to climate justice reminds me of the traditional and sacred form of tattooing in my home country in Samoa. In the Samoan context we continue to practise the tradition of tattooing *tatatau/tatau*, a practice that is truly embedded in Samoan custom. For females, the tattooing is termed *malu* and is one of the most sacred rites of passage to service *tautua* to our community. The term *malu* refers to the notions of protection and shelter, it is a *measina* – a Samoan treasure of great significance that is closely interrelated to our *fa'asinomaga*, our identity as a relational being – you are no longer one but you are now whole, connecting you as a person born out of relationships to the cosmos, the environment and to your ancestors.

 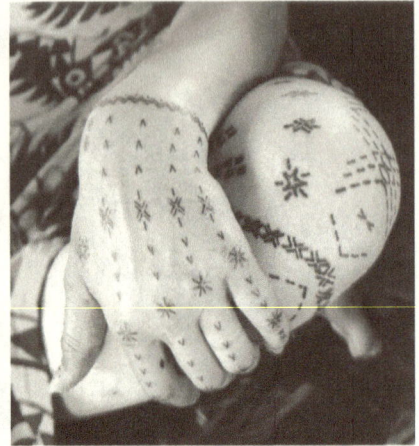

In Samoan tradition, the first step for a female in tattooing, a *malu*, starts with acknowledging her relations to her community – your *Oikos*. You recognize your intimate relations with your surroundings and therefore are conscious of your responsibility to respect, protect and care for your land. In the beginning, all of life was interconnected – we saw these relationships as sacred and it created an environmental consciousness where we were cautious of our actions to not exploit and continue to be good stewards of creation. We understood that if one suffered, we all suffered. If one was in pain then in return we too would experience the same situation.

The second step in tattooing the malu is where the process of the *tatau/* tattooing starts. It consists of marks of steel ink being tattooed at the fleshiest part of the skin high on the thighs. The deepest marks are where the pain is at its highest. In today's generation, we have noticed the ultimate failure of the neoliberal paradigm and how this has contributed to the moral crisis we as humans face today. This paradigm has introduced the concept of individualism and has birthed a culture of greed that continues to promote self-indulgence in profit and materialism through overexploitation. In the Pacific, the climate crisis continues to be a lived reality. We are a region that emits less than 1% of carbon emissions, yet we continue to bear the injustice and brunt of the climate crisis. Over the course of time, the exacerbation of rising sea levels has induced displacement and relocation for coastal villages in the Pacific. Our resources are being overexploited and raped by greed from those of a capitalist system. It is a system that continues to hide behind pretty words of 'green and blue growth', but in the end this growth still very much extracts what is treasured by us for its own profit-driven agenda. Our Pacific continues to experience the highest form of pain in terms of climate injustice – while our environment groans in agony and pain, our ancestors and our communities continue to cry in numbness as they watch their life as a whole be violently threatened.

The third step in tattooing the *malu* involves marks of steel ink being tattooed at mid-thighs. The young women here experience the cost of the ritual delivery, and this final process determines whether the ritual as a whole has been successful or not. As my father Upolu Vaai says: 'Pacific people have survived and responded to the climate crisis for decades within their cultural and spiritual dimensions and continue to still do so today, while much of the international community continues to meet challenges informed by science, Pacific communities also recognize that cultural and spiritual beliefs and practices play an essential role, all of which is informed by their own indigenous and faith spirituality and knowledge.' Although the region is commonly termed as a 'developing/ least developed' nation, we continue to show our resilience in climate adaptation through the use of our indigenous and sacred forms of knowledge. We use traditional forms of conservation methods that place taboo (*tabu*) or no-take zone protocols on areas needed to be restored. We practise indigenous rituals that promote the connection we have to ecology, burying our umbilical cord in our land. The values and ethics upheld in our spirituality guide and govern our consciousness to serve our communities wholesomely and meaningfully – sacrificing what we want for the sake of others so they (including our environment) may 'flourish' more. In the age of climate change, the Pacific has come together and created a project that provides an ecological development framework where it acknowledges the value of indigenous Pacific spirituality as an avenue for sustainable development. This project is called '*reweaving the ecological mat*'; it uses the morals of spirituality, theology and cultural identity as grounding principles to guide the world to reconciliation. A development framework does not just base climate solutions on science but acknowledges the crucial presence of indigenous and faith spirituality as a holistic way forward. The question is – how can this be delivered and be seen as a way of rethinking our Oikos to shift from being human-centric to seeing ourselves as equals to our environment? How can it change and inspire leaders to do their part in restoring wholeness in creation?

The fourth step in tattooing the *malu* signals the completion of the marks; thus begins the healing process. The completion and healing signify a renewal – a time for reflection about what its completion means and the responsibilities you now hold as a female to protect, shelter and serve the needs of your community. The *tatau* is now at its most powerful, a turnover. Our spirituality – indigenous and of faith – shares a common role as custodian to care for creation. As we journey together in our 'Vaka' canoe to climate justice it pushes us to take a moment of realization, of seeing 'where we ought to be', of repentance for the world's ecological sins. We must acknowledge that we humans are not at the centre of creation – by de-centring ourselves, we may be able to recover from the selfish pull of consumerism into which our world currently delves. Once we acknowledge that we are part of a larger community we will then be able to live efficiently and sustainably. Giving recognition to the responsibilities we hold as indigenous and Christian communities to promote intrinsic dignity and value the many. The Pacific continues to navigate through healing and recovery by amplifying its own climate frameworks that are sure to effectively work long term.

The last and final step of the *malu* tattooing practice calls for revolution – the female now celebrates. Once covered in coconut oil she is then called to stand up *tu i luga* and celebrate with her community – her family, the spirits of our environment, and her ancestors. Indigenous Pacific communities have much to offer to the world in addressing the contradictions between modern society's obsession with limitless economic growth and the ecological limits of our common home. In embracing our spirituality, being resilient in terms of adaptation, and building our own climate solutions, it does not only address our rights as indigenous people, but it reweaves an ecological narrative that restores and promotes the wholeness of life. So, it is our indigenous spirituality and rituals that mean we must stand up to the injustices of the crisis and call on leaders to commune in this fight to protect our common home. Whether leaders journey with us together in our Vaka or continue to dismiss our voices, we as Pacific indigenous peoples will continue to be the prophetic voice of the voiceless – fighting and affirming for a world that promotes the wholeness of creation and of life. Let us come together in celebration with our ancestors, our Oikos, to help shift a narrative to one that touches on the unseen trauma of indigenous people, let us fight for a future that will safeguard Mother Earth.

PART 2

Insiders and Outsiders: Struggling through History and Context

7

Palestinian Women: The Question Within the Question

MUNA NASSAR

The question of Palestine has been looming on top of the ladder of international concerns for the past 75 years. Often missing from any answers is consideration for women in Palestine, also living with the consequences of the Palestine question. We need an answer that would take into consideration issues of gender and social entitlements – admitting that without the liberation of women, the march for liberation from colonization and occupation will never be complete.

In the course of writing this chapter, the war on Gaza, 'beginning' on 7 October, is ongoing and is victim of a media coverage that condemns, that points fingers and most importantly dehumanizes the oppressed. It is a time where we witness commentators and decision-makers declare that the lives of Palestinians – both men and women, both old and young – don't matter. The Western narrative paints a picture that is far from being sensible, far from being rational and far from being just! Through my work I try to present a narrative that challenges the stereotypes about the Palestinian people in general and Palestinian women specifically.

It might seem paradoxical or even hypocritical to talk about liberation and liberating identities without bringing to the table – both literally and metaphorically – the voices of women. But feminist discourse is still an added extra in academia. As a woman delving into academic research, it feels as if it is an exclusive century-old boys' club. Hence, for me as a Palestinian, it is another layer of dominance, and would it be too farfetched if one was to say it is another layer of male hegemony oversetting the tone, producing the work and representing the reality? Rather than having a solo performance in the struggle for liberation that does not accord with their players, the reality requires an orchestra in order to achieve liberation on all fronts and from all tunes. A reimagined reality that reflects and talks to all individuals of a society, a reality where texts reflect voices rather than a voice and where equality, justice and liberation are delivered to all.

To do so, one needs a thorough understanding of the cultural and colonial history of Palestine, and by reviewing the postcolonial theory and its interaction with feminism, I aim to present in this chapter a (re)imagined projection of the future and a way forward that all the other voices who have been historically othered are included and heard. Historically and using orientalist spectacles, the Orient was seen as a feminine body that was weak and thus needed to be dominated and controlled.[1] By observing the way domination is represented as a masculine body dominating a feminine one, I intend in this chapter to analyse how Palestinian women are doubly othered, first as Palestinian and second as women. I then explore the liberative identity of Palestinian women and argue the necessity to hear all accords to achieve a liberated society both from within and beyond. In conclusion, I aim to present a reality where a binary to define each individual or group is no longer needed and where women can define their realities on their own without alluding to their movement being born as the negative of something else.

The anticolonial narrative has exposed the existing hegemonic epistemological structures as both racist and sexist, a structure that detects who can speak and who cannot.[2] It is essential to state that the practice of questioning where the women's voice was did not arise due to a Westernized context of feminism and the need to genderize everything, but due to the realization that society needs women. In the Palestinian liberation context, women have played a vital role in resisting a colonial regime and continue to promote decolonial liberation until this day. Thus, it is essential to note that the concept of feminism and women's rights and role in society is not and should not be viewed as a Western import to non-Western contexts. Moreover, context matters. The context of Western feminism differs from the context of non-Western feminism. Leila Ahmed argues that some Western feminists devalue local cultures by presuming that there is only one path for emancipating women and that is by adopting Western models, which serves as another version of hegemony and domination over non-Western contexts.[3] Beyond recognizing the contextual difference between Western and non-Western feminism, we need to understand that what women in the non-Western world demand is not to be rescued and saved. Their call is not synonymous with asking saviours – whether Western males or Western feminism – to rescue women and chaperone their movement of liberation. Gaytari Chakravorty Spivak asks what we are to think of white men saving brown women from brown men. To put it bluntly, what are we to think of white women saving brown women from brown men?[4] Thus, diluting the feminist struggle of the non-Western world to be compatible with the Western one is yet another way of obscuring the real lives and views of non-Western women and alienating their movements, and thus can be challenged on the ground of cultural imperialism.[5]

It is essential for the understanding of Palestinian women's reality to detect the real threat to their existence, and that is not Arab men, but the systematic oppression that all Palestinians suffer from, irrespective of their gender. Palestinian women do not need to be saved from Palestinian men; they need the end of the systematic oppression that strips them of their rights. Systematic oppression is the reason that women give birth on the checkpoints and often die because the medical intervention is delayed and not allowed to enter the checkpoints.[6] While I am writing this article, the war in Gaza is still unfolding in front of our own eyes. During the past 50 days, Palestinian women had to give birth in their homes without any medical interventions,[7] during a round-the-clock bombardment of the city's infrastructure, hospitals and residential neighbourhood. The war on Gaza did not only eradicate the everyday life infrastructure, but has amounted to the loss of 15,207 lives of men, women and children.[8]

The Agency of Palestinian Women

It is imperative to understand that liberation does not come in one shape or one definition, but comes through different layers. There is no straight line that one can take to arrive at liberation; each route to liberation is engraved with its own contextual impediments. So, the questions that need to be asked are: What is it like to be a Palestinian and a woman? How would a Palestinian woman speak and articulate her mind after a century-old narrative of representation done on her behalf – both internally and externally? And while Palestinians (both men and women) have endured and witnessed their agency being taken away, how would Palestinian women face the double-layered revoking of agency? And as for articulating their minds, were women able to be welcomed into the boys' club whether religiously, politically, academically or socially?

In order to answer all these questions, it is pivotal to understand the multiplicity of the voices and experiences of women, in the Palestinian context and in general. Just as one man's opinion and experience differs from another's, a woman's experience and views are different from one to another. And while the struggle for liberation from oppression imposed by a foreign hand unifies the Palestinian people – both men and women –

and is considered as essential as breathing, the march for women is longer as they still have to stand in the face of the patriarchal oppression within their context that is taking away their own agency.

The Palestinian liberation and nationalist movement has historically used a patriarchal lens. Women's roles have been understood as bearing the sons to fight the fight and resist the occupation.[9] The depiction of such a role for women is problematic – first, because it reduces the role of women to be one of a body that needs to be covered, to be governed, and most importantly to be protected. Second, it completely alienates and others women from the liberation process. Such is an implicit structure for social entitlement that is gendered and discriminatory.[10] So, it is clear that women have their own struggle within an already existing struggle against colonialism and occupation.

The (albeit patriarchal) anti-colonial liberation journey was successful in exposing the different forms of oppression both in the political and social structures of the colonial projects while also contributing to a profound social critique.[11] The postcolonial field has shown the importance of hearing the subaltern, and in recognizing the need to question the (especially Western) male-dominated source of knowledge and the hegemony over the production of knowledge.

Beyond recognizing the need for women's voices in liberation, it is crucial to highlight that women's studies, experiences or voices should be available not only in women's circles and forums but should be normalized to partake in all arenas and forums. To create a few seats for women in the government is not what is being demanded and definitely not demanded from men, as citizenship is not merely equated with voting or representation in governing institutions.[12] Instead, what is being demanded is for women to be able to represent themselves and have their own agency to voice their needs in a socially liberated society. Questions of definition and self-definition constitute the very core of political consciousness in all contexts.[13] The Palestinian cause is a great example of how important the definition of oneself is, and in that line of thought, Palestinian women value their own definition and their right for self-representation.

It is important to state that every time I speak about Palestine, I am not using the victimhood lens to talk about it. Yes, I do live under occupation; yes, my ancestors' family land was confiscated by Israel; yes, I continue to live under restricted right of movement; and yes, I still have to fight for our voices to be heard, but I can also say that all those things have made me aware of the importance of advocating for one's cause, of speaking the truth, and of asking all the hard questions, of challenging the narrative and breaking through glass ceilings. Being critical and always questioning the power dynamic stems from the fact that freedom, liberation and justice are costly and will not be handed over to you, but only by you claiming it. Thus, resisting and fighting for the agency of the Palestinian people is not only contested towards the occupation but it is also a valid demand that serves to oppose the male oppressive patriarchal system that is in place against all women.[14]

Women's Rights as Auxiliary

In contexts where countries are still fighting colonialism and are seeking liberation for themselves as people, there tends to be some sort of alienation from internal issues among people themselves. The myth permeates in Palestine that women's rights are trivial or secondary compared to other issues that the State deems to be of importance[15] and is the reason women continue to face discrimination based on their gender. In the State of Palestine, women make up 49% of the population, and to consider the rights of half of the population as secondary is a great injustice. Reasons for such low-ranking priorities and exclusion of women's rights and gender issues can vary. As analysed by Souad Dajani, the reasoning tends to be either that women are non-agents, hence the affairs of the State do not concern them, or that state affairs do not affect them.[16] In other words, there was assumed to be no gender content or consequences to political actions and the policies and power relations of the State.

This does not mean that women were not actively resisting and a part of the Palestinian liberation movement. From its inception in the 1920s, the Palestinian women's movement came out of a need for economic and social change that has paralleled resisting colonialism.[17] So, it is imperative that we see the founding of the movement not only as oppositional to the patriarchy in the Palestinian context, but as a movement concerned with the future of women and meeting their rights. It cannot be denied that women played a huge role during the first Intifada (Arabic for 'the uprising') that erupted in December 1987 and 1994, which started as a civilian mass resistance against the Israeli occupation. It has been described by commentators as an uprising that not only aimed to 'shake off' the Israeli military rule over occupied Palestine, but also was a social revolution in its own right, in which women were rebelling against the traditional places they were ascribed to by the patriarchal system.[18] And rather than viewing the active role of women to be episodic or seasonal, it should be seen as a role that has always and historically been part of the Palestinian national movement but was often dimmed and sidelined. This is not to devalue the importance of the first Intifada, as it did have a unique momentum in the women's liberation movement. Women became more aware of their rights and it encouraged women in all sectors to mobilize and to channel their organizational structure in a way that could sustain a society under siege. But more importantly, women were directly addressing issues concerning their rights and roles in the struggle for national liberation, a subject that is barely alluded to before the uprising except by a handful of committed activists.[19] Women's committees during the Intifadas organized marches and demonstrated in the streets, opposed land confiscations and were present in incidents of confrontations with the Israeli army.[20] Joost Hiltermann expands:

> women's committee activists would join local popular committee members in organizing relief or emergency services after Israeli army raids, paying solidarity visits to the families of martyrs and detainees, and providing material assistance whenever necessary. Working on behalf of prisoners and their families, they would contact lawyers, collect clothing for prisoners, and arrange prison visits via the Red Cross. Women also distributed leaflets, discussed politics openly (often for the first time), and urged people who remained unconvinced to participate in the uprising ... women were called upon to participate in popular committees and trade unions, to boycott work on strike days, to confront soldiers and settlers, and to promote a 'home economy' of locally-produced food and clothing ... women were prominent in efforts to monitor prices charged by merchants and to ensure compliance during commercial strikes and boycotts of Israeli goods, and especially in providing alternative education to children in homes, churches, and mosques after the closure of schools.[21]

Consistently, women were active economically, politically and socially during the first and the second Intifadas. However, the role that women played continued to be marginalized after the Intifadas. It was difficult to cast aside that image of women being an oasis of protection to the sons and male figures of the resistance. The pivotal role that the women played, even before the Intifadas, and continue to play until this day is yet to be recognized.[22] And as Rita Giacaman, Islah Jad and Penny Johnson have highlighted, the role women have played in the national liberation movement was an extension of their roles rather than a new role.[23]

Due to living under occupation, the lives of Palestinian women cannot be seen to be inseparable from politics and politicization. The patriarchal image of Palestinian women – where our identity is to be one of the 'mothers of the martyr' is enshrined in the Palestinian history and present, as argued by Johnson, Jad and Giacaman, as a stoical image, but it is also one that is not active in the resistance.[24] Beyond pigeonholing the role of women to be the protector of the home, or the mother, the sister, the wife of someone, the role of women should be seen as an active partner in Palestinian society at the political, the economic and the social levels.[25]

What is contested as a reality for Palestinian women and still applicable to this day, is that women have a double glass ceiling. Palestinian women are addressing gender issues and calling for women's rights while also actively engaging in the overarching struggle as Palestinian citizens to liberate themselves from occupation. More importantly, the separation of women's rights and gender issues as issues that only certain organizations are designated to work on, and which are removed from the political agenda, has made it all the more difficult to see the urgency of women's rights.[26] The double-layered glass ceiling for women is translated into a reality that if we (Palestinians) as a colonized nation were able to break free from colonial imperial bodies, we (women) still have to deal with yet another glass ceiling that aims to keep us in our place.

So how does one prioritize what question needs to be asked first? As a Palestinian woman, how do I balance out between the national question, the social question and the religious question? And at the furthest limit of the question, does asking one question eliminate all other questions? When analysing the Palestinian cause, one would get a sense that the national cause is deemed to be more important than the social cause.[27] However, it is pivotal to understand that one cause does not have to trump the other, and that both causes can exist not to be contradictory to the other but as causes of equal importance to the citizens of Palestine and to the future of Palestine. Palestinian women have worked on creating connections between the social and the national liberation cause and have made significant strides in identifying variables in their society that defined their conditions, and related issues of gender to the specific political, ideological and/or class positions of women in Palestinian society.[28]

One example I will briefly explore here. On 26 September 2019, the *Tal'at* movement was launched, where thousands of women took to the streets in 12 Palestinian cities to raise their voice against gender-based violence that women in Palestine are subjugated to. *Tal'at* means stepping out in Arabic, and it was the first Palestinian feminist movement that was able to unite women on all fronts in geographically dismantled Palestine (concerned Gaza, the West Bank and Palestinians who are Israeli citizens) and challenge the division. Their slogan vibrates against the dual oppression women in Palestine live through, 'There is no free homeland, without free women.' *Tal'at* opened a new window of opportunity for Palestinian women hoping for real social, political and religious change to make their voices heard and place a progressive feminist agenda at the core of Palestine's national emancipation – an agenda that aspires to entrench liberation as a value in all aspects of life. *Tal'at* mobilization was undertaken by Palestinian women and emerges from their lived reality under Israel's colonial regime, whose violence – being at a gunpoint from Israeli young men (or women), restricted by apartheid walls, sexually abused at checkpoints – they confront daily. It is within this context that Palestinian women struggle to end male violence and intimidation within our society. This struggle is undertaken so that women can experience safety, freedom and justice – as well as for all members of the society.

So, the duty to carry on the weight of gender and to break through the male dominance and hegemony imposed on the Palestinian national cause remains the duty of women and part of their cause.

The Resilient Identity of Palestinian Women

There will always be different and maybe contradictory ways of defining one's identity. In the case of the identity of Palestinian women, what defines it the most? Is it the struggle, the resistance or the vision of a liberated reality where Palestinians (men and women) and their land are free? How does a Palestinian, a woman and a Christian assert her identity within the context of national liberation and within the overall contest of alienation? And how have feminist liberation theologians articulated their minds in the struggle for liberation and liberating?

For Palestinian Christians, their identity is of equal importance to the culture and social fabric and structure of Palestine. Jean Zaru, a Palestinian Christian feminist theologian, has beautifully captured it through the lens of the embroidery of the Palestinian people; that is, we are an interwoven and an integral part of the whole society.[29] Being a Palestinian Christian woman, a native of the Holy Land, Zaru goes further to depict what women witness of a reality of social, economic, political and religious structures of injustice imposed on them.[30] But as for defining where Palestinian Christian women stand, Cedar Duaybis, a Palestinian Christian feminist theologian, reflects on the reality of otherness, in which the conflict is not only raging around her as a Palestinian, but also within her; a conflict between herself the Palestinian, the Christian and the woman to find her personhood alongside the 'chosen sex' inside the church.[31] Women have often been seen to be the Third World of the church (clergymen and laymen being the first two).[32] The reality of the church of the Holy Land demands a balanced functioning in which the role women can and should play isn't to be underestimated and their light should not be dimmed but should shed a brighter image of the church.

Growing up as a Palestinian Christian woman, and going to church on Sundays, I was really eager to hear how our reality of oppression would be interpreted in church. However, the reality of everyday life as a Palestinian living under occupation was never reflected in church, or even talked about in church. I felt like there was a complete separation between what we witness outside the church, and what we talk about in church. I never felt like I was putting my faith into action, but on the contrary, I felt like I was losing my faith. When you witness on a daily basis an unjust and unholy reality, how can you even hold on to faith when you live through a surrounding that completely denies your identity – first as a Palestinian, second as a Christian and third as a woman – how can you hold on to faith? However, on this journey of faith that I am still on, I have come to the realization that just as freedom is never given, women's places and voices in the church also need to be claimed, not waited for. And I, as a woman, who contemplates my context, and my role in that context, will continue to fight for my seat in the church, because the church is not only the physical space where all the men are, but it is also the people who are passionate and eager to make progress within the church and its theology/ideology.

Furthermore, it is of utter importance to highlight the interconnectedness between Palestinian women regardless of their religious affiliation. Zaru asserts the interconnectedness of both Palestinian Christians and Muslims as they have been dealt with a hegemonic agenda that usurped their rights for self-determination and existence.[33] Nadia Abboushi, another strong Palestinian feminist voice, asserts that Palestinian Muslims and Christians, both men and women, have risen consecutively together and unified against the occupation that is shown in the spirit of communion so beautifully visible in the Intifada, as Christian priests face the soldiers coming to arrest praying youths in the mosques, or as Muslim Sheikhs enter the church to pray to the one God with the Christians.[34] Furthermore, when Palestinian women address issues of injustice it is not a rare occurrence, but it is the norm. The reality of Palestinian women is one of resilience and of liberation.

The message women can contribute is one of liberation that has stemmed from their experience as women and their experience of being oppressed and othered. However, women's contributions do not and should not take off from oppression as ground zero – as a tabula rasa – but should acknowledge their history of oppression that has guided them to liberation. Moreover, the objective of the feminist critique is to serve wider society and go beyond a critique to deconstruct the problematic reality and to build societies that amplify voices within, in order to move beyond and create a more just world.

Notes

1 Edward Said, *Orientalism* (New York: Random House, 1978).
2 S. S. El-Malik, 'Intellectual Work "In-the-World": Women's Writing and Anti-Colonial Thought in Africa', *Irish Studies in International Affairs* (Vol. 24, 2013), 101–20, at p. 110.
3 Leila Ahmed, *Women and Gender in Islam: Historical Roots of a Modern Debate* (New Haven, CT: Yale University Press, 1992), 135.
4 Gaytari Chakravorty Spivak, *Can the Subaltern Speak? Reflections on the History of an Idea* (New York: Columbia University Press, 1988), 272.
5 Kumari Jayawardena, *Feminism and Nationalism in the Third World* (New York: Verso, 2016), 7.
6 https://www.unfpa.org/news/checkpoints-compound-risks-childbirth-palestinian-women#:~:text=The%20Palestinian%20Ministry%20of%20Health, the%20death%20of%20five%20women (accessed 7/03/2024).
7 https://www.who.int/news/item/03-11-2023-women-and-newborns-bearing-the-brunt-of-the-conflict-in-gaza-un-agencies-warn (accessed 7/03/2024).
8 Accurate of 2/12/2023. https://www.aljazeera.com/news/liveblog/2023/12/2/israel-hamas-war-live-israeli-bombs-rain-down-on-gaza-after-truce-collapse#:~:text=At%20least%2015%2C207%20Palestinians%20have,toll%20stands%20at%20about%201%2C200 (accessed 7/03/2024).
9 S. Younan, 'Women in the Intifada and in the Churches', in Naim Ateek, Mark Ellis and Rosmary Radford Ruether, eds, *Faith and the Intifada: Palestinian Christian Voices* (Maryknoll, NY: Orbis Books, 1992), 110.
10 Rita Giacaman, Islah Jad and Penny Johnson, 'For the Common Good? Gender and Social Citizenship in Palestine', *Middle East Report* (No. 198, 1996), 11–16, at p. 13.
11 El-Malik, 'Intellectual Work "In-the-World"', 106.
12 Giacaman, Jad and Johnson, 'For the Common Good?', 12.
13 Jayawardena, *Feminism and Nationalism*, 32.
14 S. Dajani, 'The Struggle of Palestinian Women in the Occupied Territories: Between National and Social Liberation', *Arab Studies Quarterly* (Vol. 16, 1994), 13–26, at p. 13.
15 Charlotte Bunch, 'Women's Rights as Human Rights: Toward a Re-Vision of Human Rights', *Human Rights Quarterly* (Vol. 12, 1990), 486–98.
16 Dajani, 'The Struggle of Palestinian Women'.
17 Giacaman, Jad and Johnson, 'For the Common Good?', 40.

18 Joost R. Hiltermann, 'The Women's Movement during the Uprising', *Journal of Palestine Studies* (Vol. 20, 1991), 48–57, at p. 48.
19 Hiltermann, 'The Women's Movement during the Uprising', 49.
20 Giacaman, Jad and Johnson, 'For the Common Good?', 41.
21 Hiltermann, 'The Women's Movement during the Uprising', 50–1.
22 Hiltermann, 'The Women's Movement during the Uprising', 54.
23 Giacaman, Jad and Johnson, 'For the Common Good?', 39.
24 Giacaman, Jad and Johnson, 'For the Common Good?', 45.
25 Younan, 'Women in the Intifada and in the Churches', 131.
26 Penny Johnson and Elieen Kuttab, 'Where Have All the Women (and Men) Gone? Reflections on Gender and the Second Palestinian Intifada', *Feminist Review* (No. 69, 2001), 21–43, at p. 28.
27 Randa Nasser, Fidaa Barghouti and Janan Mousa, 'Feminist Attitudes and Praxis Among Palestinian Women Activists', *Feminist Formations* (Vol. 22, 3, 2010), 146–75, at p. 149.
28 Dajani, 'The Struggle of Palestinian Women', 21.
29 Jean Zaru, 'Being Faithful Witnesses: Serving God in a Changing World', *Cornerstone* (No. 83, 2021), 1–4, at p. 2.
30 Jean Zaru, 'The Intifada, Nonviolence, and the Bible', in Ateek, Ellis and Ruether, *Faith and the Intifada*, 126.
31 Cedar Duaybis, 'Becoming Whole, The Challenge of the Palestinian Christian Women', in Ateek, Ellis and Ruether, *Faith and the Intifada*, 120.
32 Duaybis, 'Becoming Whole', 121.
33 Zaru, 'The Intifada', 127.
34 Nadia Abboushi, 'The Intifada and the Palestinian Churches', in Ateek, Ellis and Ruether, *Faith and the Intifada*, 60.

8

Justice for the Workers: Theologizing Trade Unions and Labour Movements

WILLIAM GIBSON

You would be forgiven for thinking you were at a Pentecostal revival meeting. I was in a room resembling a school assembly hall; there was standing room only and people spilled over into the hallways and additional meeting rooms. A variety of charismatic speakers took to the stage, all greeted with thunderous applause, and throughout their addresses were met with shouts of affirmation and support from the audience. The speakers were calling for a revival of solidarity, for justice to roll down and for us to renew our efforts for equality and fairness with fresh zeal. However, this was no religious revival meeting. This was a public meeting in support of railway workers on strike as part of the RMT (Rail, Maritime and Transport Workers) union in the United Kingdom.

This was my first public union meeting and one that served to galvanize my own efforts to organize in Apple, my previous place of work. Throughout the year-long process of organizing in one of the world's largest companies, I was continually confronted with situations and ideas that raised theological questions for me. Whether it was in the pastoral care and support of colleagues, the songs and liturgy of the trade union movement or the echoes of the words of Jesus and the Hebrew prophets within my religious tradition, I could not avoid the question of how theology intersects with trade unionism and wider workers' movements.

However, in my organizing efforts I discovered that trade unions, a tool for achieving justice for workers, are a double-edged sword. While the aims of the trade union movement are justice, fairness and equity for all, there is unfortunately a story of abuse of power by some within union ranks. Just this year a report was released detailing accusations of sexual harassment and bullying within the TSSA (the union for the transport and travel industries).[1] This comes not long after a similar report was published about the GMB union of which I am a member.² The problems run deeper than just individual unions but rather point to the need to tackle patriarchy and other oppressive relationships of power in all their manifestations. In this way young trade unionists have a dual task: achieving justice for workers in relation to their employer and transforming unions themselves to better reflect the values on which the trade union movement was founded.

In this chapter I will consider what it means to think theologically about trade unions and labour movements, examining the links between the Christian religion and early British trade unionists and labour activists. I will also argue for a theological ethic of solidarity that the modern church and trade union movement could participate in through collective action and fighting for justice. Finally, I will detail why an intersectional approach to trade union membership and activism is needed for young workers who are new to the trade union movement.

Christianity, Trade Unionism and Labour Movements in Britain

In this section I will discuss some influential figures and movements in the history of British trade unions and the labour movement throughout the nineteenth and twentieth centuries and the influence of Christianity upon them. Despite the avowedly secular nature of the trade union and labour movement in Britain today, many early trade unionists drew upon resources within the Christian religion to inspire and inform their activism. This is in no way an in-depth historical survey of the links between trade unionism, the labour movement and Christianity in Britain, nor is it reflective of a universal religious attitude towards trade unions; rather it serves to demonstrate that Christianity has played a part in influencing early trade unionists in a way that is informative for this attempt to outline what it means to theologize trade unions today.

One of the earliest examples of the link between Christianity and the early trade union movement in Britain is that of the Tolpuddle Martyrs. These English farm labourers, led by the Methodist lay preacher George Loveless³ and his brother James, had established a lodge of the Friendly Society of Agricultural Labourers in 1833 whose aim was to increase wages paid to workers by farmers and landowners.⁴ Trade unionism was no longer illegal as the Combinations Act of 1799, which had prohibited collective bargaining and the unionization of workers, was repealed in 1824.⁵ However, they swore an oath of secrecy,⁶ which led to them being found guilty of administering an illegal oath under the Mutiny Act and being sentenced to seven years transportation to Australia in 1834.[7] As they were sentenced, George Loveless wrote: 'God is our guide! from field, from wave, from plough, from anvil, and from loom; We come, our country's rights to save, And speak a tyrant faction's doom: We raise the watch-word liberty; We will, we will, we will be free!'[8] Loveless' commitment to improving working conditions was directly linked with his religious convictions and found expression in his organizing efforts. Additionally, the oaths taken by trade unions, like those taken by the Tolpuddle Martyrs, were deeply religious in nature. W. H. Oliver gives the example of the initiation rite of the Ashton cotton spinners where the President dwelt upon 'the power of death, the universality of sin, the transience of life, and the immortality of the spirit'.[9] Trade unions' initiation rituals and funeral practices led to them being characterized as a 'poor men's church'.[10] The Tolpuddle Martyrs serve as an example of the importance of solidarity as a central ethic in the trade union movement. After the Grand National Union led protests against the decision to transport the Tolpuddle Martyrs and wrote a petition that the MP Thomas Wakely claimed over 800,000 people signed,[11] the men were pardoned in 1836 and by 1839 all six had been returned to England.[12]

Any historical survey of the labour movement in Britain would be bereft if it failed to mention the phenomenon of the labour church movement that sprang up in the 1890s. The labour church movement was founded by John Trevor in 1891 after he resigned his post as a Unitarian minister. He believed that God was working through the labour movement, 'as once he worked through Christianity, for the further salvation of the world'.[13] The labour churches held services across Britain and at their peak boasted 50 churches;[14] they worked with other Christian organizations like the Salvation Army to raise money for workers during times of industrial action;[15] they produced a hymn book[16] and established Sunday Schools.[17] There was even a labour church service attended by five thousand people at the Bradford conference which established the Independent Labour Party.[18] Immanentism, the belief that the divine is somehow manifested in or part of the material world, was one response to the crisis of faith produced by Darwin and historical criticism and acted as a foundation for ethical socialism. Mark Bevir summarizes immanentism by stating that 'for the members of the labour church, this truth was that God existed as a presence in the spontaneous life of the world, rather than as a transcendent being who conveyed his law in a dogmatic revelation'.[19] By 1902 there were only 20 labour churches; the traditional interpretation of the labour church's rapid rise and decline is expressed by Henry Pelling who describes it as part of a 'transfer of social energy from religion to politics'.[20] However, Mark Bevir and Ken Inglis argue that there is another explanation for the movement's decline. They view the decline of the labour church as a consequence of a lack of structure and the weakness of its religious doctrines as a political theory.[21] Many of the labour church's adherents continued to have nonconformist religious convictions, like Philip Wicksteed who remained a practising Unitarian minister even after the decline of the labour churches.[22]

The labour church's preoccupation with addressing the material conditions of workers and individuals within their community is something that churches today could learn from. As with the Tolpuddle Martyrs the ethic of solidarity is evident as a primary concern within the labour church with many adherents considering 'the brotherhood of man' as their central message.[23] In arguing for a theological ethic of solidarity later in this chapter, I find solidarity to be a better Christian ethic than fraternity or brotherhood due to the patriarchal and exclusionary gendered language of brotherhood.

The final example I will give here of the link between Christianity, trade unionism and the labour movement in Britain is that of Helen Crawfurd and the Women's Peace Crusade. Helen Jack was born in 1877 in the Gorbals, a neighbourhood in Glasgow. Her father was a master baker and trade unionist, and she had a decidedly religious upbringing, also marrying a minister, 50 years her senior.[24] Crawfurd was eventually drawn to socialist and feminist ideas through encountering the deprivation and inequalities present in Glasgow.[25] Her initial activism as part of the Women's Social and Political Union and wartime activism in the Women's Peace Crusade was rich in the imagery, metaphors and biblical stories of her religious upbringing and the Scottish Reformed tradition.[26] For example, her Easter appeal in March 1918 was described as an alternative Easter service, offering 'to do homage to him who came to bring Peace on Earth and good will to men'.[27] At another meeting she drew upon John 10.10 when she stated, 'too long they had looked at Christ in the clouds; by looking and seeing Christ in our fellow men we would be doing a greater service to humanity'.[28] Crawfurd played a significant role in the political life of left-wing politics in Scotland in the early twentieth century, her politics were inspired by her religious upbringing and her conviction that collective action and solidarity could effect change.

I have provided just three examples of individuals and organizations that were part of trade unions and labour movements in Britain throughout the nineteenth and twentieth centuries. Yet even with just brief consideration of their influence and contributions it is clear they did not see a conflict between their religious faith and the left-wing politics of trade unionism, solidarity and socialism. There are many other individuals who could be mentioned, such as Arthur Henderson who was a Wesleyan preacher and was part of the establishment of the Labour Party in 1906,[29] Keir Hardie the Labour MP and trade unionist who later became a lay preacher for the Evangelical Union Church,[30] or the Wesleyan Henry Broadhurst who led the stonemasons' union and became the secretary of the parliamentary committee of the Trade Union Congress,[31] among others. Beyond individuals and organizations there is also significant crossover in art and music between trade unions and Christianity. For example, the famous American trade union song 'Solidarity Forever', written by Ralph Chaplin, follows the tune of *John Brown's Body* and the *Battle Hymn of the Republic* which are distinctly religious in their content[32] – as well as works like *The Socialist Sunday School Song Book*. I end this section with a verse from the song 'City of Light' by Felix Adler which utilizes imagery similar to that of the New Jerusalem in the books of Ezekiel[33] and Revelation.[34]

> We are builders of that City,
> All our joys and all our groans
> Help to rear its shining ramparts,
> All our lives are building stones;
> But the work that we have builded,
> Oft with bleeding hands and tears,
> And in error and in anguish,
> Will not perish with our years.[35]

However, where Christianity has played a significant role in the British trade union and labour movement in the past, today its place is more precarious. For example, in 1994 there was a clergy worker section set up in the finance and manufacturing union, which eventually became Amicus, which merged with Unite the Union and the group became the Unite Faith Workers' Branch.[36] The fact that there is a union branch for faith workers raises questions about the extent to which faith organizations have capitulated to neoliberal and capitalist ideology. Just this year Church of England clergy in the Faith Workers' Branch have raised a formal pay claim for the first time in their history due to struggling with the higher cost of living.[37] The Black Anglican theologian and clergyman the Revd Dr David Isiohoro raises concerns about the Unite Faith Workers' Branch in his book *Faith in Unions*, where he shares his personal experience of racism within the branch. He argues that the Faith

Workers' Branch centres Englishness over trade union values, evidenced by the executive committee who represent historically white churches and suffer from a lack of representation from Hindu and Muslim faith workers.[38] Isiohoro's account of racism and religious exclusion within the Faith Workers' Branch demonstrates the need for a theological ethic of solidarity and an intersectional approach to trade unionism which I will argue for in the following sections of this chapter.

A Theological Ethic of Solidarity

Dieter T. Hessel states: 'Where people are in solidarity with each other, there the law is lived. There justice is done, love expressed, community reformed. This is what it means to know God.'[39] The undergirding ethic of trade unionism and labour movements is the principle of solidarity, as the motto popularized by the Industrial Workers of the World proclaims, 'an injury to one is an injury to all'.[40] Theologizing trade unions and labour movements necessitates a consideration of a theological ethic of solidarity. As demonstrated in the previous section, religious conviction can and has in many cases inspired acts of solidarity. Solidarity is not just an act for individuals to carry out but a theological imperative for the modern church. Especially considering the Western church's involvement in colonial projects, racism, homophobia, misogyny and other intersecting relationships of power, a theological ethic of solidarity provides the church with an antidote to counteract the poison of neoliberal individualism and consumerism that is driving our current ecological crisis and increasing the economic inequalities that trade unions seek to address.

Solidarity as a theological ethic has already been argued for by several Christian denominations and theologians. Of significance, the Catholic Church set out its understanding of solidarity at the Second Vatican Council in *Gaudium et Spes* (Joy and Hope).[41] Meghan Clark summarizes the use of solidarity in *Gaudium et Spes* in three ways. First, as an interconnectedness and interdependence within the global community.[42] Second, as providing a framework for identifying our responsibilities for distant others.[43] Finally, by connecting human relationality and solidarity to the incarnation of Jesus Christ.[44] The last point on the incarnation of Christ is expressed in words of Pope Francis: 'Jesus' face is similar to that of so many of our brothers and sisters, humiliated, rendered slaves, emptied. God took on their face.'[45] This echoes the immanentism present in the labour church with its focus on Jesus the man, and 'the importance of God's presence in the world as exemplified primarily by the incarnation but also by the Church Christ left to fulfil his purpose.'[46] Biblically, the conception of the incarnation as the act of divine solidarity is present in the parable of the last judgement (Matthew 25), where Jesus radically identifies himself with the vulnerable, marginalized and excluded.[47] In this parable Jesus is asked by those deemed righteous, when they fed, clothed and visited him; he states, 'Truly I tell you, just as you did it to the least of these who are members of my family, you did it to me.'[48] A theological ethic of solidarity is therefore not just a Christian act of imitating Christ but is a location for encounter with the person of Christ through the divine act of solidarity in the incarnation. Christians encounter Christ in the face of the poor, the marginalized and the oppressed and by acting in solidarity with them they experience Christ working through them as the one who claimed that 'the Spirit of the Lord is upon me, because he has anointed me to bring good news to the poor. He has sent me to proclaim release to the captives and recovery of sight to the blind, to set free those who are oppressed, to proclaim the year of the Lord's favour.'[49]

A theological ethic of solidarity finds its clearest expression in works of liberation theology. Gustavo Gutiérrez, the well-agreed founder of the discipline, summarizes that 'all the political theologies, the theologies of hope, of revolution and of liberation, are not worth one genuine act of solidarity with exploited social classes'.[50] There is a substantial difference between a theological ethic of solidarity that only theorizes about solidarity versus one that requires action. The value of a theological ethic of solidarity should not be determined by its acceptance as a theory but rather by whether it is approved of by those whom we intend to stand in solidarity with. Rebecca Peters argues that solidarity cannot just be the showing of support through pins, t-shirts or even protests; rather, it requires engagement and relationship with the group that you intend to show solidarity with.[51] She states that solidarity 'represents a bond between people that calls for loyalty, compassion, and companionship, a bond rooted in the agape love of the Christian tradition'.[52]

Considering the theological solidarity ethics presented by Hessel, Peters, Gutiérrez and the Second Vatican Council, among others, it appears that they contain some common features; these include:

1 Relationship with a marginalized group and awareness of interconnectedness and privilege.
2 Personal and communal action taken in partnership with the group or individuals you intend to act in solidarity with.
3 Commitment to systemic change, through the means of politics, prayer and collective action.

4 A theological grounding in the incarnation of Jesus as the divine act of solidarity.

Using this ethical framework, I conclude that it is necessary that Christian action for justice must include acts of solidarity. This is also true for the work of trade unionism; it is possible to engage in trade union activity with the sole motive of improving one's individual terms and conditions of employment. However, solidarity, particularly in neo-colonial nations such as the UK and USA, not only looks at our individual circumstances but also recognizes the interconnectedness in our employment relationships with marginalized groups globally. For example, retail workers in the UK when acting on this ethic of solidarity will seek to unionize for the improvement of their terms and conditions and for their colleagues both locally and globally. Recognizing the ways in which workers in a company's supply chain can experience oppressive work practices and that until justice is achieved for all workers whether in supply, production, sales and support then it has not been achieved at all. One example relevant to the UK context is that of pay gap reporting where there is a legal requirement for companies with more than 250 members of staff to produce a report on their gender pay gap; however, no such legal requirement exists for racial pay gap reporting. This year the Trade Union Congress called upon the government to introduce racial pay gap reporting.[53] The Office for National Statistics has shown that in some cases white British workers earn more than racial and ethnic minorities for doing the same job in the UK.[54] The lack of required racial pay gap reporting makes bridging this gap more difficult. White trade unionists campaigning for racial pay gap reporting demonstrate what it means to act in solidarity and the necessity of an intersectional approach, especially because racial and ethnic minority women are often doubly affected by racial and gender pay gaps – men earned more than women in all but three ethnic groups in 2019.[55]

An Intersectional Approach to Trade Unions and Labour Movements

This theological ethic of solidarity also requires us to take an intersectional approach to the work of trade unionism and labour movements, recognizing that class, although central, is not the only characteristic to be considered when locating individuals in their relationship to power. In the UK people under the age of 35 make up 36.8% of employees but only 24.1% of union members.[56] Despite this, young workers were three times as likely to work in sectors where their jobs were more at risk during the Coronavirus pandemic, including work in the food, entertainment, recreation and arts sectors.[57] Women represent 56.8% of union members and union density has been greater among women since 2002; in part this is due to higher female employment rates in the public sector.[58] Yet despite this representation, women continue to experience sexual harassment and misogyny within trade unions – the spaces designed for solace from work are not safe for women. This is exactly why an intersectional approach that incorporates an ethic of solidarity is so necessary for trade unions. Trade unions are rightly focused on issues of class, including but not limited to 'objective resources, esteem and deference commanded by social roles, education, moral values, style of life, taste, and caste'.[59] Yet this focus can also become a stumbling block leading to a lack of awareness of relationships of power such as gender, race, religion, sexuality and more. Joerg Rieger acknowledges the ways in which an ethic of solidarity can benefit us here when he says, 'solidarity along the lines of the hegemony of class needs to be informed by solidarity along the lines of gender, sexuality, race, ethnicity, nationality, and so on.'[60] An intersectional approach that utilizes an ethic of solidarity would not only focus on the improvement of working conditions for workers in neo-colonial nation states but also fight for and stand with global workers who are exploited in production and manufacturing as well as in extraction of raw materials. It would also take account of the ways in which the climate crisis plays a role in these relationships of power, acknowledging the fact that reducing consumption, pushing for climate reparations and holding companies to account on their supply chain are necessary acts of solidarity. These acts of solidarity would be following on the path of the immanentists mentioned earlier and their belief that 'God was present equally in all',[61] as well as the incarnational approach argued for by Pope Francis, who expanded solidarity to include all of creation in a 'new and universal solidarity'.[62]

Trade unions remain a useful tool for tackling and addressing inequalities and achieving justice for workers. Collective bargaining is still one of the most effective ways of closing the gender pay gap, protecting workers' rights and achieving justice in the workplace. However, new trade unionists unfortunately face a battle on two fronts, one for justice in their workplace and one for justice within the trade union and labour movement. There also remains a clear divide between trade unions' effectiveness in the minority world and in the majority world. In countries where workers' rights are weakened or are close to non-existent, acts of solidarity are required from those in a position to act.

Conclusion

There is a clear history of Christianity intersecting with the trade union and labour movement in the UK. This is evident in the lives of individuals, in labour churches, the independent Labour Party and trade unions. This history is often not acknowledged and even though the modern trade union movement is avowedly secular there remains a need for people of faith to adopt a theological ethic of solidarity to be able to further causes of justice and peace. Activism and theology without solidarity remains a performative endeavour that often serves to validate individuals in positions of privilege rather than benefiting those who are marginalized and in need of justice. A theological ethic of solidarity requires relationship, individual action and a commitment to systemic change; for those who call themselves Christians it is substantiated by the divine act of solidarity in the person of Jesus Christ. This theological ethic of solidarity must take account of intersectionality if it is to be of any benefit to the global community. Acts of solidarity and a trade unionism that focus solely upon issues of class without acknowledging intersecting power structures can too easily lead to further marginalization for those who already bear the brunt of capitalism's brutality.

Notes

1 https://www.tssa.org.uk/news-and-events/tssa-news/independent-inquiry-report-published (accessed 8/03/2024).

2 The Monaghan Report, https://www.gmb.org.uk/news/independent-investigation (accessed 8/03/2024).

3 For a more in-depth consideration of the influence of Methodism in the British labour movement refer to R. F. Wearmouth, *Methodism and the Struggle of the Working Class* (Leicester: Edgar Bakes, 1954); R. F. Wearmouth, *The Social and Political Influence of Methodism in the Twentieth Century* (London: Epworth Press, 1957); and David Hempton, *Religion and Political Culture in Britain and Ireland from the Glorious Revolution to the Decline of the Empire* (Cambridge: Cambridge University Press, 1996).

4 Jane Holgate, 'Faith in Unions: From Safe Spaces to Organised Labour?', *Capital and Class* (Vol. 37, 2, June 2013), 243.

5 Clare Griffiths, 'From "Dorchester Labourers" to "Tolpuddle Martyrs": Celebrating Radicalism in the English Countryside', in *Secular Martyrdom in Britain and Ireland: From Peterloo to the Present*, ed. Quentin Outram and Keith Laybourn (London: Palgrave Macmillan, 2018), 60.

6 W. H. Oliver, 'Tolpuddle Martyrs and Trade Union Oaths', *Labour History* (Vol. 10, May 1966), 5–12.

7 Griffiths, 'From "Dorchester Labourers"', 61.

8 Holgate, 'Faith in Unions', 243.
9 Oliver, 'Tolpuddle Martyrs', 10.
10 Oliver, 'Tolpuddle Martyrs', 8.
11 Griffiths, 'From "Dorchester Labourers"', 61.
12 Ibid.
13 John Trevor, *My Quest for God* (London: Labour Prophet Office, 1897), 241.
14 Mark Bevir, 'The Labour Church Movement, 1891–1902', *Journal of British Studies* (Vol. 38, 2, April 1999), 234.
15 Holgate, 'Faith in Unions', 245.
16 K. S. Inglis, 'The Labour Church Movement', *International Review of Social History* (Vol. 3, 3, 1958), 450.
17 Inglis, 'The Labour Church Movement', 458.
18 Inglis, 'The Labour Church Movement', 445.
19 Inglis, 'The Labour Church Movement', 224.
20 Henry Pelling, *The Origins of the Labour Party, 1880–1900* (London: Macmillan, 1954), 139.
21 Inglis, 'The Labour Church Movement', 449; and Bevir, 'The Labour Church Movement', 219.
22 Bevir, 'The Labour Church Movement', 220.
23 Bevir, 'The Labour Church Movement', 225.
24 Lesley Orr, 'If Christ could be Militant so could I', *Kirchliche Zeitgeschichte* (Vol. 31, 1, 2018), 29.
25 Orr, 'If Christ could be Militant', 30.
26 Orr, 'If Christ could be Militant', 41.
27 Report by Chief Constable of Edinburgh to Secretary for Scotland of meeting held on 29 March 1918, *National Records of Scotland*, HH31/34/9.
28 *Kirkintilloch Gazette,* 1 March 1918.
29 Holgate, 'Faith in Unions', 244.
30 Ibid.
31 Ibid.
32 Ralph Chaplin, 'Solidarity Forever', in *Little Red Songbook,* 9th ed. (Chicago: Industrial Workers of the World, 1915).
33 Ezekiel 40—44.
34 Revelation 21—22.
35 Felix Adler, *The Socialist Sunday School Song Book* (The National Council of British Socialist Sunday School Unions, 1957), 7.
36 David Isiohoro, *Faith in Unions: Racism and Religious Exclusion in the Faith Workers Branch of Unite the Union 2017–2020* (Eugene: Wipf and Stock Publishers, 2022), 12.
37 'Church of England clergy demand pay rise for first time in history', *The Independent,* Last Modified 19 June 2023, https://www.independent.co.uk/news/uk/church-of-england-unite-church-commissioners-b2360240.html (accessed 8/03/2024).
38 Isiohoro, *Faith in Unions,* 110.
39 Dieter T. Hessel, 'Solidarity Ethics: A Public Focus for the Church', *Review of Religious Research* (Vol. 20, 3, Summer 1979), 254.
40 William Dudley Haywood, *The Autobiography of Big Bill Haywood* (New York: International Publishers Co., 1929), 186.

41 'Gaudium et Spes', Vatican, 7 December 1965, https://www.vatican.va/archive/hist_councils/ii_vatican_council/documents/vat-ii_const_19651207_gaudium-et-spes_en.html (accessed 8/03/2024).

42 Meghan J. Clark, 'Pope Francis and the Christological Dimensions of Solidarity in Catholic Social Teaching', *Theological Studies* (Vol. 80, 1, 2019), 102–3.

43 Ibid.

44 Ibid.

45 Clark, 'Pope Francis', 112.

46 Bevir, 'The Labour Church Movement', 222.

47 Clark, 'Pope Francis', 112–23.

48 Matthew 25.40 NRSV.

49 Luke 4.18–19 NRSV.

50 Gustavo Gutiérrez, *A Theology of Liberation* (Maryknoll: Orbis Books, 1973), 388.

51 Rebecca Todd Peters, 'Reflections on a Theology of Solidarity', *The Ecumenical Review* (Vol. 67, 2, July 2015), 230.

52 Ibid.

53 'Make ethnicity pay gap reporting mandatory – TUC', BBC, last modified 25 April 2023, https://www.bbc.co.uk/news/uk-politics-65315793# (accessed 21/02/2024).

54 'Ethnicity Pay Gaps: 2019', Office for National Statistics, https://www.ons.gov.uk/employmentandlabourmarket/peopleinwork/earningsandworkinghours/articles/ethnicitypaygapsingreatbritain/2019#:~:text=In%202019%2C%20the%20median%20hourly,its%20narrowest%20level%20since%202012 (accessed 8/03/2024).

55 Ibid.

56 'TUC Equality Audit 2022', TUC, 18 October 2022, https://www.tuc.org.uk/EqualityAudit2022?page=2 (accessed 8/03/2024).

57 'TUC Young Workers', TUC, 12 June 2020, https://www.tuc.org.uk/news/young-workers-three-times-more-likely-be-employed-sectors-where-jobs-are-most-risk-tuc#:~:text=Of%204%2C352%2C000%20UK%20workers%20aged,for%20workers%20older%20than%2025 (accessed 8/03/2024).

58 'TUC Equality Audit 2022'.

59 Dov Cohen, Faith Shin, Xi Liu, Peter Ondish and Michael W. Kraus, 'Defining Social Class Across Time and Between Groups', *Personality and Social Psychology Bulletin* (Vol. 43, 11, 2017), 1531.

60 Joerg Rieger, *Theology in the Capitalocene: Ecology, Identity, Class and Solidarity* (Minneapolis: Fortress Press, 2022), 11.

61 Bevir, 'The Labour Church Movement', 235.

62 Francis, '*Laudato Si*' (24 May 2015), 14, https://www.vatican.va/content/francesco/en/encyclicals/documents/papa-francesco_20150524_enciclica-laudato-si.html (accessed 8/03/2024).

9

'This is my Story, this is my Song': Queer Presbyterians, Provocative Questions, Practical Politics, and a Case for Church History in the Development of Theologies of Justice

DAVID BRANDON SMITH

I became and remain Presbyterian largely because I believe the church needs a form of governance that does not rest upon the assumption that theology is a finished product pre-packaged by our faithful forebears and thus stale by the time we unwrap it or, worse, ship it off to be consumed by a hungry world. Indeed, 'Theology [and church governance, by extension] at its best allows matters of substance to remain works in progress.'[1] It is for this reason that queer Presbyterians and their allies have spent the last five decades challenging systemic oppression in and beyond the church while mostly operating within time-tested patterns of Presbyterian engagement.

American Presbyterians have long displayed a tendency to ask provocative questions. Such broad assertions and the topics included under the interpretive paradigms they generate rarely withstand scrutiny in matters of detail and scope, but the history of my tradition and of Christianity, in general, can, indeed, be summarized via reference to the questions raised and responses given at specific times and places. Such questions, in turn, and from the perspective of the *longue durée* (the long term) of history, can define eras, or at least historians' interpretations of key developments within given timespans. Questions like those I will raise in this chapter as a way of contextualizing mainline American Presbyterianism's 50-year struggle over the inclusion, ordination and marriage of LGBTQIA+ Christians, clarify the open relationship between intra-, inter- and extra-ecclesial developments: that is, the relationship between the Presbyterian Church, the churches and the world. Such provocative queries may also shed 'more light' on how those who aim to develop new theologies of justice can draw wisdom from the church's story as embodied in its history.

'Do you sincerely receive and adopt the essential tenets of the Reformed faith?'

Just as action on most ideological and political debates in the United States is mediated through the legal framework that flows out of the nation's constitution, since independence, American Presbyterians have addressed similar questions through the lens of polity principles that are presently enshrined in their churches' forms of government (constitutions). In the Presbyterian Church (USA), my home denomination, the questions that have defined different eras live on as theologically and historically grounded principles of ecclesiastical order. Within its representative, democratic and constitutionalist framework, no debate has so rocked the church over the past 50 years as that which has raged over the inclusion, ordination and marriage of Presbyterians whose sexual orientation and/or gender identity differs from assumed norms.

The church's discursive history has been folded into the questions that would-be ordinands must answer in the affirmative before assuming their offices. Teaching Elders (pastors/ministers of word and sacrament), Ruling Elders (elected from within congregations to govern and provide spiritual oversight of the church) and Deacons (elected from within congregations and guided by the 'Session' – body of Elders – in carrying out the church's ministries of compassion, witness and service) are asked a series of questions during their ordination services, each of which has its own developmental history. The third in the series of nine 'Constitutional Questions' (the ninth differs based on the office to be assumed) reads as follows:

> Do you sincerely receive and adopt the essential tenets of the Reformed faith as expressed in the confessions of our church as authentic and reliable expositions of what Scripture leads us to believe and do, and will you be instructed and led by those confessions as you lead the people of God?[2]

This question, especially the clause about the 'essential tenets of the Reformed faith' and the notion that ordinands are to be 'instructed and led by' (rather than 'obedient to') the church's confessions, exemplifies the relationship between what one might call 'religious freedom' or 'freedom of conscience' and the 'confessional nature' of the Presbyterian Church, especially when it comes to its policy regarding ecclesiastical offices.[3] It also bears witness to some of the discursive strands that have defined the ecclesial life of North American Presbyterians from the colonial era to the present.

'Whose side are you on?'

In July of 1620, a Reformed pastor named John Robinson issued a proclamation to a group of Dutch Pilgrims aboard the *Speedwell*, which was bound for the shores of the 'new world'. Robinson proclaimed, 'For I am very confident the Lord hath more truth and light yet to break forth out of his Holy Word.'[4] Over a century after Robinson issued his proclamation, amid what is often (though not without controversy – more than a few have called it an 'interpretative fiction')[5] described as the First Great Awakening (from the 1730s to late 1740s), revivalists, including many Presbyterians, again drew upon the biblical imagery of 'light' to describe the Spirit's movement in the world.[6] Revivalists came to be called 'New Lights', while traditionalists, who spurned such 'enthusiasms', were called 'Old Lights'. Lest they, and those who study them, be accused of falling in with the spiritual trends of their time, the Presbyterians who engaged in the Old/New Light debate are described as New or Old 'Siders'.

In colonial New England, as well as in the mid-Atlantic, where Presbyterians were more dominant, the Old/New Light or Old/New Side dispute did not create entirely 'new divisions among the clergy but followed contours formed prior to the actual outbursts of revivals'.[7] That said, one's answer to questions like 'Whose Side are you on?' could define everything from one's understanding of salvation to devotional practices. Moreover, while there were as many differences of opinion on the great social issues of the day within the two primary camps/sides as between them, one's stance on revival may have had a lot to say about everything from one's place of birth, economic status, or even stances on the abolition of slavery, public morality, temperance, and gender equality in education.[8]

'Shall woman preach?'

Presbyterian self-questioning continued as the tides of revival ebbed and flowed. Amid what is often termed the Second Great Awakening (from the 1790s to the 1840s), churches split over the advent of a new stir of revivalism. One of the new groups to emerge out of older denominations in the opening decade of the nineteenth century was the Cumberland Presbyterian Church. Having been rebuked by higher judicatories for licensing ministers who failed to meet the church's ordination standards, Presbyterians in the Cumberland River Valley began organizing themselves independently. In February of 1810, they established a new denominational communion at an independent presbytery meeting in Dickinson, Tennessee.[9]

Generations later, as a continuation of the revivalist tradition of ordaining ministers that others might consider unqualified, on 5 November 1889, in the waning moments of a Nolin Presbytery meeting, this small group of Southern Presbyterians made history: they licensed and ordained Louisa Mariah Layman Woosley (1862–1952) to the ministry of word and sacrament. Throughout her life, Woosley sought to model humility in the acceptance of her role in the pulpit, but, as Marie Linnie Hudson writes, her 'ordination did not simply set her apart for ministry; it transformed her into a symbol of women's equal partnership with men in the leadership of the church'.[10]

While her years of service had endeared her to her own presbytery, the larger bodies of the small denomination, which, as we have seen, had been formed around the right of presbyteries to ordain and install ministers, were less enthusiastic. The 'event of Woosley's ordination divided the church over the question of the authority and role of women according to scripture and the Constitution of the church'.[11] In 1891, as a response to the backlash prompted by her ordination, the embattled minister asked and answered a question of her own in a book titled, *Shall Woman Preach? Or The Question Answered*.[12]

The fact that at least enough Cumberland Presbyterians saw fit to join the passionate minister in responding affirmatively to her question attests to Woosley's gravitas and pastoral presence. Yet, despite such developments among the Cumberland group, American Presbyterianism's major Northern and Southern branches, which had split during the US Civil War, would not remove official barriers to the ordination of women as Ruling Elders until 1930.[13] It was not until the passage of 'Overture B' in May 1955 and its ratification by the majority of presbyteries in 1956 that the way was cleared for Margaret Towner (b. 1925) to become the first

Presbyterian woman in the Northern Church to answer constitutional questions then asked of pastoral ordinands. Southern Presbyterians beyond the Cumberland fold would have to wait even longer to see a woman ordained to the ministry of preaching, but even in that community, Woosley's question was answered in the affirmative when Rachel Henderlite (1905–91) was ordained in 1965.

'What is your Christianity?'

Women were not the only group of Presbyterians to pose provocative questions in the eighteenth, nineteenth and early twentieth centuries. Just as few twenty-first-century debates in the US and around the world can escape what W. E. B. Dubois defined as 'the problem of the color line',[14] seemingly straightforward questions of church law and doctrine have been indelibly marked by the struggle over the institution of chattel slavery. In the years after US independence, as the first General Assembly of the PCUSA gathered in May of 1789, Presbyterians officially condemned slavery and called their co-religionists to 'work toward abolition'.[15] Unfortunately, this statement, which, given its early date, might strike modern readers as prophetic, was more an act of virtue signalling than a concrete policy proposal.

In the centuries that followed, the 'slavery question' would divide Christian communities along sectional (North/South) lines, even as other doctrinal disputes split the church. Around the time of what is commonly called the 'Old School–New School Controversy' (distinct though descended from the New/Old Side debates referenced above), various Black Presbyterians rose to prominence in the church. A leader among them was America's first Black seminary graduate (Princeton Theological Seminary, Class of 1828), Theodore Sedgwick Wright (1797–1847).

Some of Wright's many provocative questions were recorded in a July 1837 issue of *The Colored American*. Amid debates over mission efforts, the admittance of slaveholders to communion, and the mistreatment of people of colour at the Lord's Table, the pastor of the First 'Colored' Presbyterian Church of New York City demanded,

> What is your Christianity? Where is your consistency in talking about the heathen, traversing the ocean to circulate the Bible everywhere, while you frown upon them at the door? What is your Christianity? How do you regard your brethren? How do you treat them at the Lord's Table?[16]

These rhetorical questions and the unspoken questions behind them were designed to poke at the church's nervous system: they play on the missional ethos in ways that might grate against modern sensibilities, but they reflect Wright's passionate refusal to permit the separation of the church's spiritual mission of bearing witness to salvation in the world from its call to work for justice in society.

The 'doctrine of the spirituality of the church' which, in its more radical expressions, posited that the church should concern itself exclusively with spiritual rather than social or political matters, would not rise to prominence in intra-Presbyterian debates until several decades after Wright posed the questions cited here.[17] Nevertheless, many within the church of his day felt they could carry out the gospel's commission without challenging either the institution of chattel slavery in the South or the unequal treatment of Black Americans in the North. Wright had little patience for such notions; spiritual freedom, of which the mistreatment of his fellow Black Presbyterians at the Lord's Table made a mockery, was meaningless if not accompanied by concrete engagement alongside those who worked tirelessly to extend structural freedoms to the enslaved and the marginalized.

'Shall the fundamentalists win?'

As I have already hinted, following the outbreak of the US Civil War, the nation's largest Presbyterian bodies would also be torn asunder. In 1861, both the New and Old School Presbyterians of the South split from their co-religionists in the North to form their own churches. The Southern schools then united with one another into the Presbyterian Church in the Confederate States of America, which would remain separate from its Northern counterpart (and largely segregated along racial lines) long after the war's end. After the nation's reunification, the Southern church continued its separate existence as the Presbyterian Church in the United States (PCUS), which was distinct from the United Presbyterian Church in the United States of America (UPCUSA) in the North – a church that was, itself, a union of two previously distinct branches of Northern Presbyterianism. It would not be until 1983, 122 years after their separation, that the largest Northern and Southern Presbyterian bodies would reunite into the PC(USA).

Yet, as the points charted thus far might suggest, the process of self-questioning among Presbyterianism's largest branches was not paused between 1861 and 1983. By the late nineteenth century, the next great intra-Presbyterian conflict was already brewing. The so-called 'Fundamentalist–Modernist' controversy, which became an all-out schismatic brawl when questions about church governance and ordination policy emerged at the centre of the conversation, can be introduced via reference to the titles of two sermons preached by pastors at a high point of the dispute. In 1922, the theologically liberal preacher, who was then serving as the pastor of the First Presbyterian Church of New York City, Harry Emerson Fosdick (1878–1969), issued one of the formative practical-theological questions of his era when he asked his beleaguered congregation, 'Shall the Fundamentalists Win?' In response to the sermon's publication and circulation, Clarence E. Macartney (1879–1957), the 'moderate/loyalist'[18] pastor then serving Philadelphia's Arch Street Presbyterian Church, retorted with his own question in a sermon titled, 'Shall Unbelief Win?'

While those expressing fundamentalist perspectives eventually left to found what is known today as the Orthodox Presbyterian Church – hardly the last intra-Presbyterian schism of the twentieth century – theological moderates/denominational loyalists and liberals found a way to move beyond questions about who would and should 'win' in the major doctrinal disputes of the era. They answered the question of whether it was possible to maintain unity amid theological diversity with a reluctant but (eventually) adamant, 'yes'.

After years of work, the so-called 'Swearingen Commission' of the Northern General Assembly issued its 1927 report. The commission upheld a long-standing precedent of Presbyterian polity when it concluded that the church's higher bodies (like the General Assembly) could not force their interpretation of essential and necessary articles of Reformed faith on presbyteries in a general way, but only in specific cases. Therefore, if an ordaining or installing body (presbyteries for teaching elders, congregations for ruling elders and deacons), through the leading of the Holy Spirit, affirms that a person is called to and qualified for the ministry, it has the right to ordain that person. This right applies regardless of where the ordinand falls on the spectrum from fundamentalist to liberal, so long as that person affirms their belief in the church's confessional standards, possesses the requisite educational qualifications, has their examination sustained by the ordaining body, and is willing to fulfil all constitutional obligations of their office.[19] The higher governing bodies of the church could review specific cases that raised concerns about a particular officer's confessional fidelity or pastoral practice, but all previous bans (including the infamous 'Doctrinal Deliverance of 1910')[20] on the ordination of people holding (or not holding) specific beliefs on the so-called 'fundamentals of the faith' were thenceforth null and void.

'Unite with the Northern Presbyterian Church?'

Reunion between the church's Northern and Southern branches was anything but a foregone conclusion in the decades leading up to the uniting assembly in 1983. Following vitriolic debates over the ordination of divorced people and women from the 1930s to the 1950s, the 1960s were characterized by a struggle over the church's engagement with the Civil Rights Movement and the desegregation of many Southern congregations. In the Presbyterian world, these disputes can be summarized by referencing yet another question. Upset by the attempts of leaders in the Southern church to reunite with the more racially progressive Northern Presbyterians and thus to accept the universal application of their desegregation policies, stances towards the empowerment of women in church leadership, and the initial stages of discussion around human sexuality, a Southern lawyer and Presbyterian Ruling Elder, Chalmers W. Alexander, composed an article that asked and answered a question of his own: 'Unite with the Northern Presbyterian Church? No!'[21]

'Is anyone else out there gay?'

While debates about civil rights for Black Americans, feminist movements, and reunion continued in full swing, Presbyterians were confronted by yet another question, which finally gets us to the heart of this chapter. High-level debate over the full inclusion of gay, lesbian and bisexual Presbyterians in the church's life began at least as early as 1966 when the Northern church's Council on Church and Society initiated a study on 'Sexuality and the Human Community'. Following quickly on the denomination's initial self-questioning, 'the 1970s witnessed a notable acceleration of study and debate',[22] which, like many disputes before it, 'often took on legislative forms that centered on ordination'.[23]

David Baily Sindt (1940–86), a Presbyterian minister and social worker who was ordained by the Northern church in 1965, had subsequently come out as gay and was then denied an opportunity to take up a pastoral call by the presbytery within the bounds of which he felt called to serve. Though he had since taken a job at the Illinois Department of Children and Family Services, Sindt made his way to the General Assembly of his church in the summer of 1974. As if attempting to challenge the church's tradition of fastidious adherence to decency and order with an equally traditional (and inherently Presbyterian) disregard for presumptive impositions on free expression, Sindt climbed up on his chair in the middle of the assembly hall and held up a poster that asked a question; 'Is anyone else out there gay?'[24]

The next 50 years of the church's common life would be largely defined by its collective struggle to answer the questions behind this question – queries that echo those of countless generations of Presbyterians in other times and places. Specifically, the community asked itself, can openly LGBTQIA+ people be members of Presbyterian congregations? Can they be ordained as Teaching Elders, Ruling Elders and Deacons? Can they be married in the churches they call home? The church answered the first question about membership affirmatively in 1978 (North) and 1979 (South). After a series of advances and setbacks, all of which were defined by intense battles over church law and polity, the second question on ordination was finally answered affirmatively in 2011, and the third about marriage was answered with a 'yes' in 2015.

It is worth noting here that these answers apply only to the majority of Presbyterian congregations that remain part of the Presbyterian Church (USA). That church's decisions do not apply to those with whom it has not been historically affiliated or to groups (like the Orthodox Presbyterian Church) that split from the larger body amid disputes in the first half of the twentieth century. The policies referenced here also do not apply to the second largest US Presbyterian body, the Presbyterian Church in America (PCA), which was established (mainly in the South) in 1973 amid consternation over the prospect of reunion between the Northern and Southern churches, the ongoing practice of women's ordination, biblical inerrancy and the ratification of the Confession of 1967, which condemned racial segregation and called for reconciliation. The decisions on ordination and marriage also do not apply to the Evangelical Presbyterian Church (EPC), which split from the PC(USA) in 1981 following debates over substitutionary atonement and the requirement that church officers participate in the ordination of women. Finally, the decisions on ordination and marriage do not apply in the congregations that left the larger body to form the Evangelical Covenant Order of Presbyterians (ECO) in 2012 in direct response to the affirmative decision on the ordination of LGBTQIA+ clergy.

Though their passionate advocacy came at great personal and relational cost, from the very beginning of their intra-ecclesial movement, many queer Presbyterians advocated for their place at the table from within the church's historic discursive patterns and systems of governance. From the outside looking in, such an approach opens those who employ it to criticism for what might appear to be an *atheological* use of practical politics. Such critiques are based on a fundamental misconception, namely that American Presbyterian polity functions parallel to and distinct from the church's theology. In fact, every detail of the church's governance is derived from and interwoven with its confessional identity and a theologically grounded commitment to freedom of conscience. For Presbyterians, internally diverse churches, like pluralist societies, need laws that are administered collectively by democratically elected gatherings of 'presbyters' (that is, elders or mature leaders of any age), not by appointed individuals at the top of hierarchies.

Like Woosley, Wright and others before them, LGBTQIA+ people of faith posed provocative questions, not only through pens, paper and posters but also by practising 'ministries of presence'. They embodied their calling by simply, yet profoundly, being who they were as Christians who happened to be queer and as queer people who happened to be Christian. As Sindt wrote before he set out for the 1974 General Assembly, 'I suggest that we focus our initial efforts nationally on a "ministry of presence" ... to work for change within the denomination, not attack it from either within or without.'[25] Queer Presbyterians and their allies also drew upon their church's history when they, like the 'New Lights' of the First Great Awakening, labelled many openly affirming churches 'More Light Congregations' from 1978 onward.

Pro-inclusion groups like the Covenant Network of Presbyterians, which was founded in 1997 and considered 'moderate' when compared to the More Light wing to their left, took a page out of Theodore Sedgwick Wright's book. They emphasized the historic Presbyterian understanding of the church as a covenantal community where salvation, and thus unqualified inclusion around the Lord's Table, is an unmerited gift of grace bestowed by a sovereign God, not a privilege to be dispensed to some who are deemed worthy by a self-congratulatory ecclesiastical hierarchy. They also argued passionately for the removal of bans on gay and lesbian ordination (themselves products of late twentieth-century political debates in the broader society) based on the balance struck between freedom of thought and confessional fidelity in the early eighteenth century and codified by the Swearingen Commission Report of 1927.

Presbyterian Questions, Practical Politics and Church History

As with any approach to the writing of history that strives to hold together the perspective of the *longue durée* with a recognition of the vital role played by moments of crisis or decision, especially within well-connected social sub-groups, the questions raised here only point to some of the issues that defined the eras covered so briefly. The questions posed in this chapter reveal discernible, though non-linear, patterns of intra-Presbyterian engagement on divisive questions that were identified, recycled and practised by subsequent generations. These patterns were exemplified in the struggle over LGBTQIA+ inclusion, ordination and marriage in ways that are distinct but related to previous disputes. In the second half of the twentieth century, questions raised by individuals and groups of believers awakened the church's governing bodies to a theological crisis that strained the relationship between freedom and perceived tradition. The crisis that emerged prompted calls for a decision. Though the specifics of the questions raised differed from those faced by the church in the past, the way the communion asked and answered them was not new: the political process involved in creating a church that was inclusive and affirming of LGBTQIA+ membership, ordination and marriage reflected the events that followed the church's internal reckoning with revivalism, slavery, civil war, racism, gender equality and theological expressions of modernity.

In response to the crisis evoked by new questions, parties and factions emerged (or at least realigned to absorb new discursive elements), both within the church itself and the broader movements calling for change; some in this emergent period advocated for the development of collective and clear-cut identities (like many that eventually converged into the 'Covenant Network' camp), while other groups embraced their otherness and practised a politics of transgression, parody and anti-assimilation (like those who gradually consolidated into the 'More Light Churches Network').

Both approaches, and the convergences between them, when judged simply on the ability of the groups that employed them to achieve their stated aims, had merits, and each was essential to removing barriers to the full inclusion of LGBTQIA+ people in the church. The full inclusion of queer believers in my faith community can thus be described as the consequence of broader and ongoing intra-, inter- and extra-ecclesial developments, which compelled people of faith to ask and try to answer emergent questions together. The current state of affairs in the denomination is a result, at least in part, of both provocative acts like holding up a poster that asked, 'Is anyone else out there gay?' and a willingness to pose equally daring but comparatively complex questions about the proper application and historical-theological foundations of church law.

In the preceding volume in the present series, *Young, Woke and Christian: Words from a Missing Generation*, Josh Mock penned a chapter titled 'Queer, Christian and Tired: Why I'm no Longer Talking to Cishet Christians About Sexuality'. Josh's historical and theological reflection raised profound methodological questions. Like the Presbyterians I referenced in the foregoing pages, Josh also raised a question; this time, it was directed at queer Christians. Josh wanted to know, 'How many lives must be lost, how many queers rejected, how much grace denied before we accept that assimilation, dialogue, apologetics, and compromise will not bring us the freedom we deserve?'[26]

I genuinely resonate with this question and the pain behind it. Yet, I wonder, as a gay Christian, Presbyterian minister of word and sacrament, and church historian, if there is a danger in conflating all the terms referenced in this provocative query. I also wonder whether it is credible to suggest that things like dialogue, apologetics and compromise (at least on non-essentials and within ecclesio-political systems) have failed. Indeed, the (transitory?) failure of such efforts is evidenced in many of the communities Josh referenced *but not in mine*.

Arguments for historical inevitability based on a newly minted and precariously maintained status quo rarely hold up when scrutinized. However, the persistent practice of ministries of presence, calculated political manoeuvring, and a willingness to delve into the *minutiae* of policy, law and the church's history of complex but often brave questioning of social norms, linked with uncomfortable compromises, the endurance of soul-crushing setbacks, and a willingness to entertain (and rebut) offensive questions, changed my church. I can say from experience that these practices are changing other communions as well. Perhaps the sacrifice for which such methods call is not worth it, but I suppose that raises a question that everyone must answer for themselves.

Though few of the church's most influential provocateurs espoused gradualist schemes, many of their queries took decades or even centuries to answer in the affirmative, and each of the answers given is undermined by the schisms that accompanied them. Even so, the result of the church's self-questioning – and it is a self-questioning because queer Presbyterians challenged the church from *within* – has had an impact on the lives of countless people around the world. From the Christians who can now come to church and be fully embraced by a community without worrying whether they or their children who are baptized into the faith will be loved and nurtured throughout their lives, regardless of how they identify or whom they love, to the ministers who can serve the church while loving their partners without fear of losing their jobs, to the entire community, which can now benefit from the unapologetic life and witness of people who are called and qualified to preach the good news of love and justice to a hurting world, these questions have been asked and answered.

Change in the church and the churches, like change in the world, may require concerted effort and practical politicking; it may also necessitate a willingness to compromise on methods and throw every liberative nonviolent option on the table. Furthermore, as Sindt might remind us, those who would develop new theologies of justice must also recognize that our battle is not truly with 'the Church' – as if we were somehow attacking it from without, but with factions that have exerted power over it: to give the church (as a spiritual body *and* institution) over to the well-meaning but uninformed, the bigots or pietistic charlatans is, at least for many of us, to sell our baptismal rebirthright. And, at least for this cantankerous American Presbyterian, *that ain't happnin*. To accept that we must stand outside the church or our religious traditions and target them from beyond is to fall prey to the life-denying myth of queer-Christian non-existence, which so many in the church *and* the 'queer community' have tried to impose upon us.

Instead, by drawing on the discursive history of my own tradition, I have tried to make the case that we must take up the challenge to look deeply into our churches' histories, to view those histories and the discursive patterns that shaped them as resources in the struggle for justice, not merely as hindrances to inclusion and affirmation. All readers of the historical record should strive to minimize the violence they do to the past by imposing anachronistic paradigms upon it. However, to build solidarity with those who have gone before us, queer Christians and students of the church's story ought to ask new questions of history that, perhaps, can reveal knowledge that others may have overlooked or intentionally obscured.

What are the stories within the church's story that have been written in invisible ink, and how might we build solidarity with those who have gone before us by working with the Spirit to shed 'more light' on the shadowy corners of faith? For me, as an adopted heir (more on that below) to the American Presbyterian tradition, solidarity with the Christian past might arise through the act of retelling the stories of bold Presbyterians of the past – faithful people who advocated for a balance between freedom of conscience and the imposition of creedal dogmatism in the early eighteenth century and those who bore witness to revival while honouring tradition in the late eighteenth century and throughout the nineteenth. Perhaps it will also mean joining with Wright, Woosley and Fosdick in asking bold questions of the church regarding its complicity in slavery and racial segregation, along with its frequent unwillingness to heed God's word when proclaimed from the mouths of women and tendency to surpass both scripture and tradition in placing limits on the church's doctrinal diversity. Through their concerted efforts, these people of faith, like David Baily Sindt and the other queer Presbyterians who followed in their footsteps, did change their church – an institution that was, despite its waning influence amid today's denominational decline, once considered by many to be 'the most powerful ecclesiastical body in America'.[27]

'This is my story, this is my Song'

Let me conclude by offering what might read like a confession, especially since I have emphasized my experience as a member of the Presbyterian fold. I have been a Presbyterian for most of my adult life, but I grew up as a Southern Baptist. Whether I sang along with the sonorous tones of our choir director at church or at my great-grandmother's house on Sunday afternoon, many a weekend during my teenage years was accompanied by good old-fashioned hymn singing. One of the gospel tunes that comes to mind when I recall that time in my life is 'Fanny' Jane Crosby and Phoebe Knapp's 1873 hymn, 'Blessed Assurance'. As I write, I hear the refrain. It wells up from within me; my mind is flooded with memories of people I long to see again and echoes of a faith to which I cannot help but cling:

> This is my story, this is my song,
> Praising my Savior all the day long.
> This is my story, this is my song,
> Praising my Savior all the day long.

The church's story – the story of pain and prayer, of freedom and obedience, of justice and joy, is my story, and its unending song of praise and gratitude is the song of every queer person who calls the church home. The discursive histories of our traditions provide ample evidence of human fallibility, but they are also well-springs of resources for liberation. And so, I challenge readers to look deeper into the church's story, not only with an eye toward diversities of gender and sexuality, but to the broader discourses around liberation, freedom and inclusion that continue to shape who we are as people of faith. It is time to stop yielding our claim on the Christian tradition (and its claim on us!) to those who would suggest we are doing something entirely new; it is time to debunk the myths and reclaim our place in the history of the church's self-questioning as we continue working within our communities to embrace transformative theologies of justice.

Notes

1 John Wilkinson, 'Peace, Unity, and Purity and the Presbyterian Church's Fifty-Year Journey on Human Sexuality', in *Interpretation: A Journal of Bible and Theology* (Vol. 74, 3, 2020), 275–88, at p. 286.

2 Presbyterian Church (USA), *Constitution, Part II: Book of Order* (Office of the General Assembly: Louisville, KY, 2023), W-4.0404c.

3 I have traced the development of these questions and others in greater detail in David Brandon Smith, '"Calling the Question": The Role of Ministries of Presence and Polity Principles in the Struggle for LGBTQIA+ Inclusion, Ordination, and Marriage in the Presbyterian Church (USA) and its Predecessor Denominations', *Religions* (Vol. 13, 2023), 1119.

4 Robert Ashton, *The Works of John Robinson: Pastor of the Pilgrim Fathers with a Memoir and Annotations* (London: Snow, 1851).

5 See, for example, Jon Butler, 'Enthusiasm Described and Decried: The Great Awakening as Interpretative Fiction', *The Journal of American History* (Vol. 69, 2, 1982), 205–325.

6 Jonathan Edwards was perhaps the most influential writer to employ this imagery.

7 Harry S. Stout, 'The Great Awakening in New England Reconsidered: The New England Clergy', *Journal of Social History* (Vol. 1, 1, Autumn 1974), 21–47, at p. 41.

8 See Butler, 'Enthusiasm Described and Decried', 305–6 for an introduction to this complex discourse.

9 L. Thomas Smith, Jr, 'Cumberland Presbyterian Church', in *Tennessee Encyclopedia* (Tennessee Historical Society Online, 8 October 2017).

10 Mary Linnie Hudson, *Shall woman preach? Or the Question answered: The ministry of Louisa M. Woosley in the Cumberland Presbyterian Church 1887–1942* (PhD Dissertation, Vanderbilt University, University Microfilms International: Ann Arbor, MI, 1992), 34.

11 Ibid., 35.

12 Louisa M. L. Woosley, *Shall Woman Preach?– or the Question Answered* (Caneyville: self-published, 1891).

13 Presbyterian Historical Society, 'Timeline of Presbyterian History in America'.

14 W. E. B. Dubois, *The Souls of Black Folk*, Oxford World Classics (Oxford: Oxford University Press, 1903), 3.

15 James H. Smylie, *A Brief History of the Presbyterians* (Geneva: Louisville, 1996), 87.

16 Quoted in Bella Gross, 'Life and Times of Theodore S. Wright, 1797–1847', *Negro History Bulletin* (Vol. 3, 9, 1940), 133–8, at p. 135.

17 This doctrine is especially important if one is to understand the debates round

the so-called 'Gardner Spring Resolutions' at the onset of the US Civil War. See Smith, 'Calling the Question'.

18 Most would describe Macartney as a 'fundamentalist', or at least a 'conservative', but his thoughts developed over time, and his style of churchmanship should be distinguished from those on his right.

19 This final point was not clarified by the Swearingen Commission's report but by a case that drew upon the principles outlined by it. In Maxwell v. Pittsburgh Presbytery, the Permanent Judicial Commission of the General Assembly (GA-PJC), which is like an intra-Presbyterian Supreme Court, decided that W. W. Kenyon's ordination was invalid because he refused to participate in services of the ordination of women to the church's offices, which was his constitutional obligation as an officer of the church. The Kenyon case is foundational to the formation of the Evangelical Presbyterian Church (EPC), referenced below.

20 Amid an earlier phase of debate between fundamentalists and modernists, which came to a head in 1910, the General Assembly issued a 'Doctrinal Deliverance', which, according to the Swearingen Report, should have only held advisory power but was applied as an authoritative statement on matters of doctrine. A (transient) victory for the denomination's right wing, the statement demanded that candidates for ordination affirm what are known as the 'five fundamentals'.

21 Chalmers W. Alexander, 'Unite with the Northern Presbyterian Church? No!' in *Southern Presbyterian Journal* (Vol. 6, 15 July, 1947).

22 Wilkinson, 'Peace', 277.

23 Ibid.

24 See R. W. Holmen, *Queer Clergy: A History of Gay and Lesbian Ministry in American Protestantism* (Cleveland, OH: Pilgrim, 2013), 352.

25 Ibid., 353.

26 Josh Mock, 'Queer, Christian and Tired: Why I'm no Longer Talking to Cishet Christians About Sexuality', in Victoria Turner, ed., *Young, Woke and Christian: Words from a Missing Generation* (London: SCM Press, 2022), 48.

27 Alice Adams, *The Neglected Period of Anti-Slavery*, in Gross, 'Life and Times', 135.

10

The Myth of the Gospel: Trump, Politics and the Crisis of the Evangelical Church

NATHAN DEVER

In 2006, sitting before thousands of evangelical pastors gathered for the inaugural 'Together for the Gospel' conference in Louisville, Kentucky, Al Mohler, president of the Southern Baptist Theological Seminary, the flagship seminary of the largest Protestant denomination in the US, was asked if fidelity to the gospel could ever require Christians to 'betray America'.[1] Responding confidently, Mohler stated that 'we should be prepared to betray any earthly kingdom' for the sake of Christ; a response that was met with wild applause from the audience.[2] And as this conference – one organized by four prominent evangelical leaders representing different, often competing denominations – had been conceived with the specific goal of highlighting the power of 'the gospel' to foster a transcendent spiritual unity, Mohler's response fitted the moment perfectly. His unwavering response made clear the position of the many evangelicals he represented. Nothing, including politics, could ever negate a Christian's responsibility to first be faithful to 'the gospel'. And continuing to be held on a biannual basis, in the years that followed, the conference proved to be hugely popular, with regular attendance reaching over 12,000. But despite the notion of 'gospel' unity that animated the conference, for Mohler, and many other evangelicals, when confronted with the rise of Donald Trump and the moral conundrum of whether or not to support him, this sentiment of other-worldly allegiance, so appealing in theory, proved to be much harder in practice. For in the years to come not only would Mohler go on to do the exact opposite of what he preached – in 2016 deeming evangelical support for Trump a betrayal of Christian witness, before publicly supporting Trump himself in 2020[3] – but the entire Together for the Gospel conference itself, breaking apart internally, was also scrapped. Holding its final gathering in 2022, which Mohler and other original founders were not a part of, the atmosphere was very different from that of 2006.[4] Marked by a constant lament over the rise of 'political' division at the expense of 'gospel' unity, talks at this final gathering tellingly had titles such as 'What does together for the gospel mean when we are so divided?' So what should we take away from this story, and what significance might this have for questions of theology and justice within the American Evangelical Church today? While there are a whole host of conclusions and observations that could be made, for the purposes of this chapter I want to highlight two. These are, first, that the Evangelical Church of the Trump era, wracked by painful divisions, is in crisis, and second, that the driver of this crisis is widely understood to be rooted in the rise of politics within the church.

The Crisis of Trump-era Evangelicalism

Let me begin with some personal reflections on the most obvious of these observations: that the Evangelical Church in the United States is in crisis. As someone who grew up within the church, and someone who remains deeply connected to it today, this is not an observation that I make with glee. Like so many others who grew up within the church, as I have got older, my personal beliefs have shifted significantly; a process that has often been painful. But even as my beliefs no longer resemble those that I grew up with, I can't help still thinking of myself as an evangelical. Of course, there is a certain amount of cultural cachet that could be derived from shedding this label in some circles. I could join the many others who call themselves 'exvangelicals' and go on to recount some story of 'deconstruction'. But personally, there is something that I find off-putting about this. It is not that I think there is anything wrong with those who embrace this label, or who are helped by processing their experience through such narratives. Rather, my discomfort is more to do with a lack of confidence in my own ability to somehow 'transcend' the effects of the environment that I grew up in. For better or for worse, as I have often explained to friends and family, I have been formed as an evangelical 'object'. And yet, since 2016, a year in which the community that I grew up in, and which I continue to have so many connections to, became synonymous with support for Donald Trump, my proximity to evangelicalism, already tenuous, has felt increasingly strained. And today, as the moral rot at the heart of the church becomes more and more evident, and the community descends further into irreversible schism, my feelings of unease about calling myself an evangelical have only intensified.

But ironically, even as this unease has been catalysed in large part by my feelings of frustration watching the church so quickly embrace Trump, today what I find myself most exasperated by is actually not evangelicalism's many Trump apologists, but rather its scattered gang of Trump-opponents. For while I can at times appreciate their intentions, I am increasingly frustrated by what I believe to be the fundamentally counterproductive approach to politics that often undergirds their opposition. It is a political theology that suggests the problematic notion of the church's 'spirituality' as a remedy to the present crisis of its 'politicization', a suggestion that yields nothing more than a cosmopolitan authoritarian politics of unity no better suited to meet the challenges of the present moment than the Trumpian vision it opposes. Therefore, in this chapter, as I consider the crisis of Trump-era evangelicalism, a topic that has been written about extensively, I hope to add a new critical perspective to this ongoing conversation by critiquing the language of the 'moderate' evangelicals ostensibly opposed to Trump which we so often uncritically praise. Something that I hope might, in a small way at least, gesture towards an alternative, more self-critical discourse of resistance that those who choose to remain within the church might possibly consider.

The Politicization Narrative

In the wake of Trump's rise, many frustrated evangelicals have lamented what they perceive to be the 'politicization' of American evangelicalism, a process presented as the Faustian prioritization of the 'political' over the 'spiritual'. Narrated as a slow-burn transformation that began with the rise of the Religious Right in the 1970s, and culminated in 2016 with the evangelical embrace of Donald Trump, according to its critics at least, this new politicized evangelicalism is merely a hollow shell of its former self. It is a movement that has traded Christian witness for political power, subordinated religious identity to political identity, and which has ultimately dissolved itself in the toxic acid of political partisanship. And certainly, when considered in light of the above example of the Together for the Gospel conference's rise and fall, this narrative would seem to be a perfect fit. Whereas in a pre-Trump world evangelicals could gather together in a big-tent manner for the sake of 'the gospel' – presented as the locus of the church's unifying 'spiritual' identity – in the Trump era 'political' divisions made this impossible. But even as there is an undeniable commonsense appeal to this narrative, I want to suggest that it is wrong, and that the crisis of contemporary evangelicalism is not the politicization of the Evangelical Church but in fact, the exact opposite – its depoliticization. And therefore, what the present moment calls for, I believe, is not to discourage the church's politicization, but rather to encourage it.

From the outset though I want to acknowledge that there are many legitimate reasons that one might be dismissive of the general idea that I am suggesting: that we should want the Evangelical Church more invested in politics. This is particularly true when considered in light of *who* or *what* is most often meant by terms such as 'the evangelical church', 'evangelical' or 'evangelicalism' in the United States. For though there are many churches and denominations that might be justifiably labelled 'evangelical',[5] given the broader political dynamics in which it has developed, the tone and tenor of the Evangelical Church, and the broader cultural framework of evangelicalism to which it has given rise, has been historically, and remains presently, dominated by the perspective of conservative straight white men.[6] This structural reality has made the Evangelical Church a useful political ally for those engaged in the kind of grievance-driven, racist, homophobic and misogynistic politics of nostalgia[7] that has so long been a fixture of US politics and which Donald Trump's political vision so effectively capitalized on. And in light of this fact, one might reasonably wonder if Donald Trump – or someone like him – is really anything more than the natural endpoint of 'politicized' evangelicalism. This is not to say the sole cause of it, but indicative of its vision nonetheless. And if this is the case shouldn't we conclude that politicizing evangelicalism runs counter to the pursuit of realizing a more just and equitable society? Shouldn't evangelicals, as religious people, stay in their lane and be more focused on spiritual matters? Perhaps.

Of course, to answer these questions affirmatively, one would certainly find oneself in good company, for this would be to arrive at the conclusion that dominates current analyses of Trump-era evangelicalism. Indeed, as it has become standard for commentators to root today's crisis in the rise of the Religious Right and the Moral Majority in the 1970s, teleological readings of evangelical history that terminate with Trump have become the norm. As one commentator wrote in a 2022 article published in *The Atlantic* entitled 'How Politics Poisoned the Evangelical Church':

> Evangelical leaders set something in motion decades ago that pastors today can no longer control. Not only were Christians conditioned to understand their struggle as one against flesh and blood, fixated on earthly concerns, a fight for a kingdom of this world – all of which runs

directly counter to the commands of scripture – they were indoctrinated with a belief that because the stakes were getting so high, any means was justified. Which brings us to Donald Trump.[8]

What such observers conclude is that evangelicals + Politics = Trump. And far from simply being the perspective of outside observers, this same narrative has been adopted with arguably even greater force by Trump-era evangelicalism's internal critics. In fact, among such voices it is now almost something of a trope in their unending analyses to make some statement about the church having forgone its legitimate spiritual aims for the pursuit of illegitimate political ones. For example, as historian and self-described '#NeverTrump' evangelical Thomas Kidd writes, 'the desire of many white evangelicals to reestablish political influence is at the root of their identity crisis today.'[9] Exemplifying the teleological tendency mentioned above, as Kidd puts it, over the last half century 'republican insider evangelicals' have cynically 'abetted the politicization' of evangelicalism. A process in which proximity to worldly power has slowly 'clouded' evangelicals' judgement and 'distracted' them from their 'spiritual' mission. And this process, by uncritically wedding the church to the Republican Party, has inexorably led to the moral confusion that is evangelical support for Donald Trump.[10]

For understandable reasons, these are voices that we love to amplify. We love to feel that we are giving voice to the morally courageous dissenting figures who stand alone within a church awash in hypocrisy. And reflecting this, since 2016 there has been a constant stream of flattering profiles on evangelical 'resisters' published in popular media outlets. But in presenting the current crisis in this way and amplifying the voices of those that we perceive to be the more palatable, 'moderate' evangelicals, what is often being put forward, even if this is not stated directly, is not just a historical narrative, or an objective analysis of the present, but the outlines of a political theology.[11] I suggest this is a dead end that simply gives cover to those who would – if not explicitly support Trump – paper over the disturbing views widespread within the church that his rise has made so clear.

The Politicization Narrative as Political Theology

So what is the political theology suggested by the politicization narrative? Since at its core this narrative rests on the assumption that 'the political' and 'the spiritual' exist as distinct antithetical categories wherein the church's responsibility is to protect the latter from the corrupting influence of the former, what it suggests is the normativity of a kind of two-kingdom political theology. According to this paradigm, taken in a very general sense, while worldly affairs and spiritual affairs are both legitimate means through which God exercises authority, the church's concern is primarily with the latter. The church's authority and mission are firmly grounded in the spiritual, not worldly, kingdom. For, in contrast to the institutions of the worldly kingdom that are concerned with temporal actions that play no part in salvation, the church's concern is stewarding 'the gospel'. The spiritual message is of eternal importance and, within the wider evangelical tradition, is explicitly about the importance of 'faith' over 'works'.[12] Thus, for the church to take an institutional stand on a 'political' matter *as the church* would be to confuse the authority that God has established between these two kingdoms and imperil the purity of 'the gospel' by implying that salvation is somehow contingent on something other than faith alone.[13] Supplying the framework that makes the politicization narrative theologically legible then, since, within a two-kingdom paradigm 'the church' as the domain of the gospel, and 'the world' as the domain of politics, are cast as antithetical realms that must remain separate to protect the purity of 'the gospel', it becomes logical to speak of their combination as a corruption; the 'politicization' of the church.

But why is this a dead end? The most obvious place to start in answering this question is to note, as many have done before, that a two-kingdom paradigm can facilitate a dangerous dualism that separates belief from action – 'the spiritual' from 'the political'. As political theologian Joshua Ralston has written on this point, such a distinction between belief and action runs the risk of vindicating 'quietism and passivity' in the face of worldly evil.[14] And indeed, as others have pointed out with regard to the development of American evangelical identity specifically, this mode of thinking has 'forged the way towards [a] divided self' that yields an 'empty politic',[15] a disposition in which a division between the spiritual and the political allows the worldly actions of evangelicals to escape the scrutiny that their personal beliefs would seem to demand. For in the context of a theology that defines ultimate responsibility in terms of *beliefs* rather than *actions*, it becomes possible to look past any human act as long as one's internal 'beliefs' are in order. This reveals the counterproductive nature of anything that might reinforce this 'divided self' – such as the politicization narrative's suggested return to an authentic 'spiritual' evangelical practice – as it reveals the dangers not of combining, but of *separating* spiritual identity and political identity. But while this point is certainly important and a useful place to begin, it is important that we push even further. This paradigm, in reality, does not just legitimize a mode of existence in terms of this 'divided self' – a passive act of guiding one towards conformity with a natural reality – but the way in which it actually *produces* and defines the 'natural' categories according to which 'the self' is to be divided. It assumes the power to define 'the gospel'.

Here, by defining 'the gospel', I mean the ability to authoritatively define the legitimate bounds of Christian social responsibility – the parameters of the 'divided self' – by declaring, based on one's own reading of scripture, what issues are core 'gospel' issues, and what are secondary 'political' issues – which issues the church can and must speak to and those on which it can remain silent. This act of depoliticization, akin to the modern discourse of secularism that is itself a cousin of two-kingdom theology,[16] derives power from invisibility as it produces 'authoritative settlements of religion and politics while simultaneously claiming to be exempt from this process of production'.[17] In practice, recognizing the ostensibly *natural* distinction between the spiritual and the political is not as neutral or as simple a process as it might seem. Rather than making this determination with reference to a clearly prescribed 'natural order' evident to all from a plain text reading of scripture, this determination instead relies on the contingent perspective of the interpreter whose opinion then becomes the normative reference for a prescribed 'natural order' – 'the gospel' – to which others must conform.

Therefore, what this paradigm does is further embed power within the hands of those who already have it. Separating 'religion' and 'politics' – what a Christian is and is not required to do – depends on their own definitions. Those who are already afforded epistemic privilege are rendered epistemological sovereigns able by definition to govern, declaring issues that *they* believe Christians should mobilize around as 'gospel' issues while forestalling action around other issues by declaring them to be 'political', all the while claiming that such views originate outside of themselves.

And indeed, demonstrating with striking clarity the concrete power of this authority, it is through just such a move, deployed within a general narrative of politicization, that the Evangelical Church in the United States has repeatedly over the course of its history delegitimized calls for action on pressing matters of justice. It is how church leaders in the nineteenth century delegitimized calls for institutional opposition to slavery, calling them 'fanatical attempts' to divide the church over a 'political' issue that was a matter neither of 'faith' nor of 'gospel order'.[18] It is how evangelical leaders in the twentieth century delegitimized calls for action on civil rights, defining such acts as 'political' and thus a distraction from the 'spiritual need' which 'the gospel' addresses.[19] And disturbingly, it is the way in which today, facilitated again by the logic of the politicization narrative, so many within the church are suggesting we should respond to the challenges of the present as they write longingly for a return to an imagined purer 'spiritual' evangelicalism.

Beyond Politicization

Returning once more to the case of Together for the Gospel, we can see a clear example of what the politicization narrative and its implicit political theology look like in practice. At its final gathering in 2022, during a discussion entitled 'protecting Christian freedom when everything is politicized', Presbyterian theologian Kevin DeYoung commended the doctrine of 'the spirituality of the church' as a means of confronting the 'politicization' of the church. As DeYoung explained, it is not that Christians can never speak on matters of politics but that the divisions of the present are symptomatic of people going far beyond the general principles that are clear in scripture. Illustrating his point, while the Bible makes clear that something like racism is wrong, DeYoung noted, it does not have anything to say on specific matters of policy to combat racism. Therefore, while it is right for the church to oppose racism in a general sense, to bring discussions of particular programmes of action into the church would be illegitimate and divisive. A wiser course of action for Christian leaders, therefore, is to remain silent on such specific points in order to preserve unity and protect the gospel. As the conference's attendees were reminded repeatedly over the course of this final gathering, the 'foundation of the unity' that the church enjoys is 'the gospel that we proclaim'; a message that 'has a definite content to it' and that leaders cannot simply 'redefine every generation'. Thus, what we see encouraged as a means of confronting the crisis of the Trump era, when viewed through the political theology of the politicization narrative – the standard narrative of the 'moderate' evangelicals who oppose Trump – is a call to a suppressive form of two-kingdom theology that reinforces the epistemic privilege of the majority as it calls on Christians, in the face of 'political' division, to be quiet and pursue an authoritarian unity premised on 'the gospel' that makes division itself, rather than the underlying issues that drive it, the enemy.

In reality, this unity, just like the idea of an uninterpreted 'gospel' that it is based on, is a myth, and the political theology of the politicization narrative must be rejected. The church has always been a worldly, political institution, and the repeated attempts to escape this fact through depoliticizing appeals to notions of its 'spirituality' cannot change this. Such notions are, as history shows us, no less dangerous a form of nostalgia than that which animates Trump's slogan of 'Make America Great Again'. Therefore, rather than attempting to run from the fact that its presence has an impact on the world around it, that actions matter, and that politics is not a derivative activity but the means by which community is formed and deformed, the church must be pushed to confront its political existence. Rather than allowing it to hide behind the depoliticizing smokescreen of spirituality, it must be actively politicized and forced to sit with the impact and reality of its presence as a human institution. True resistance, then, must be premised on a politics of epistemic humility, rather than sovereignty; one that defines 'the gospel' in community with the downtrodden and marginalized, rather than at their expense.

Notes

1 Collin Hansen, *Young, Restless, Reformed: A journalist's journey with the New Calvinists* (Wheaton, IL: Crossway Books, 2008), 109.

2 Ibid.

3 Issac Chotiner, 'How the head of the Southern Baptist Theological Seminary came around to Trump', *The New Yorker* (2020), https://www.newyorker.com/news/q-and-a/how-the-head-of-the-southern-baptist-theological-seminary-came-around-to-trump (accessed 22/03/2024).

4 Kate Shellnutt, 'T4G Conference will end in 2022', *Christianity Today* (2021), https://www.christianitytoday.com/news/2021/october/t4g-together-for-gospel-ends-al-mohler-dever-duncan.html (accessed 22/03/2024).

5 Isaac B. Sharp, *The Other Evangelicals: A story of liberal, black, progressive, feminist, and Gay Christians, and the movement that pushed them out* (Grand Rapids, MI: Eerdmans, 2023).

6 Molly Worthen, *Apostles of Reason: The crisis of authority in American evangelicalism* (New York: Oxford University Press, 2016), 3–5.

7 Robert P. Jones, *The End of White Christian America* (New York: Simon & Schuster, 2017), 82.

8 Tim Alberta, 'How Politics Poisoned the Evangelical Church', *The Atlantic* (2022), https://www.theatlantic.com/magazine/archive/2022/06/evangelical-church-pastors-political-radicalization/629631/ (accessed 22/03/2024).

9 Thomas S. Kidd, *Who is an Evangelical?: The history of a movement in crisis* (New Haven, CT: Yale University Press, 2019), 91–2.

10 Ibid., 1, 93.

11 Ibid., 155.

12 Joshua Ralston, *Law and the Rule of God: A Christian engagement with sharīʿa* (Cambridge: Cambridge University Press, 2022), 191.

13 Of course, two-kingdom theology is a varied and rich tradition which extends far beyond the rudimentary framework outlined here. Moreover, it is not universally accepted within American evangelicalism. Even so, as evangelical political thought tends to operate within the broader parameters of what Miller calls 'normative secularism', it continues to play an outsize role in defining the grammar of evangelical political discourse. See David VanDrunen, *Natural Law and the Two Kingdoms: A study in the development of Reformed social thought* (Grand Rapids, MI: Eerdmans, 2010); Jonathan Leeman, *Political Church the Local Assembly as Embassy of Christ's Rule* (Downers Grove, IL: IVP Academic, 2016); Daniel D. Miller, 'American Christian nationalism and the meaning of "religion"', *Method & Theory in the Study of Religion* (Vol. 34, 1–2, 2021), 64–85, doi:10.1163/15700682-12341533.

14 Ralston, *Law and the Rule of God*, 194.

15 David Fitch, *The End of Evangelicalism?: Discerning a new faithfulness for mission: Towards an evangelical political theology* (Eugene, OR: Cascade Books, 2011), 85.

16 Winnifred F. Sullivan et al., eds, *Politics of Religious Freedom* (Chicago, IL: University of Chicago Press, 2015), 19.

17 Elizabeth Shakman Hurd, *The Politics of Secularism in International Relations* (Princeton, NJ: Princeton University Press, 2019), 16.

18 Southern Baptist Historical Library and Archives. Proceedings of the Southern Baptist Convention 1845, http://media2.sbhla.org.s3.amazonaws.com/annuals/SBC_Annual_1845.pdf (accessed 22/03/2024).

19 Jerry Falwell, *Ministers and Marches* (1965) (The Jerry Falwell Library), https://liberty.contentdm.oclc.org/digital/collection/p17184coll4/id/4090 (accessed 22/03/2024).

11

A Step Forwards or Backwards? Reflections on Homelessness, Housing and Politics in England from 1945 to the Present

IAN ROWE

> The British people are compassionate. We will always support those who are genuinely homeless. But we cannot allow our streets to be taken over by rows of tents occupied by people, many of them from abroad, living on the streets as a lifestyle choice. *Suella Braverman, former UK Home Secretary, 4 November 2023*[1]

The UK is one of the wealthiest countries in the world and London in particular is one of the world's most prosperous cities. The landmarks of Big Ben, Tower Bridge and the Houses of Parliament are recognized around the world. It is the place that many celebrities across the world call home. But despite this level of wealth, London, and England more widely, has a huge and often ignored issue – homelessness.

According to the UK homelessness charity Shelter, 271,000 people are recorded as being homeless in England, including 123,000 children. That equals 1 in every 208 people living in England without a home.[2]

Before beginning to understand homelessness, we have to appreciate two very important factors. The first is that the experience of becoming and being homeless is different for each person. Tragically, however, a large part of what happens when you become homeless is that you become dehumanized. It is important to remember that every person is an individual and I don't pretend to talk for all homeless people or their experiences. The second thing to realize is that, like many issues in the UK, knowing exactly who is responsible for housing and homelessness is complex and confusing. Broadly speaking, local government (often called councils or local authorities in the UK) are responsible for housing and homelessness in a framework defined by their national government with that being either the Welsh, Scottish, Northern Irish or the Westminster government (for England). Increasingly power is being devolved to some English regions such as in London with the Greater London Authority, which covers the 32 boroughs of London (but not the City of London), and at times these levels of government also play a part in housing and homelessness policy. In this chapter I will be talking mostly about issues and framework that affect England and in particular London.

When approached to write this chapter I almost said no. I wondered what I could bring to this discussion, not only because of my lack of a PhD or even a Masters but also whether my voice needed to be heard. Read the news, turn on the TV or go on social media and you'll find someone like me telling you what I think. There isn't a shortage of white, able-bodied, straight, Western men giving you opinions on stuff they often don't know much about. But since you are reading this, I must have changed my mind. I decided to use this as a platform to hopefully promote voices you wouldn't usually see in these publications. So, I will attempt to talk about something that in many ways I don't know much about, homelessness. Yes, my day job is a caseworker at a large English homeless charity based in London but helping the homeless is a job and passion instead of my daily reality. The few of you who know me might find me saying that slightly ridiculous. 'Ian,' you might say, 'you've worked for a homeless charity for three years.' This is true, I have worked since October 2020 for a major homelessness charity in London. But unlike the many clients I have tried to help I have never been homeless; unlike them I have never worried about my next meal or whether I was going to survive the night. So, it's important to know that I'm not going to try and speak for the lived experience of the thousands of people who sleep rough on the streets of London – I can't do that. I'm also not going to give you a definitive history of housing in London (or the UK more widely).

Instead, what I am going to do is explain what legally defines homelessness and what temporary accommodation is; then I'm going to explain why the use of temporary accommodation is increasing. Then it's onto a whistle-stop tour of social changes and economic changes that have impacted the UK since 1945. This latter part will be informed by and interwoven with a conversation I had with a colleague who has lived experience of street homelessness. As I said earlier, this chapter isn't a definitive history of housing or homelessness, but I hope that it will spark some questions about what justice looks like for some of the most vulnerable people in British society.

Defining What is Meant by Homelessness in England Today – 2024

So, what defines someone as homeless in England today? We can find the answer in the 1996 Housing Act which defines someone as homeless if they satisfy one or more of the following conditions:

- They have no accommodation available to occupy.
- They are at risk of violence or domestic abuse.
- They have accommodation but it is not reasonable for them to continue to occupy it.
- They have accommodation but cannot secure entry to it.
- They have no legal right to occupy their accommodation.
- They live in a mobile home or houseboat but have no place to put it or live in it.[3]

As I quoted at the start of my chapter, 271,000 people are recorded as fitting into one of these categories. This doesn't mean that 271,000 people are sleeping on the street (often known as rough sleeping). They are housed in what is called temporary accommodation (TA). This is provided by local government as a temporary measure while the council works with them to resolve their homelessness on a longer-term basis. Getting into TA is often a challenge because a client will usually have to have been defined as being priority need. This means that they are seen as more vulnerable than an average person – if they aren't deemed as priority need the council may offer extremely limited help and no accommodation at all.[4] So this accommodation is by definition occupied by more vulnerable people within English society. However, it is often dirty, overcrowded and at times dangerous, with there being usually no council or support staff on site. It can also be far from a person's community due to there being limited availability in many areas – this is particularly acute in London. The suggestion that it is temporary is often a misnomer, for 68% of people live there for over a year. Unsurprisingly, living in this environment has a negative medical impact, with 63% of residents saying it has affected their mental health and 51% saying it has harmed their physical health. It also negatively impacts people's ability to access and attend healthcare appointments and increases social isolation.[5] Despite the obvious shortcomings and issues with TA, when I was working with rough sleepers in London getting a client into one of these bedspaces was seen as a great outcome. We had managed to prove the client was priority need and entitled to more council support compared to most clients who had to stay in the accommodation we provided because there was often no alternative. Therefore, you end up with many of the most vulnerable in English society housed in often totally unsuitable accommodation for long periods and if you aren't defined as being vulnerable enough you get even less help.

It's important to remember that this 271,000 statistic does not include the 'hidden homeless' who, partly due to the fragmented nature of government support in the UK, do not know what to do when threatened with, or experiencing, homelessness. This results in people beginning to 'sofa surf' where they will stay with a series of friends, or family members, so they don't end up on the streets. It is really difficult to know how many people are in this situation due to the temporary and informal nature of the arrangement of this accommodation. In 2019 the homeless charity Crisis estimated it to be 71,400 a night.[6] The rising costs of rents and other living costs over the past four years in England means that it is reasonable to predict that this has increased since. Even when these people do try to access support, they can find it a real challenge, because the local councils who provide this support have had their budgets cut since 2010. These cuts have resulted in local authorities' spending power, the amount of money they have to spend, dropping by 17.5% between 2010 and 2020. This has recovered somewhat recently, but their spending power was still 10.2% below 2009 levels in 2022.[7] This reduction in the amount of money local governments have in their budgets means that it has been increasingly difficult for them to fund temporary and other forms of accommodation, resulting in some councils aggressively 'gatekeeping', where they put up barriers to access support, such as long wait times on the phone. Additionally, many housing and council offices have closed to the public. Historically these were spaces where homelessness people could go and 'present' to the council and request assistance. The closure of these offices was often as a response to the pandemic, but as of November 2023, many of these offices have not reopened unless by prior appointment, resulting in vulnerable people having to advocate for themselves in a complex system that is under considerable strain. Other support services such as the Citizens' Advice Bureau are also being inundated with requests for help leading to long waiting times and staff burnout. Finally, I have not discussed here the reasons why people become homeless but it's important to remember that it affects all aspects of society – just look at the rates of repossessions that have increased across all areas since 2022.[8]

How is England in this Crisis?

Smaller budgets mean councils are limited in how they can support homeless people because, unlike in the 1970s, they do not own large stocks of property. This limits their ability to provide the accommodation and support needed. A large reason for why councils do not own large property portfolios is because since the 1980s the UK has systemically sold off its government housing stock (almost always called council housing) under a policy called 'right to buy'. The history of this policy is complex; it was a divisive issue when introduced and is still contested in UK politics today. During the 1980s, the then Conservative government allowed council tenants to buy the properties they lived in. They were able to do this at below market prices and tenants were entitled to discounts depending on how long they had lived in the property. This resulted in a huge transfer of property ownership from the state to individuals, a trend that has continued to this day, helped by the fact that 'right to buy' is still government policy, with many within the current government wanting to expand this to include housing associations.[9] Given that housing associations are some of the few organizations that still build any kind of social housing, allowing them to be sold to tenants means that this problem will only get worse.

In London 300,000 properties have been sold since the introduction of 'right to buy'. The income generated from this huge sell-off was not, however, used to build new properties. In the last decade around 23,000 homes were sold and just 14,000 houses were built with the money raised by these sales.[10] This is a reduction of 9,000 homes owned by councils across the city, and many of these former council properties were, and continue to be, purchased by their council tenants who then rented them out on the private rented market. This was and is often done at much higher rents, with the profits going to the new landlord, instead of the local council. The result of all this is that councils now have very few properties to offer to vulnerable members of their community. This increases waiting times for those living in TA and often forces others to live in privately rented accommodation.

The lack of government investment and regulation has also led to increasing rents in the private rented market. Due to there not being enough houses built since the 1970s (along with other policies) house prices have risen with demand, meaning they are increasingly unaffordable for a large proportion of the population. However, the motivation to change this is limited by three powerful vested interests. First, home owners want their house to increase in value because when they sell it, they will make a profit. Second, construction companies, which are private companies, need to maximize their profits. This means that if house prices are high, they don't want to flood the market with more homes, because that would mean they would get a lower return on their investment per house. This group has benefited hugely from the current housing crisis. Research shows that in 2008 the amount paid in dividends from the nine largest housebuilders peaked at £464 million and by 2017 that number had reached £1.8 billon.[11] Third, and finally, local residents often object to housing being built in their local communities, due to concern it will overwhelm public services, or that people from outside their community will change it, so they mobilize to stop developments happening.[12]

Increasingly high prices to buy property results in people being forced to rent, or stay with family longer, as they save to get on the housing ladder. This, coupled with people buying properties so they can rent them out, rather than living in them, pushes up rent prices even further, particularly in London. Since the 1980s the UK has deindustrialized and become more of a service-based economy. This shift has been hugely beneficial to London, with its financial services industry in particular becoming increasingly important. This increase has not been met with sufficient homes being built, and has resulted in people being forced into the more expensive private rented market. The shortage of housing in essence prices out the poorest in society. The government does provide support for those on the lowest incomes, or unemployed, through the social security system. For many people this is through a benefit called Universal Credit (UC), which as of November 2023 gives £368.74 a month to unemployed single adults over 25, for their utility bills, council tax, transport, food and other costs. Most people are also able to claim help with their housing through UC and the amount they receive depends on their age and location. However, like many social security systems around the world, UC is often complicated to navigate. To slightly oversimplify it, the major issue is that the government has, for most claimants, capped the total amount that can be claimed. As of November 2023, the amount for a single adult is £1,413.92 in London and £1,229.42 outside London.[13] These amounts sound sufficient, but because of the huge shortage of housing, rents often exceed these limits, meaning that no matter how hard someone looks, they are unable to find a property that the government is willing to fund. Accordingly, this forces people to make difficult decisions and often means they have to leave London, or move to different parts of the UK, where they may have no community, and often little support.

My Conversation with Winston – Complicated Progress?

Hopefully you now appreciate some of the issues facing those experiencing homelessness in the UK, as well as some of the issues within the wider housing market and why we are in this position. As I said earlier, I don't want this chapter to just include my voice, so before writing I decided to talk to one of my colleagues. I spoke to Winston (not his real name), an older Black man who has been working in the sector for a long time, who has also experienced homelessness himself, along with drug and alcohol addiction. I would love to spend the rest of the chapter retelling our conversation but my word count will limit me in what I am able to say. So instead of transcribing our conversation, I thought I'd pick out themes he touched on, give them context and reflect on them. It's important to note that these reflections are my own and don't represent Winston's views.

A more socially progressive society?

When I spoke to Winston what struck me is how much Britain has changed since the mid-1960s and how, in many ways, we are still fighting the same battles for progress. The first thing he said about his experience of growing up as a child in south London was that British society was racist. He talked of how other children, families and the state defined him by his race and he was made to feel he did not belong in British society. Winston spoke of how the racism and the abuse were seen as normal occurrences within a family and society and nothing out of the ordinary. This made me reflect on whether this is the same experience people from a similar working-class minority background have in British society today. The answer I came to was that it is complicated. You can see racism across British society today – just take housing. Recently there was a case in Rochdale, Greater Manchester where a child died due to exposure to mould. His family weren't taken seriously when they raised the matter with the local council because of assumptions the council made about their 'lifestyle' from culture clashes with the family's Sudanese heritage. This is an obvious case of racism in modern Britain, a society that looks very different from the one of the 1960s.[14]

The beginnings of a legal framework to protect minorities and promote equality started with a wave of legislation in the late 1960s. These were either aimed at decriminalizing expressions of people's identities or ideas, such as with homosexuality in 1967, or criminalizing discrimination or prejudice due to someone's gender or race, such as the Race Relations Act of 1965.[15] This began a trend that has continued into modern British society with the state increasingly moving to protect minority groups. Again, this is oversimplification with progressive policies often coming in fits and starts – and of course, legal change does not mean that societal views suddenly change overnight.

A good example of this change to legal rights and to some extent societal views is the progress of gay rights over the past 60 years. Until 1967 in England and Wales 'homosexual acts' were criminalized and a person could be prosecuted for being gay.[16] This 1967 Act passing was undeniably progress, with gay men able to legally be in a relationship with a partner of their choosing. However, partial decriminalization did not mean that gay men weren't convicted under other pieces of legislation as the gay activist Peter Tatchell argued in *The Guardian* newspaper in 2017 on the fiftieth anniversary of the law.[17] It also did not mean that suddenly the British public were tolerant and accepting of gay people. Even by 1989 40% of Britons still felt homosexual relationships between consenting adults were morally wrong. However, by 2019 this figure had fallen to 13%[18] and a right-wing Conservative government even introduced gay marriage in England and Wales in 2014.[19] These statistics and the introduction of gay marriage show clearly that the UK is a very different place from 1989, let alone 1963, meaning that in a legal sense, and increasingly a societal one, people are more accepted as they are. However, progress is always under threat. The recent government report into London's Metropolitan Police which found it to be institutionally racist, sexist and homophobic, as well as the recent debates over trans rights, shows us that this consensus might be fragile.[20]

A more economically conservative country?

To return to Winston, in our conversation he also talked of the ease of getting a council house with his partner in his 20s, paid for by the huge salary she could obtain as a secretary and how he was able to find work in a factory with his grandmother with little difficulty. It is easy to contrast this to the UK of today where people often struggle to make ends meet, living standards are falling and the cost of living is rising. When we look back 60 years to 1963, just before the beginning of social changes in British society, we find a Britain much more economically left wing, because in 1963 Britain was still governed by what is often called the postwar consensus. As with most of my chapter, this idea was contentious then, and is still hotly disputed today, but broadly speaking from 1945 to 1979 the UK adopted a mixed market model of capitalism. This meant that some parts of the economy were owned and directed by the state and some by private companies. There was also broad agreement on a large well-funded welfare state, which included a National Health Service (NHS) which was (and still is) free at the point of use, and paid for through taxation instead of private insurance.

There was also a general acceptance of state intervention in markets, with a good example being the housing market. In the postwar period there was a housing shortage, the destruction caused by wartime bombing, twinned with a desire to continue slum clearances, meant that new housing was needed. Governments, both of the centre right and of the centre left, recognized this and initiated large-scale public housing programmes. Housing production reached 354,130 units under a Conservative government in 1954 and 425,830 in 1968 under a Labour government.[21] The quality of this housing is often debated, with many properties being high-rise apartment blocks of dubious quality and design, often leading to problems such as mould. Local authorities also quickly gained a reputation for low-quality and unreliable maintenance of the properties they owned. The sudden change from more communal slum living, to more isolated living within tower blocks also often led to people feeling more socially isolated and lonely. However, this large-scale building effort meant that families could for the first time enjoy some of the basic necessities of life, such as an indoor toilet.

This postwar consensus was not to last however, and there was a growing mood within the Conservative Party that the social and economic strife of the 1970s showed that British society and economic policy was failing. This led them to believe that the state, far from being an enabling force within society, was instead a restrictive one. This meant that after the Conservatives under Margaret Thatcher came to power in 1979 a movement away from state ownership began, with an increasing emphasis on the individual. Previously owned public corporations such as coal, steel and telecoms were privatized, trade union activities were restricted, regulations on numerous industries such as banking were loosened, and taxation was lowered. This shift away from collectivism was cemented by 1987 when Mrs Thatcher proclaimed in an infamous interview with *Women's Own* that 'there is no such thing as society' but instead there are individuals and families.[22]

This again brings us back to housing. As I have argued earlier in this chapter, the right to buy effectively destroyed the UK social housing market, and is one of the main causes of the housing crisis we are experiencing today. Looking at the numbers, between 1953 and 1977 the total amount of housing built per year only dipped below 300,000 in three years: 1958, 1959 and 1974.[23] However, since 1980 the total number of houses built each year has never been above 250,000 despite the UK population rising from around 56 million in 1980 to 67 million today.[24] This shows us that despite Mrs Thatcher extolling the virtues of property ownership it has become an increasingly distant dream to many people in British society.

A Just Society?

It is dangerous in many ways to see the past as a better place – we can never go back, no matter how much we might want to. I was born in 1995, so never experienced the full employment and large stocks of council housing of the 1960s. I grew up with the ideas of markets being the driving force of the economy and that the government's job was to get out of the way to enable economic growth. On the other hand, unlike my father who grew up in the 1960s and 70s in Edinburgh, I never experienced seeing nuns being spat at in the street. That's not to say that it was perfect – calling someone gay was an insult until I was around 15. But the society and community I grew up in was objectively much more tolerant. So that brings us back to the question I have asked so many times in this chapter – is England, and the UK more widely, a more just society today than it was 60 years ago? I think it's an impossible question to answer; it seems, to me at least, that British society has given rights with one hand and taken away security with another.

This contradiction reminds me of another theme that I've come back to over and over again, the dire state of the housing market in England today. In my most recent role as a caseworker with rough sleepers in emergency accommodation, an important part of the job was to understand the clients' support needs.[25] This meant I spent time trying to build trust, get them to open up and offered support with issues they may have been facing such as mental ill health, domestic violence, substance misuse or shame about their sexuality. I then offered support and referred clients to other services to try and help them on the road to recovery. This work was tough and often had limited success but at times I did feel that I was actually helping someone change their lives for the better. From my limited understanding of Britain 60 years ago, this would not have happened and it is very likely that the person would have been judged instead of supported. This does not mean, however, that modern British society is without judgement – just look at the quotation at the start of this chapter – but it does mean that places exist for people to get help and express their true identity.

However, when it came to actually solving their homelessness, actually moving them into a property, the options were very limited. I spent a lot of time fighting with councils to assess my clients and agree that they had responsibility for them. I spent a lot of time telling clients that they would have to 'be realistic' about where they could live, and to expect very little from their landlords despite paying huge rents. I spent a lot of time sending in referrals and was often told that my client didn't meet a certain criterion, so they were not eligible for help. It is hard to say with certainty that if I was doing my job in 1962 instead of 2022 that it would have been easier to house my clients. But the systematic cutting of council budgets, the selling off of council homes and the fact we are on our fifteenth housing minister since 2010[26] makes me think it must have been better.

So, a more just society? I'll leave that up to you.

Notes

1 You can find her post from X (Twitter) in full here: https://twitter.com/SuellaBraverman/status/1720730450556006714 (accessed 22/03/2024).

2 A very detailed article on temporary accommodation was posted on 11 January 2023 on Shelter's website: https://england.shelter.org.uk/media/press_release/at_least_271000_people_are_homeless_in_england_today#:~:text=New%20research%20from%20Shelter%20shows,England%20are%20without%20a%20home (accessed 22/03/2024).

3 Shelter have a great legal part to their website about homelessness: for the list of legislation, see https://england.shelter.org.uk/professional_resources/legal/homelessness_applications/homelessness_and_threatened_homelessness/legal_definition_of_homelessness_and_threatened_homelessness#reference-3 (accessed 22/03/2024); the original legislation can be found at https://www.legislation.gov.uk/ukpga/1996/52/section/176 (accessed 22/03/2024).

4 Shelter, 29 September 2023 – this is a whole portal on Shelter's website about priority need: https://england.shelter.org.uk/housing_advice/homelessness/priority_need/who_has_a_priority_need (accessed 22/03/2024).

5 Shelter, 11 January 2023 (see note 2 above).

6 This statistic is taken from a report from B. Sanders, S. Boobis and F. Albanese, *'It was like a nightmare': The reality of sofa surfing in Britain today* (London: Crisis, 2019), https://www.crisis.org.uk/ending-homelessness/homelessness-knowledge-hub/types-of-homelessness/it-was-like-a-nightmare-the-reality-of-sofa-surfing-in-britain-today/ (accessed 23/05/2024).

7 Institute for Government article, 10 March 2020, by Graham Atkins and Stu-

art Hoddinott, https://www.instituteforgovernment.org.uk/explainer/local-government-funding-england#:~:text=Local%20authority%20'spending%20power'%20%E2%80%93,%25%20below%202009%2F10%20levels (accessed 22/03/2024).

8 UK Government, 'Mortgage and landlord possession statistics: January to March 2023', https://www.gov.uk/government/statistics/mortgage-and-landlord-possession-statistics-january-to-march-2023/mortgage-and-landlord-possession-statistics-january-to-march-2023 (accessed 22/03/2024).

9 For more information about the government policy to expand right to buy to housing associations, see UK Parliament, 'A Voluntary Right to Buy for Housing Association Tenants', 26 September 2023, https://commonslibrary.parliament.uk/the-right-to-buy-in-england/ (accessed 22/04/2024).

10 Press Release, London Mayor, 2022, https://www.london.gov.uk/press-releases/mayoral/mayor-hails-success-of-right-to-buy-back#:~:text=The%20Mayor%20of%20London%2C%20Sadiq,homes%20back%20into%20public%20ownership (accessed 12/04/2024).

11 Tom Archer and Ian Cole, 'The financialisation of housing production: Exploring capital flows and value extraction among major housebuilders in the UK', *Journal of Housing and the Built Environment* (Vol. 36, 2021), 1367–87.

12 There are interesting discussions about these topics on *New Statesman* YouTube channel, in particular the video, 'The housing market crash is just beginning'. The BBC also explored this in their two-part documentary *Britain's Housing Crisis: What Went Wrong?*

13 You can find the amounts for universal standard allowance at https://www.gov.uk/universal-credit/what-youll-get and the benefit cap amounts at https://www.gov.uk/benefit-cap/benefit-cap-amounts (both accessed 22/03/2024). These websites will be updated if the amount changes but the figures I have quoted are correct as of December 2023.

14 Robert Booth, 'Landlord admits it made assumptions about family in mouldy Rochdale flat', *The Guardian*, 22 November 2022, https://www.theguardian.com/society/2022/nov/22/landlord-assumptions-family-mouldy-rochdale-flat-borough wide-housing (accessed 22/03/2024).

15 UK Parliament, 'Race Relations Act 1965', https://www.parliament.uk/about/living-heritage/transformingsociety/private-lives/relationships/collections1/race-relations-act-1965/race-relations-act-1965/ (accessed 22/03/2024).

16 It wasn't until 1980 in Scotland and 1982 in Northern Ireland that homosexuality was legalized.

17 For other pieces of legislation used to prosecute gay men after legalization and for a brief exploration of the 1908s Conservative government's approach to gay rights, see Peter Tatchell, 'Don't fall for the myth that it's 50 years since we decriminalised homosexuality', *The Guardian*, 23 May 2017, https://www.theguardian.com/commentisfree/2017/may/23/fifty-years-gay-liberation-uk-barely-four-1967-act (accessed 23/03/2024).

18 Bobby Duffy, 'How British moral attitudes have changed in the last 30 years' (Policy Institute, Kings College London, 2019), https://www.kcl.ac.uk/policy-institute/assets/British-moral-attitudes.pdf (accessed 23/03/2024).

19 Scotland also introduced gay marriage the same year and it was introduced in Northern Ireland in 2020.

20 Baroness Casey of Blackstock DBE CB, 'An independent review into the standards of behaviour and internal culture of the Metropolitan Police Service', March 2023, 257, 285 32, https://www.met.police.uk/police-forces/metropolitan-police/areas/about-us/about-the-met/bcr/baroness-casey-review/ (accessed 23/03/2024).

21 Colin Wiles, 'Look back in anger', *Inside Housing*, 23 October 2013, https://www.insidehousing.co.uk/comment/look-back-in-anger-37554 (accessed 23/03/2024).

22 Margaret Thatcher interviewed in *Woman's Own*, 23 September 1987, https://www.margaretthatcher.org/document/106689 (Accessed 23/03/2024). This is a very interesting article and I recommend reading the full transcript.

23 Statista Research Department, 'New homes completed by private companies, housing associations and local authorities in the United Kingdom (UK) from 1949 to 2022', 6 November 2023, https://www.statista.com/statistics/746101/completion-of-new-dwellings-uk/ (accessed 23/03/2024).

24 D. Clark 'Population of the United Kingdom from 1871 to 2021', 23 November 2023, https://www.statista.com/statistics/281296/uk-population/ (accessed 23/03/2024).

25 Just to give this a little more context, from October 2021 to May 2023 I worked as a caseworker with rough sleepers who stayed in a hotel run by a large homeless charity. We would provide them with a hotel room and then conduct intensive casework and move them on to different accommodation options. At the time of writing I still work in the field but now have a more specialist role with clients usually in temporary accommodation or social housing.

26 Brian Wheeler, 'New housing minister Rachel Maclean will be 15th since 2010', *BBC News*, 9 February 2023, https://www.bbc.co.uk/news/uk-politics-64555909 (accessed 23/03/2024).

PART 3

Disrupting Theology, Theory and Thinking

12

An Essay That Is Already Belated: Some Notes on Holocaust and the Recovery of Witnessing

DAVE KORN

> In a catastrophic age ... trauma itself may provide the very link between cultures. *Cathy Caruth*

To provide *a holding for a crisis* through a discussion of American letters: such was to be my aim in this paper, but in the face of the materials I fled into my solitude and longed for an ivory tower in which to forge a work of pure theory that had absolutely no relevance whatsoever to society. This however proved harder than you might expect, like a missing bullet, a bench by the road; so here is what I came up with instead.

bell hooks found in theory a *'location for healing'*:

> Let me begin by saying that I came to theory because I was hurting – the pain within me was so intense that I could not go on living.... I found a place of sanctuary in 'theorizing', in making sense out of what was happening. I found a place where I could imagine possible futures, a place where life could be lived differently.[1]

Making sense out of things and imagining different possible futures – these functions are happily shared by imaginative literature, whose complex rational-affective entanglement of memory and imagination can weave cognitive frameworks that establish a holding for unspeakable grief by facilitating special forms of access to elements of the collective consciousness that may not be amenable to so-called non-fiction accounts or to statistics. Literary fiction, and in fact all art, makes possible the exploration of many diverse ways of being in the world – modes of existence, some that are, some that have been, and some that have never been.

Thus in the context of art, pain and the revolutionary imagination, let us (re)mark that regarding a generation's efforts to construct a viable future, any capacity to actualize the liberatory potential of dream and theory may prove contingent upon establishing a proper relationship to the past and what dwells there 'that is impossible to psychically metabolize'.[2] To dwell on it is anathema to survival; and yet to rush away from the worst, which may be necessary to do, may also be to abandon certain responsibilities, as Toni Morrison writes of the American context. It has been posed 'that America was not *another* place, a *new* start in history, but just the giant theatre where everyone's drama was played out with greater openness'.[3] So what holds for America may hold for the human race. 'There is a necessity for remembering the horror,' Morrison holds of the American past, 'but of course there's a necessity for remembering it … in a manner in which the memory is not destructive.'[4] Though her books brim with violence and conflicting tensions, they arguably approach such heights of non-destructivity as they powerfully model the paradoxical interplay between the effacing force of the dissociative impulse and the simultaneous imperative to speak the truth aloud. 'The conflict between the will to deny horrible events and the will to proclaim them aloud is the central dialectic of psychological trauma,' writes Judith Herman in 'Crime and Memory' in *Trauma and Self*.

The ordinary human response to atrocities is to banish them from consciousness. Certain violations of the social compact are too terrible to utter aloud: this is the meaning of the word *unspeakable*. Atrocities, however, refuse to be buried. As powerful as the desire to deny atrocities is the conviction that denial does not work. Our folk wisdom and classic literature are filled with ghosts who refuse to rest in their graves until their stories are told, ghosts who appear in dreams or visions, bidding their children, 'Remember me.' Remembering and telling the truth about terrible events are essential tasks both for the healing of individual victims, perpetrators and families, and for the restoration of the social order.[5]

The ordinary human response is to forget; atrocities, however, refuse to be buried. To disregard the past then is to risk the invocation of a haunting: the evocative acquires the function of a stay against forgetting – an incitement to remembrance: some evidently malevolent disruptive force who makes demands, appears and withdraws, counteracts any living of life that is predicated on denial. 'Our folk wisdom and classic literature are filled with ghosts who refuse to rest in their graves until their stories are told.' Such tales may harbour the unbearable tension that arises when 'the imperative to tell the story … is inhabited by the impossibility of telling'.[6] Two tiny hand prints appear in the cake. In one tale suffused with what Cathy Caruth has called the 'haunting power'[7] of trauma, the collective American unspoken is brilliantly rendered as fictional fantastic presence, a ghost that haunts a character in a literary work. It harbours a wound that repels as it compels: 'Outside a driver whipped his horse into the gallop local people felt necessary when they passed 124.'[8] Within the universe she weaves, Morrison expertly models the psychological tension between the forces of repression and the necessity for remembering.[9] The action of the difficult narrative, though the work is wrought of a 'complex fragmentation of time',[10] takes place years after slavery was 'abolished', so it serves to further underscore the enduring nature of the 'historical' wound.

> *Beloved* was so powerful to me, not so much because of the story, which in very Morrison-like fashion one knows very early on, rather it is the anguish of slavery, that lingering emotional suffering that she evokes in the writing. And frankly I do not think there are enough non-fiction books written that try to talk about this anguish – this Black people grief that is so profound – it has made us wordless. In very negative reviews of *Beloved* ... both reviewers liken it to holocaust literature, specifically to literature of Jewish experience that emerged from the Nazi tragedy. While they see this similarity as negative, I see it as a crucial attempt to impress upon the reader's consciousness that the experience of slavery here was, for African-Americans and their descendants, a holocaust experience – a tragedy of such ongoing magnitude that folk suffer, anguish it today.[11]

Swapping definite for indefinite article, hooks appropriates the proper noun, suggesting an affinity based in the shared experience of ongoing anguish. In Morrison's ability to bear witness to this anguish, her work can be said to function as a form of testimony.[12] In this sense she counteracts the distorting, obliviating power of an unspeakable event or experience during which it becomes no longer possible to be authentic witness to the truth of what happens. As Dori Laub writes: 'This collapse of witnessing is precisely, in my view, what is central to the Holocaust experience.'[13] Now the definite article indicates a historical particular, while the truth retains universal application. Jill Matus comments on 'the way in which Morrison's novels function as a form of cultural memory and how, in their engagement with the African American past, they testify to historical trauma'.[14] In this sense, the works can be said to constitute a 'resurrection of witnessing'.[15] Hence a work of literary fiction contributes to the crucial task that will be faced by any nation harbouring a history of atrocity.

The works of Toni Morrison contribute powerfully to this process with respect to the American shadow. But what kind of language could contain that by which one has been rendered *wordless*? The very fabric of *Beloved* is fractured into flashback and plotpoint, repetitions and resistance, the text *performing* the incomprehensibility of the trauma it narrates 'through, for example, gaps and silences, the repeated breakdown of language, and the collapse of understanding'.[16] 'The narrative enacts a circling or repetition around the traumatic event. In this way it accords significantly with psychoanalytic accounts of traumatic repetitions,' writes Matus.[17] The structure of the novel embodies its own paradoxes, and may by turns approach and evade, may provoke and resist the reader's efforts to understand, a mechanism by which the structure of the text itself comes to mirror the patterns of the human psyche. While such techniques are the province of creative rather than critical prose, a critic might mimic the practice of conspicuous omissions, repetition and patterning, withholding information, unveiling perplexities, deferring to the intent of the material itself to resist the reader's efforts to deploy their own prejudiced frameworks for understanding. Such a critic might cautiously elect to elucidate certain aspects of a text while deliberately leaving others obscure – *reveal a little but conceal far more*, as Nietzsche said of skin. *For the woodshed when the horsemen came.* Of the wound at the book's heart. 'It's so buried in the text you can barely find it.'[18] Though, as bell hooks said, you know it to begin. In the foreword prefacing later editions Morrison at least orientates the reader so that the disorientation is by design:

> I wanted the reader to be kidnapped, thrown ruthlessly into an alien environment as the first step into a shared experience with the book's population – just as the characters were snatched from one place to another, from any place to any other, without preparation or defense.[19]

The survivors of holocaust experience show the traumatogenic tells[20] that follow catastrophic violations of safety and security: a severely compromised sense of safety and security; perpetual hypervigilance to threat; ostracization from larger community; crisis of history and memory; the repetition of the trauma manifests itself in life in perplexing fashion, periodically returning in the form of so-called traumatic re-enactments,[21] which may be triggered by minor or major provocations and may lead to disproportionately catastrophic retribution; and so forth. One can admire how a novelist incorporates accurate insights from trauma theory into a work of fiction, while setting aside any geopolitical resonance.

We have already noted that the interdependent aspects of a healing process together occur at a rate over an amount of time which may render diminutive the attention span of the public, which may have long since rebranded the survivors of atrocity and shifted cause. For survivors and their descendants, outside perception that has the power to bear witness also has power to convolute, further compounding the trauma. The dynamics of being ostracized are modelled in *Beloved* as Sethe is rejected by the community, and indeed, 'deep down many traumatized people are even more haunted by the shame they feel about what they themselves did or did not do under the circumstances'.[22] Being shunned by the community can only establish the isolation in which PTSD now festers.[23] Fortunately, in the fictional case the seclusion is not absolute, and while she is boycotted and isolated by many, with Denver's and Paul D's support, Sethe is able to begin confronting the apparition.

Late in the narrative, a tragic climax occurs when Denver rallies the neighbourhood women for interventive exorcism. As Sethe and something demonic stand in the doorway facing the singing women who have gathered in the yard, Sethe spots behind them, below the 'definite green of the leaves', an approaching horseman. Actually, he is coming to give Denver a ride to work; but Sethe absolutely loses it and viciously attacks. Though fortunately Denver and the women are able to subdue her. *Damn crazy woman try to stab him with a ice pick*. What has just happened, why this excessive and totally inappropriate violence? Van der Kolk discusses research indicating 'that traumatized people have a tendency to superimpose their trauma on everything around them'.[24] The reader, and fortunately Denver, shrewdly apprehend that Sethe has been triggered by the apprehension of a horseman coming. Another repetition, but with two crucial differences: that this time Sethe takes the action that could not be taken under the circumstances; and that this time the community is able to successfully intervene to prevent violence. So effectively does the artist transmit what van der Kolk has called 'the inner truth of the experience'[25] that the reader is drawn up into the spectacle of violence directed against an innocent in a powerful dramatic climax which, like Greek tragedy, evokes pity and terror in the spectator, cathartically purging those emotions.[26] Classical and psychoanalytic notions of catharsis differ in that for the Viennese, release is not necessarily evoked through art but involves 'the discharge of previously repressed affects connected to traumatic events'.[27] Modern theorists have argued that in the event of inescapable crisis, unable to utilize the stress hormones produced, the body becomes frozen in fight-or-flight mode, the threat response system stuck in a hyperactivated state. Intriguingly, a growing body of research provides evidence to suggest that using various methods to initiate a discharge of this pent-up emotional energy can effect what Pierre Janet termed 'the pleasure of completed action', contributing viscerally to a sense of deep personal resolution and proper integration of the traumatic experience.[28] To dramatize this process in a work of art is to exploit the insights furnished by Aristotle on the effective deployment of tragedy to provoke a cathartic response in the spectator. That 'the discharge of previously repressed affects connected to traumatic events' can be skilfully triggered through literary representation of dramatic spectacle is demonstrated in the works of novelists such as Toni Morrison, whose work stands in precise relation to Greek tragedy.[29]

Late in the narrative, isolated in the house, bonds having broken down, even Denver having been driven out, Sethe cherishes Beloved, who saps Sethe like a succubus. In the house, she is breaking chunks of ice to cool Beloved when she hears singing. She drops the ice pick into her apron pocket and 'Together they stood in the doorway'; the voices of Denver and the women she has gathered are 'a wave of sound wide enough to sound deep water and knock the pods off chestnut trees'.[30]

> Sethe feels her eyes burn and it may have been to keep them clear that she looks up. The sky is blue and clear. Not one touch of death in the definite green of the leaves. It is when she lowers her eyes to look again at the loving faces before her that she sees him. Guiding the mare, slowing down, his black hat wide-brimmed enough to hide his face but not his purpose. He is coming into her yard and he is coming for her best thing. She hears wings. Little hummingbirds stick needle beaks right through her headcloth into her hair and beat their wings. And if she thinks anything, it is no. No no. Nonono. She flies. The ice pick is not in her hand; it is her hand.[31]

In this astonishing and subtle sequence, we witness a complex cognitive distortion characteristic of trauma dramatized through the actions of a character in a novel. Why does Sethe viciously attack a man who has come to give Denver a ride to her new job? The characteristic post-traumatic cognitive distortion lies precisely in 'that the impact of the traumatic event lies precisely in its belatedness, in its refusal to be simply located, in its insistent appearance outside the boundaries of any single place or time'.[32] For Sethe, the experience of the past continues to recur, repeatedly superimposing itself upon the present. 'His black hat wide-brimmed enough to hide his face but not his purpose.' In fact, Sethe mistakes both the identity and the purpose of this friendly figure. In a jarring discrepancy between experiences of realities, she lives the moment as a re-enactment of the moment when she spots the horsemen approaching, a vision intimately entangled with the catastrophic woodshed buried in the book's heart, *where it would be safe* ... Incredibly, the novel invites us to consider how apparently incomprehensible violence may spring from a belated re-enactment of a previous trauma: this bewildering experience Morrison deftly dramatizes in Sethe's apprehension of a horseman and the violence of her response. Another repetition, but with two crucial differences. This time, instead of the worst thing, Sethe directs aggression against the one she experiences as 'coming for her best thing', thus taking the action she could not take under the circumstances – albeit *belatedly*, and therefore still *misdirecting* the aggression against innocence; and yet that crucially, this time the community is able to witness and intervene. The somatic experience of acting out the apparently proper response while having her own post-traumatic aggression safely contained by the community provides a cathartic release for Sethe – and for the reader who dares to share in the experience. A similar or analogous affective discharge may apparently be achieved through retaliatory aggression when art, and when community, are able to provide adequate holding and containment. Such holding and containment must derive externally to the situation, from 'someone who could step outside of the coercively totalitarian and dehumanizing frame of reference in which the event was taking place, and provide an independent frame of reference through which the event could be observed'.[33] Insofar as the international community proves unable or unwilling to effectively provide such frame of reference for atrocity, this can be said to constitute a global collapse of witnessing, a baseline of international complicity in the intercultural, intergenerational transmission of holocaust.

American literature has been engaged in a process of reckoning. *Vergangenheitsbewältigung* can suggest 'public debate within a country on a problematic period of its recent history ... where "problematic" refers to traumatic events that raise sensitive questions of collective culpability'.[34] In her engagement with history and memory, Toni Morrison's body of work makes it possible to explore such questions within the safe holding environment of art. 'Bearing witness to the past, Morrison's novels can also be seen as ceremonies of proper burial, an opportunity to put painful events of the past in a place where they no longer haunt successive generations.'[35] Thus a literary text can facilitate *adaptive transmission* of a holocaust experience. When adaptive transmission of one's experience becomes impossible, maladaptive forms of transmission may occur.

That *never again* must apply to all peoples at all times – who can claim to be in a superior position? In the aftermath of atrocity, evolving affinities may transform in complex and non-intuitive ways, undermining the ability of simplistic binaries to function as absolute categories of judgement. It has been pointed out that 'we have an unrealistic expectation of how traumatized peoples will behave'.[36] In a strange complexity of logic, sometimes maladaptive transmission of experience proves not so easily stemmed. In the case of America, in the beat after the bombs, metabolizing concentration, colonially carved up, misused – what folks sought was the right 'to be a human being, to be respected as a human being, to be given the rights of a human being in this society, on this earth, in this day'.[37] A universal struggle, it was natural to express 'Afro-American solidarity with the oppressed people of the world', as did *The Black Panther* in 1969,[38] the same paper that released a poem called 'Enemy of the Sun'[39] under the name of George Jackson, a Panther and a(nother) Black man who died in police custody. The intentional 'mis-attribution' of the work of a Palestinian poet to a Black revolutionary has been called 'a powerful illustration of kinship in the practice of revolutionary political solidarity',[40] suggesting too the complex of contradictory affinities between America and the Holy Land.

Faced with recurring violations of human dignity like those to which the poets bear witness, resistance movements branch swiftly into conflict over method. By his later years, Malcolm X was willing to let the dominant culture choose: The Ballot or the Bullet:[41] 1964, the same year Dr King released *Why We Can't Wait* with his 'Letter from a Birmingham Jail' on non-violent direct action, and Nelson Mandela stood trial in Pretoria and proclaimed he was prepared to die for the ideal of a democratic and free society. After police in Sharpeville had fired live ammunition into a crowd of thousands, difficult questions were raised about non-violent resistance in the face of overwhelming violence. Archbishop Desmond Tutu conceded that perhaps 'Nonviolence presupposes a minimum moral level,'[42] indicating that the context of resistance determines its proper methods. Dr King called the South African massacre 'A tragic and shameful expression of man's inhumanity to man',[43] and issued a grave warning to America, on whose own non-violent demonstrations Malcolm X's position was clear:

> I don't go for non-violence if it also means a delayed solution. To me a delayed solution is a non-solution. Or I'll say it another way. If it must take violence to get the Black man his human rights in this country, I'm *for* violence exactly as you know the Irish, the Poles, or Jews would be if they were flagrantly discriminated against.[44]

Dr King, on the other hand, believed that violence could only ever beget violence, and held that his opponents failed to appreciate the radical difference between non-resistance and non-violent resistance:

> I'm talking about a very strong force, where you stand up with all your might against an evil system, and you're not a coward. You are resisting, but you come to see that tactically as well as morally it is better to be nonviolent. Even if one didn't want to deal with the moral question, it would just be impractical for the Negro to talk about making his struggle violent.[45]

Such rhetoric can produce strong emotion and has been held controversial in part because it raises the theoretically inflammatory question about the use of violence as method to eliminate violence. Perhaps the best response comes from Angela Davis, interviewed in California State Prison, asked by a white reporter whether she approved of violence: 'You ask me whether I *approve of violence*? I mean, that just doesn't make any sense at all.'

In the struggle toward justice, violent and non-violent methods share an intent 'to create such a crisis and foster such a tension that a community that has constantly refused to negotiate is forced to confront the issue'.[46] The tactical aspect of non-violence may be often and critically overlooked by those who have been taught to view non-violence as a limitation rather than a stratagem. Advocates of non-violence hold it to be not only less destructive to the opposition but most of all *more practically effective* at achieving urgently needed change to fundamental structures within a given society. Throughout his life King remained steadfast on this point, also drawing attention to the 'international potential of nonviolence',[47] a force that half a century later we are just barely beginning to tap as we establish the proper methods determined by our utterly unprecedented interconnected global context. Malcolm also emphasized the need for international involvement. He too remained steadfast even as he moved in the direction of compromise, a fact that mobilized extremists.[48] Five days before assassination by multiple gunshot wounds, he stated the aim:

> to come up with a program that would make our grievances international and make the world see that our problem was no longer a Negro problem or an American problem but a human problem. A problem for humanity. And a problem which should be attacked by all elements of humanity. A problem that was so complex that it was impossible for Uncle Sam to solve it himself and therefore we want to get into a body or conference with people who are in such positions that they can help

us get some kind of adjustment for this situation before it gets so explosive that no one can handle it.[49]

If 'theorizing' dwells in the act of making sense of things and imagining different possible futures, then Malcolm's appeal belongs to the category. He wants to 'make the world see' the *specific* problem as a *human* problem relevant to 'all elements of humanity', and he appeals for external involvement: in other words, he calls for witnessing and intervention. These have already been identified as protective elements in *Beloved*; and for Caruth, in the aftermath of holocaust the act of witnessing itself becomes an intervention: permits a 'passing out of the isolation imposed by the event: that the history of a trauma, in its inherent belatedness, can only take place through the listening of another'.[50] An end of post-traumatic isolation upon a recovery of witnessing: so *Beloved*, Malcolm X and the literature of atrocity establish a kernel of agreement. In the novel, the effective emergency response, the one that is successfully able to prevent violence, is the one that is able to accurately appraise the situation and take interventive action with absolute sensitivity to the inner experience of the aggressor and the targets of aggression. When binaries break open into polygonal complexities (or, when certainty is disrupted by many-sided realities) that demand deeper nuance, deeper listening, deeper sensitivity to commonality in the shared experience of catastrophic loss, than can be found in the blunt force gesture of being 'against' entire communities of human beings, then we urgently require a form of witnessing and intervention that is predicated on the denial that certain lives are less worthy of being grieved than others.[51] The denial that certain lives are as worthy of being grieved is a gesture not fundamentally different from that collapse of witnessing that has been named central to the experience of holocaust. We say this because faced with the international spectre of perpetuating holocaust, the narratives we uphold determine the range of our possibilities for response. To read violence as a response to trauma is neither to justify violence nor is it to assert the inevitability of violence; it is a notion that fundamentally belongs to the activity of theorizing.

Notes

1 bell hooks, 'Theory as Liberatory Practice', *Yale Journal of Law and Feminism* (1991).
2 Maria Yassa, 'The Inner Crypt', *The Scandinavian Psychoanalytic Review* (Vol. 25, 2, 2002), 83. *Metabolize* is glossed: 'to know, think, verbalize, symbolize and thereby transform into a bearable aspect of the subject's experiential world'.

3 Umberto Eco, *On Literature* (London: Vintage, 2006), 256. Eco is quoting Cesare Pavese in 1947.

4 Danille Taylor-Guthrie, ed., *Conversations with Toni Morrison* (Jackson: University Press of Mississippi, 1994), 247–8.

5 Charles B. Strozier and Michael Flynn, eds., *Trauma and Self* (Lanham: Rowman & Littlefield, 1996), 4.

6 Cathy Caruth, ed., *Trauma: Explorations in Memory* (Baltimore: Johns Hopkins University Press, 1995), 65.

7 Ibid., 4.

8 Toni Morrison, *Beloved* (London: Vintage, 2016) (first published 1987), 5.

9 Morrison: 'And it was the struggle, the pitched battle between remembering and forgetting, that became the device of the narrative', *Mouth Full of Blood: Essays, Speeches and Meditations* (London: Vintage, 2020), 324.

10 Henry Louis Gates and Anthony Appiah, eds, *Toni Morrison: Critical Perspectives Past and Present* (New York: Amistad, 1993), 357.

11 bell hooks, *Yearning: Race, Gender, and Cultural Politics* (Boston: South End Press, 1990), 216.

12 In Shoshana Felman's terms: 'the process of the testimony – that of bearing witness to a crisis or a trauma', Caruth, *Trauma*, 13.

13 Ibid., 65. Dori Laub, dual-national psychoanalyst and sociologist who has produced a powerful body of work on Holocaust and testimony.

14 Jill Matus, *Toni Morrison* (Manchester: Manchester University Press, 1998), 1.

15 Ibid., 2.

16 Christa Schönfelder, *Wounds and Words: Childhood and Family Trauma in Romantic and Postmodern Fiction* (Bielefeld: Transcript Verlag, 2013), 31.

17 Matus, *Toni Morrison*, 112.

18 'which is precisely what one wanted it to be', Morrison, 'Toni Morrison: Beloved', National Visionary Leadership Project (NVLP) (2004), interview, https://www.youtube.com/watch?v=RP6umkgMRq4 (accessed 21/02/2024).

19 Morrison, *Beloved*, xii.

20 For an extended discussion of the symptomatic indications of trauma, see *The Body Keeps the Score* (London: Penguin Random House UK, 2014), in which researcher Bessel van der Kolk argues eloquently for a conceptualization that comprehends the enduring impact of traumatic experience. 'We have learned that trauma is not just an event that took place sometime in the past; it is also the imprint left by that experience on mind, brain, and body', 24.

21 On the compulsion to repeat – a way of coming to know a traumatic experience belatedly – Erikson comments: 'In all of these cases, so Freud concluded, the individual unconsciously arranges for variations of an original theme which he has not learned either to overcome or to live with: he tries to master a situation which in its original form had been too much for him by meeting it repeatedly and of his own accord.' *Childhood and Society* (New York: W. W. Norton & Co, 1950), 189–90.

22 Van der Kolk, *The Body Keeps the Score*, 15.

23 An experience of isolation may be both cause and effect of trauma, whereas 'Traumatized human beings recover in the context of relationships', ibid., 252.

24 Ibid., 18.

25 Ibid., 51.

26 See κάθαρσις in Aristotle's *Poetics*.

27 American Psychological Association, *APA Dictionary of Psychology* (2023), https://dictionary.apa.org/catharsis (accessed 21/02/2024).

28 Van der Kolk, *The Body Keeps the Score*, 261. Van der Kolk calls Janet 'the first great explorer of trauma'. In these pages he discusses the somatic, 'body-based' therapies of Ogden and Levine.

29 For a discussion of *Beloved* and *Medea* that remains sensitive to the complexities involved in such a comparison, see e.g., Shelley P. Haley, 'Self-Definition, Community and Resistance', *Thamyris* (Vol. 2, 2, 1995).

30 Morrison, *Beloved*, 308.

31 Ibid.

32 Caruth, *Trauma*, 8–9. Caruth calls this idea 'the central Freudian insight into trauma'.

33 Dori Laub in Caruth, *Trauma*, 66.

34 From the Duden lexicon, accessed via Wikipedia. As ever, the German language has a word for what others cannot easily name. The beautiful and fraught word itself harbours tensions identical to the ones it arouses in public debate; see also Theodor Adorno, 'Was bedeutet: Aufarbeitung der Vergangenheit?' ('What is meant by "working through the past"?'), a lecture delivered 9 November 1959 at a conference on education held in Wiesbaden. Available in Theodor W. Adorno, *Critical Models: Interventions and Catchwords,* trans. Henry W. Pickford (New York: Columbia University Press, 1998).

35 Matus, *Toni Morrison*, 2.

36 Edward Said et al., *Freud and the Non-European* (New York: Verso, 2003), 77. Jacqueline Rose quoting Judge Richard Goldstone on the subject of the Albanians of Kosovo.

37 Malcolm X, in 1964. Printed in *By Any Means Necessary: Speeches, Interviews, and a Letter by Malcolm X* (New York: Pathfinder Press, 1970), 56.

38 The beautiful graphic full-page artwork of Emory Douglas, in *The Black Panther* (Vol. 2, 19, 4 January 1969).

39 *The Black Panther* (Vol. 7, 5, 25 September 1971).

40 Greg Thomas, 'Blame It on the Sun', *Comparative American Studies: An International Journal* (Vol. 13, 3, 2015), 236.

41 Printed in *Malcolm X Speaks: Selected Speeches and Statements* (Grove Press, 1990). 'The ballot or the bullet explains itself.' Cf. Frederick Douglass on the three boxes upon which the liberties of the American people were dependent: 'the Ballot-box, the Jury-box, and the Cartridge-box …', *The Life and Times of Frederick Douglass: From 1817–1882* (London: Christian Age Office, 1882), 333.

42 William Raspberry, 'The Violence of Apartheid', *The Washington Post*, 1 December 1985.

43 Letter to Claude Barnett, 1960.

44 *The Autobiography of Malcolm X* (New York: Grove Press, 1964), 367.

45 *The Autobiography of Martin Luther King, Jr.* (Intellectual Properties Management in association with Warner Books, 1998), 266. Cf. Einstein's 'militant pacifism' and Judith Butler's 'aggressive nonviolence'.

46 Martin Luther King, *Why We Can't Wait* (New York: New American Library, 1964), 79.

47 'Let My People Go', *Africa Today* (Vol. 12, 10, December 1965), 10.

48 Cf. Yitzhak Rabin.

49 'Not Just an American Problem, But a World Problem' (address at Rochester, New York, 16 February 1965).

50 Caruth, *Trauma*, 11.

51 See Judith Butler on grievability, *The Force of Nonviolence: An Ethico-Political Bind* (New York: Verso, 2021).

13

Reimagining Hindu Liberation Theology in India with Raimon Panikkar

SHRUTI DIXIT

Around six decades after Independence, Raimon Panikkar, the interfaith thinker, went ahead to proclaim that India was not entirely liberated even after Independence. He said,

> After pursuing 'modern development' with neither the excuse nor the handicap of colonial rule, sixty-five years of independence in the Indic subcontinent are sufficient to demonstrate that the path of modernization India has taken has not delivered the promised liberation.[1]

The reason that Panikkar puts forth for this failure is simply the fact that we are collectively treading in the wrong direction. Panikkar explains this mistaken path in his work, 'Indra's Cunning', which forms a part of his second volume on Hinduism, forming a long essay divided into three sections. It is essential to note that Panikkar's ideas as presented in this volume were first recorded in his 1955 *Letter from India*. He later returned to his work almost 50 years later to provide new insights into India's state after the said 'modernization'.[2] The first section introduces the modern predicament of Indic society by providing several examples of the current situation that vary from multiple social challenges, farmers' plight, problems faced by Adivasis and Dalits to the unrest of students, artists, intellectuals and so on. The second section looks deeper into the Indic situation to argue that the incompatibility between the cosmology of the traditional person in India and the cosmology of technological India is one of the major reasons behind the disconnect. Lastly, the third section is a call for awakening: Panikkar introduces what he actually means by Indra's cunning and how Indians, and the world at large, must adopt his crafty ways to save themselves from the predicament. While this chapter will continue mentioning more about Panikkar's thoughts on how India is in a continual state of ferment since Independence,[3] and build the argument using his ideas, it is necessary to highlight some things that will be elementary in the discussion that this chapter is going to initiate.

Panikkar makes use of the myth of Indra primarily for two reasons. On the one hand, Panikkar wants to highlight the importance of the divine dimension and how we cannot eliminate it and look at the world through a two-dimensional lens, as the modern individual is usually bound to do. His use of the myth of Indra – Indra being a Vedic God – does not have any Sanskritic inclinations. Panikkar believes that the Vedic narrative does have a 'wider resonance and can divest itself up to a certain extent of particular connotations'. On the other hand, this is an attempt by Panikkar to show how a myth can be cross-cultural and be used beyond its original context to create new meaning. According to him, myths have a saving power and 'only a new myth can save us'.[4] In this chapter, I will use the myth of Indra as Panikkar does and examine how it could be used to liberate us in the present times.

Furthermore, Panikkar's focus is on India when he presents his thesis. He even says that it could be extended as a problem faced by the entire subcontinent. The centre of attention of my chapter are Hindus; not just because of the fact that Hindus constitute the majority population in India but purely due to the dynamic change in the understanding of Hinduism and the interpretation of Hindu Liberation Theology that I intend to propose through this chapter.

In addition to this, the unrealized liberation that Panikkar is speaking about in 'Indra's Cunning' is a liberation from the idea that the modern standard of living can be universalized, given its difference from the traditional reality of an Indian and an Indian psyche. It is a liberation from the idea that this world is ruled by powerful humans and does not have a divine backing. It is a cosmotheandric realization that asserts the existence of different cosmologies pertaining to tradition and technocracy. And while talking about the alternatives to achieve this liberation, Panikkar mentions the need for a religious transformation, a relearning of our traditional values in order to understand why the discord exists. My idea of Hindu Liberation Theology is inspired by this idea of the requirement of a radical change, in other words, a profound transformation. This chapter is an attempt to propose a new interpretation of Hindu Liberation Theology where I stress the need for liberation from the present conception of what it means to be a Hindu.

Theology (or not) in the Hindu Tradition

The only significant work written till now on Liberation Theology in an Indian context is Rambachan's *Hindu Theology of Liberation: Not-Two is Not One*, strongly rooted in the Advaita theological tradition and reflects on the need for a liberation theology based upon it. The book is divided in two parts. The first part deals with the interpretation and analysis of the Advaita theology and a discussion based on its fundamental teachings. The second uses this Advaita foundation to theologically respond to some of the contemporary issues in the Indian context such as patriarchy, homophobia, anthropocentrism, childism and caste. By using the ideas of Advaita, the book proposes ways in which the 'Advaita tradition offers a holistic liberation that has implications for our economic, political, and social relationships.'[5] Prof. Rambachan asserts that the list of issues is not exhaustive and there might be other issues that need to be considered when we think about Liberation Theology in the Hindu context. This chapter can be called an extension of the work carried out by Rambachan in his seminal book.

One of the most pertinent questions that must be addressed before we delve into the major argument that this chapter brings is whether there is anything called Hindu Theology. Can we understand Liberation Theology in the context of Hinduism and India? Hinduism is mostly mentioned in terms of a philosophy rather than a theology; theology being a Western term.[6] But the terms are synonymous and are often used interchangeably by many scholars of Hinduism. I would argue that to use the terms in the case of a study on Hindu tradition, it is essential to see what school of philosophy (Darśana) is used to carry out the interpretative work.

In his essay *Hindu Theology as Churning the Latent*, Jonathan Edelmann comprehensively engages with the question of what can be considered Hindu theology as well as strongly arguing the need for the term 'Hindu theology'. He does this by juxtaposing his understanding of theology with that of philosophy in Hinduism. According to his interpretation, theology and philosophy have a lot in common but they are distinct in some terms. While theology is an interpretation of a text – wherein the text is considered sufficient to understand the truth, which is usually about the knowledge of God or related divine subjects – philosophy approaches any text through the means of logic, reasoning and argumentation. The sole purpose of philosophy might not be to understand the divine. But these definitions do not work for studies in Hinduism as the characteristics of theology and philosophy put forth by Edelmann often overlap. This is the reason behind the long-standing discourse on whether Śaṅkara, Rāmānuja, Mādhava and others can be called philosophers or theologians. Edelmann stresses the need to introduce the category of Hindu theology in the academic world to 'give a space for the existing constructive work in Hinduism' that currently forms a part of other disciplines such as Hindu Studies, Religious Studies, Indology, and Philosophy.[7] Hindu theology, then, comes to be understood not just as pure scriptural exegesis but any work of scholarship that aims to discover the divine aspects of the universe through varying methods. Prof. Chakravarthi Ram-Prasad also mentions the fundamental nature of the exegetical work in the field of Hindu theology in today's times, given the divine authority of *śruti*.[8] In addition, in his *A Hindu Theology of Liberation*, Rambachan highlights that one of the primary concerns of theology has always been the interpretation of revelation and if theology is understood in these terms, then all of Śaṅkara's work can be understood as theological. Panikkar also contends that Śaṅkara and many others can be seen as theologians as they have dealt with matters of ultimate concern by relying on the divine revelatory texts more than on logic, reason and argumentation.

Rambachan's usage of 'Hindu theology' in his work is entirely different from how theology is used in a Christian context. Based on these discussions, we can conclude that the term 'Hindu theology' can be employed for scholarly work in Hinduism that includes scriptural exegesis to unravel knowledge of the Absolute and bring forth the ways the divine forces interact with the cosmic and human elements.

Although Hindu theology can exist through some modifications in the hermeneutical understanding of the term theology, when it comes to intellectual discussions based on Hindu tradition, several scholars have indicated the futility of settling on either theology or philosophy to signify a kind of study. These classifications are not applicable in Hinduism as they are not regarded as mutually exclusive and intend to find answers to metaphysical issues. In fact, as noted by Ram-Prasad, the aspects on which the text focuses decides whether the study is theological or philosophical.[9] Panikkar writes,

> Whether we choose to call it theology or philosophy, *brahmajñāna* or *darśana*, however, this universal wisdom has always aspired to be comprehensive knowledge, to represent a complete vision of the ultimate problems of reality.[10]

Liberation Theology (or not) in the Hindu Tradition

Rambachan's 2015 book is still the most significant work on Hindu theology of liberation. And it is for this reason that Rambachan recognizes his work as a product of interreligious learning emerging out of a dialogue with the existing works on Liberation Theology in other traditions.[11] There are multiple ways in which a theology of liberation can be generated in the Hindu tradition. When we talk about liberation in the Hindu context, it firstly refers to *moksha* – liberation from *samsāra*, the cycle of life and death. In this case, liberation is only possible after death, but Vedānta also talks about *jīvanmuktī*, which can be simply understood as liberation while living. This type of *moksha* is possible when a person attains the knowledge of *brahman* (*brahmavidya* or *brahmajñāña*) during their lifetime. A person does not need to leave their body in order to achieve liberation from reincarnation. The Hindu texts such as the *Upanishads* talk about these understandings of liberation in great detail. In the scholarly space of Liberation Theology, liberation is seen as an emancipation from suffering and injustice – liberation from the 'systemic evil' which is visible in various forms such as economic, social, political, psychological and so on. Camila Vergara talks about the crisis that democracies all over the world are going through because of a systemic corruption, which is a result of growth in oligarchic powers.[12] The idea of systemic corruption that Vergara mentions can be a subject of a project of Liberation Theology that is focused on politics but is supported by religious texts. This chapter does not employ that methodology. In Rambachan's words,

> For the liberation theologian, religion and justice are inseparable. The practice of justice in human relationships is the highest expression of the religious life.[13]

Hindus generally talk about liberation from the structures of caste and patriarchy, among many other topics. There have been several studies over time that focus on how these systems can be proved as being the cause of many evil happenings in the society, and how religious ideals can be used to liberate people from them. There are undoubtedly multiple issues that have been at the centre of liberation theologians' attention but what seems the most pertinent at this point of time is the change that Hinduism has undergone through these centuries and how it has affected the dynamics of people's lives in India.

Panikkar clearly pointed out, and it can be viewed as prophetic to some degree, that 'A new religious wave is spreading throughout the world, but in many cases it is shortsighted, fundamentalist, revivalist, and exclusivist.'[14]

Hinduism has always been recognized for its evolutionary character. The lack of a scripture and a canon allows the fluidity that one can see in the Hindu tradition. Unfortunately, the pluralistic and all-encompassing structure of Hinduism is often overlooked in the mainstream discourse of today's India where there is a strong initiative to maintain a singular understanding of Hinduism – one that is far removed from its ancient ideals. There are several reasons behind this transformation in Hinduism. First, one can attribute this change to adherents forgetting that Hinduism 'is merely a foreign label invented for the purpose of grouping together a bundle of religions (or religious traditions)'.[15] Second, the discord between the traditional way of living and the modern standard set by the westerners and introduced through technology. Third, the construction and upsurge of Hindu nationalist ideology. Although Panikkar was writing about it in 1993, he clearly mentioned the way in which 'the symbol of Hindutva offers a unifying myth;[16] a reality that has become distinctly evident in the present times through various social and political movements. Panikkar highlighted that '[c]hange is a modern category, improvement a traditional symbol, and growth a natural event'.[17] Hindus need to realize that there has been a change, a negative shift, in the idea of how a Hindu comes to be defined. The shift is visibly not an evolutionary growth that can be interpreted in terms of an imperative requirement given the sociological and technological developments.

The transformation is ideologically motivated and considers India synonymous with Hinduism. This has resulted in an increase in cases of religious intolerance all around India and even beyond. Many Hindus in India are swayed by the idea that they have a dominant right or claim over their country and forget what being a Hindu traditionally means. The path that they have chosen is wrong when judged by Hindu traditional parameters in the sense that it is not spiritually guided but politically informed and ideologically motivated. The question that needs to be answered is how Hindus can liberate themselves from this predicament.

A Way Towards Hindu Liberation Theology

As Panikkar highlights,

> The first step toward liberation consists in recognizing that it is all merely Indra's temptation – the temptation to believe that the universe is ruled by Man – by us, the elites, the masters of history, the scientists, the shapers of the world. This is his cunning. We still do not realize this, and carry on devising reforms.[18]

While on the one hand, this statement is a reflection on how people neglect the omnipresence of God and the way the divine works in unfolding every other moment, on the other hand, the statement is hinting at the myth of Indra again. Liberation requires us to be conscious of cosmotheandrism. Panikkar coined this term in his work *The Cosmotheandric Experience* wherein he views reality as three dimensional. Everything that exists is constitutive of the divine, human and earthly. To put it in his words,

> The cosmotheandric principle could be formulated by saying that the divine, human and the earthly – however we may prefer to call them – are the three irreducible dimensions which constitute the real, i.e., any reality inasmuch as it is real. It does not deny that the abstracting capacity of our mind can, for particular and limited purposes, consider parts of reality independently; it does not deny the complexity of the real and its many degrees. But this principle reminds us that the parts are parts and that they are not accidently juxtaposed, but essentially related to the whole.[19]

The divine, human and earthly as parts cannot exist individually as they are inherently connected to one another. The cosmotheandric principle brings to light how reality, as we see it, is not what we have constructed through our limited human power, but is a result of the mutual endeavour of the divine, cosmic and human. Hence, people cannot presume that they rule the universe by being completely unmindful of the divine faculties surrounding them, by being forgetful of their primitive roots.

What is the alternative? Panikkar contends that in order for a profound transformation to take place, the world/great religions need to 'relearn from tribal and/or minor religions' and 'rediscover chthonic, telluric, and mythical values'.[20] There is a need to revisit the *śruti* and *smriti* to remind oneself of the traditional meaning of being an Indic human being. Although Hinduism is not dependent on scriptures as other monolithic religions, there has been an unfortunate overlooking of the holy texts in the case of Hindu tradition due to the probable efforts to adapt to the modern way of lifestyle. To be human, one must acknowledge one's roots; one must relearn the Hindu way of living and liberate oneself from the obsessive drive of transforming the Hindu tradition. This reinterpretation of the *sanātana dharma* into a religion that offers no space for dialogue cannot be a unifying myth for the liberation of Hindus in India. 'The validity of the sanātana dharma does not depend upon a rigid and unchangeable social and doctrinal structure, but upon an everlasting claim that it is (the) right dharma.'[21]

Here, I call all Hindus to return to *The Bhagavad Gita* where Krishna affirms

अहमात्मा गुडाकेश सर्वभूताशयस्थितः ।
अहमादिश्च मध्यं च भूतानामन्त एव च ॥ १०-२० ॥

This can be translated as 'I am the self, Gudakesha, situated in the hearts of all creatures, just as I am the beginning, the middle, and the end of creatures.'[22]

The verse is a reminder for all to remember that Lord Krishna does exist in all creatures, and we must be mindful of that. It is important to realize that being a Hindu is foremost about the knowledge of the Absolute and its immanence as well as transcendence. The myth of Indra must be invoked here as done by Panikkar to free ourselves from following the religion of man, when in fact the Hindu tradition is a religion that is characterized primarily by the all-pervasive divinity.

To conclude, I would like to stress the argument made by Rambachan on the essentiality of granting reality to the world if we want to propose a liberation theology at all.[23] Looking at the world as an illusion and only the *brahman* as real (according to Advaita Vedanta) leads to the belief that all problems pertaining to the human world are non-existent and do not require serious attention. He emphasizes the need to look at the world as a visible articulation of the fullness of *brahman* as it is not necessary 'to deny the reality and value of the many to affirm the infinity of the one'.[24] Interestingly, Panikkar also mentions this in his argument on why most people do not take initiatives to bring about change. He writes:

> Most traditional religions, especially Asian dharmic conceptions of life, tend to consider this material world as temporary, fleeting, if not downright illusory. In this context, therefore, if external things do not go

according to our wishes and expectations, it is more realistic for us to adapt and seek inner contentment than to fight a losing battle.²⁵

Panikkar understands this to be a result of the conflict of cosmologies. Furthermore, along with granting reality to the world, it is equally important to accept the presence of multiple realities to liberate ourselves from falling into a linear interpretation of Hinduism. Hindu Liberation Theology, as presented in this chapter, is a theology that displays how Hindus need to be saved from themselves. The liberation is from a suffering that Hindus are inflicting on themselves (and others) due to their own forgetfulness of their traditional ideals and beliefs. Religion is deeply ingrained in our society and it is not uncommon that at times, religion tends to hinder the growth of humans by getting misconstrued for multiple reasons. If religion needs a transformation today, we must be up for it. If a religion and its followers need liberation from the piling misinterpretations, we must be willing to relearn.

Notes

1 Raimon Panikkar, 'Indra's Cunning', in *Opera Omnia Hinduism Part 2* (Delhi: Motilal Banarsidass, 2019), 275. As argued by Panikkar, this idea was also the major argument present in the special issue of *Daedalus*, 'Another India', published in autumn 1989, especially noted in the works of Ashis Nandy and Rajni Kothari.
2 Ibid., 273.
3 Ibid., 290.
4 Ibid., 276.
5 Anantanand Rambachan, *A Hindu Theology of Liberation* (Albany, NY: State University of New York, 2015), 8.
6 Theology was coined by Plato as an alternative term to Philosophy, meaning not only that it was connected to religion, but in his understanding it was true religion itself, which was a constant preparation for death. See Panikkar, 'Foundation of the Indic Philosophy' in *Opera Omnia Hinduism Part 2*, 223.
7 Jonathan Edelmann, 'Hindu Theology as Churning the Latent', *Journal of the American Academy of Religion* (Vol. 81, 2, June 2013), 427–66.
8 Chakravarthi Ram-Prasad, 'Reading the *Ācāryas*: A Generous Conception of the Theological Method', *Journal of Hindu Studies* (Vol. 7, 1, May 2014), 98.
9 Ibid., 106.
10 Panikkar, 'Foundation of the Indic Philosophy', 221.
11 Rambachan, *Hindu Theology of Liberation*, 4.
12 Camila Vergara, *Systemic Corruption: Constitutional Ideas for an Anti-Oligarchic Republic* (Princeton, NJ: Princeton University Press, 2020).
13 Rambachan, *Hindu Theology of Liberation*, 5.
14 Panikkar, 'Indra's Cunning', 358.

15 Ibid., 355.
16 Ibid., 339.
17 Ibid., 293.
18 Ibid., 371.
19 See Raimon Panikkar, *The Cosmotheandric Experience* (Delhi: Motilal Banarsidass, 1998), 60.
20 Panikkar, 'Indra's Cunning', 360.
21 Raimon Panikkar, *The Unknown Christ of Hinduism: Toward an Ecumenical Christophany* (Maryknoll, NY: Orbis Books, 1981), 6.
22 W. J. Johnson, *The Bhagavad Gita* (New York: Oxford University Press, 1994), 46.
23 Rambachan, *Hindu Theology of Liberation*, 7.
24 Ibid., 8.
25 Panikkar, 'Indra's Cunning', 294.

14

Exposing Selfish Motivations Disguised as Justice: Questioning the Narrative of the Miracle of Cultured Meat

ARVIN GOUW

Meat consumption leaves a massive carbon footprint that is unsustainable in light of the climate change problem. There are several alternatives to land-based animals, such as plant-based foods, sea-animal meat, and cultured meat. Of the three, cultured meat leaves the smallest carbon footprint and eliminates the taking of life altogether. The industry is attracting millions in funding from the US. This chapter will discuss the advantages and disadvantages of cultured meat from multiple religious perspectives, especially Christianity and Hinduism. Advantages include the alleviation of animal suffering and the reduction of carbon footprint, which might very well be acceptable to both Hindus and Christians. For example, Christopher Bryant of the University of Bath has reported that of the 730 Hindus surveyed, 65% would eat cultured goat and 68% would eat cultured chicken, but only 20% would eat cultured pork and 19% would eat cultured beef. Despite these advantages, there are several issues that this chapter will push religious people to carefully consider. Disadvantages include the capitalism of cultured meat, the lack of discussion of overconsumption, and lack of discussion of the treatment of animals in general. For example, Shaukana Rishi Das, the director of the Oxford Centre for Hindu Studies, considers cultured meat as an example of human arrogance. Regardless of the advantages and disadvantages, religious and non-religious perspectives on a novel technology such as cultured meat, and a common problem such as climate change, provide a novel approach to combat systemic injustices that lead to climate injustice. However, this chapter also contextualizes and questions this approach, exposing its complicitly with a neo-capitalist ideology that privileges choice over justice, and presents a simpler, and seriously overlooked, alternative to tackling climate disaster.

Introducing the Problem

The problem of climate change has been going on for decades and there are no signs of it slowing down as discussed annually in UN COP conferences. There have been multiple attempts by various groups to address this problem – hardly a single problem for it has multiple causes that are interrelated: conventional agriculture, mining, thawing of the permafrost in the frozen Arctic, landfill, forest burning, crop burning and many others.

Since climate change is a complex phenomenon involving scientific and socioeconomic factors, there are many ways to narrate it. Being a Christian from Indonesia, my narrative of the problem will be more sea-based. This is a narrative that is not often heard. Most climate change narratives are very land-based.

Let's start with the causes of climate change. Factories and technologies that use fossil fuels emit greenhouse gases that trap more heat and increase temperature in the atmosphere. This increased temperature causes the land to become dry, making it more difficult for plants to grow. The drought causes more floods, which in turn cause more droughts. This comes down to the water cycle. The same heat that evaporates more water vapor off the oceans also sucks it out of the first metre of topsoil and makes the droughts hit more quickly and more deeply, and last longer. For a long time people said, 'Well, it's kind of funny, kind of hard to believe that it's causing more flooding and more drought,' but it definitely is. That is the pattern the scientists have told us about for a long time.

One might think that more carbon dioxide would make plants grow better, but this is not true. Major crops like wheat, barley, rice and potato – grown in projected 2100 carbon dioxide levels (540–958 ppm) have 6–15% less protein than those grown in current carbon dioxide levels (315–400 ppm), significantly reducing their nutritional value. High carbon dioxide concentrations cut levels of key nutrients such as iron, zinc, calcium and magnesium by 5–10% in most plant species.[1] Currently, about 2.4 billion people get at least 60% of their zinc and iron from staple crops like wheat, rice and potatoes. This means most crops have fewer essential minerals per calorie and become less nutritious.[2] Experts project that as the climate crisis makes crops less nutritious, an additional 25 million children under five will be at risk of malnutrition by 2050.[3]

Reduction of crop growth in turn causes a reduction in food supply for animal farming. In addition, agriculture and farming in themselves contribute to climate change independently. In effect, decreased food production causes famines that disproportionately harm the poor more than the rich. This causes socioeconomic as well as political instability. Massive immigration from tropical and dry areas to subtropical areas has taken place due to climate change. But migration will not solve the problem, because the increased temperature is expanding from the tropical areas to the subtropical areas as well. Along with the increasing hot zone from the tropics to the subtropics come all the pests and diseases. For example, wheat rust is a crop blight currently present in many countries throughout Africa and the Middle East. One of the most dangerous strains of wheat stem rust threatens 90% of current wheat varieties grown worldwide.[4] As another example, Alfatoxins are moulds that can affect plant crops and raise the risk of liver damage, cancer and blindness, as well as stunting foetuses and infants. Aflatoxins are spreading to more areas as a result of shifting weather patterns, with approximately 4.5 billion people in developing countries exposed each year, though the amounts are largely unmonitored, and the numbers are rising.[5]

We have a global problem, not just a tropical problem. This is not a trivial problem and its severity is quantifiable. In the United States alone, the Inflation Reduction Act addresses these climate change issues with several provisions aimed at increasing land-based carbon sinks and making the soil more fertile in the process, and forestry. Almost $20 billion is for agricultural conservation, including environmental quality incentives. Almost $5 billion is for regional conservation partnerships. More than $3 billion is for conservation stewardship programmes. Almost $1.5 billion is for agricultural conservation easements, and $1 billion for technical assistance for agricultural conservation. More than $2.5 billion is for coastal resilience in agriculture.[6]

The solution to such a land-based narrative is to fix the problems on the land. Some of the solutions include less fossil fuel use, use of more efficient agriculture, reduce agriculture and farming, grow more trees to reduce the greenhouse gas emission. All these efforts have been put forward and unfortunately they are not yet making a dent in the climate change problem. But this might just be changing very soon due to the development of a novel technology called cultured meat.

The Magic Bullet: Cultured Meat (CM)

What is cultured meat (CM)? Cultured meat is basically a lab-grown meat. In many ways, lab-grown meat is better than plant-based meat when it comes to alleviating climate change because plant agriculture still takes up a lot of land area which is becoming more and more difficult to facilitate due to population increase as well as decreased fertile land due to global warming. On the other hand, CM grow in giant bioreactors that hold gallons of culture media (food for cells to grow the meat) to allow the CM to grow.

A single definition of CM does not suffice, because it does not clearly explain the process that is involved in growing meat in the lab. Culturing meat means culturing cells. These cells come from the foetuses of any animal that we want. So the first step in creating CM is to harvest some cells from our animal of preference (cow, pig, chicken etc.), then culture those cells in the laboratory until they grow. The way to make cells grow in the laboratory is by putting these cells in physiological temperatures and feeding them with 'media' that contain nutrients that they need (glucose, glutamine, lipids, amino acids etc.). Once you have enough cells, then they can be 3D-printed to make whatever shape you want, whether for a burger patty or a ribeye steak.

There are clear advantages to CM because of this process. First, minimal animal suffering takes place because there is no longer any need to slaughter an animal. Second, this process uses much less water compared to standard farming because in farming cows, for example, you need to water the grass to grow to feed the cows, but you also need to provide water for the cows. With global warming, you need more water to grow grass and to provide drinking water for the cows. Third, CM requires much less land when compared to animal farming; the reason being that CM grows in bioreactors, which are giant cylinders that stay in a factory laboratory. Fourth, culturing CM requires a lot less energy both in terms of fossil fuels and electricity. The operational energy needs of an animal farm consume much more energy than the management of a CM laboratory.

Climate change causes food shortages that are exacerbated by increasing world population. CM seems to be able to solve both problems simultaneously. Not only that, CM may decrease climate change directly because according to United Nations Food and Agriculture Organization (UN FAO), agriculture contributes one-third of greenhouse gas emissions, of which 65% are from beef and dairy cattle production. In summary, CM alleviates animal suffering, reduces 78–96% of the greenhouse gas footprint, decreases land use by 99%, and reduces water use by 82–96%.

Then why isn't everybody eating CM?

Unless you live in the Silicon Valley area, you probably won't see cultured meat very frequently. There is obviously some pushback from people with regards to consuming CM. There are many reasons why people have been reluctant to consume CM, but for the purposes of this chapter I want to explore some responses from religious communities. Religious communities are very diverse and it is impossible to include all of them, but the sampling done here is to portray the variety of responses both against and for CM.

Hindu Perspectives on CM

Rita Sherma is the founding Director and Associate Professor at the Center for Dharma Studies at GTU Berkeley, and she expresses some concerns. First of all, 'there is the problem of desiring meat of other sentient beings which is not considered conducive to spiritual advancement'. Second, 'there is no need for CM, because there are many other options. For example, Indian food has a variety of delicious food created from protein sources derived from various plant-based sources such as lentils, legumes, milk solids (paneer) etc., which provide flavour and satisfaction for those who like the flavours.'[7] Third, from the viewpoint of diverse religious ethics, we may cause moral injury to ourselves by engaging in the slaughter and consumption of other sentient beings. She argues that this is being researched by studies that look at brutality to animals and trace the trajectory to more serious crimes – to crimes against other humans.

Shaunaka Rishi Das is the Director of the Oxford Centre for Hindu Studies. He is a lecturer and Hindu Chaplain to Oxford University. He believes that from a Hindu perspective, using an animal's cells to make meat constitutes an example of human arrogance. Rishi Das explains that Hindus mostly abstain from meat. They also do not subscribe to the Western principle of dominion over non-human beings. 'It's an entirely different philosophical starting point,' he says. 'It's not: I am the master of you. It is: I am your servant. I am the servant of nature. I am the servant of animals.'[8] Even if the animal is not killed, he says, humans are still asserting that its cells are theirs to use. Theologically this is highly problematic.

Christian Responses to CM

Christians vary in their responses to cultured meat, but they can be located within the larger context of a Christian holy war against obesity. This is a predominantly American phenomenon, but it is not without a global impact. Fundamentalist Christians are by far the heaviest of all religious groups, according to one study.[9] This can be seen by the popular books written on Christian diet.[10] They share similar contents, and here's an example from Don Colbert:

> Did Jesus actually teach anything about nutrition or how we should eat? My contention is that He did – not necessarily by what He said, but by what He did. There are hundreds of examples throughout the Bible of practices related to healthy eating. Jesus embodied them fully in his lifestyle. Even casual readers of the Bible know of many stories that refer to food as part of, or the main focus of, the story. Jesus taught key spiritual principles using a number of food analogies. He also participated in biblical feasts and celebratory meals. At the Last Supper, He instituted a ritual that involved food as the most sacred memorial of His death. The medical and scientific facts confirm it. If we eat as Jesus ate, we will be healthier. He is our role model for good habits in eating, exercising, and living a healthy, balanced life.[11]

Some of these Christian diet books are targeted towards women where the idea of women being slim for their husband is presented as a good Christian thing to do.[12] The conflation of Christianity and a woman's body image did not go unnoticed and several Christian theologians have responded to the problematic narration of weight loss and gender.[13] It has been shown that Christians may be more susceptible to obesity due to American church behaviour which includes festivities involving communities celebrating with food. This runs in conjunction with the gender role of women in food preparation while the men simply run the show and eat.

Thus, for Christians who subscribe to CM in an attempt to lose weight, we must be careful not to participate or buy into the narrative of the Christian war against obesity. Obesity is depicted as a vice, due to excess of consumption, to a sin of greed. This is how obesity is perceived in both the general population as well as among Christian communities. The problem of incorporating such a narrative is that Christians are then lending further ammunition to the secular narrative that obesity is a vice. Obesity has been associated with various kinds of discrimination. Discrimination happens at schools where schoolteachers consciously and unconsciously regard obese children as slow, lazy and stupid. Obese employees are also discriminated against at work, having difficulties in climbing up the corporate ladder. The American phenomenon of acceptance of CM among Christians demonstrates a complex set of intersectionalities between obesity, discrimination, patriarchy and religion.

Non-religious Considerations Regarding CM

Non-religious considerations regarding CM have often been ignored by religious communities. Here I would like to focus specifically on the economics behind CM. The problem of the CM industry is not its feasibility or pricing. The price of the first CM burger was $330,000 in 2013, but in 2020 the first restaurant ever to serve lab-grown chicken sold it for only $23. This dramatic difference happens due to advances in science as well as the economy of scale. The development of CM is largely driven by the entrepreneurial ecosystem, where funding for CM was less than $0.3m in 2015 but became over $160m in 2020.[14]

Despite the great advantages of CM, I would like to raise some concerns that revolve around the business of CM itself. Whenever one sees an exponential increase of funding for a certain technology in less than a decade, one must be cautious of the implications of such a strong economic driving force. More specifically, the narrative that is being sold here is that CM solves the problem of climate change, obesity and animal suffering all at once. Yet, one cannot help but question whether this narrative is too good to be true.

I would argue that CM is an American solution that is being exported globally. When we look at global consumption of meat, the United States, Europe, Latin America and Australia are leading with over 165g per person per day in 2019.[15] On the other hand, Africa, the Middle East, India, Indonesia and Japan show some of the lowest meat consumption in the world at below 40mg per person. As Rita Sherma points out above, meat consumption is simply not a concern for most Indians, which constitute the third largest population in the world. Now when we look at the kinds of meat that are being consumed, chicken is the predominant source of meat globally.[16] Beef consumption is highest in the United States. Pork consumption is highest in China. Yet, beef is the predominant CM that is currently being developed. This makes sense because almost half of CM companies in the world are founded in the United States, and more specifically in the Silicon Valley area of California, and the rest of them are predominantly located in the global North.[17]

Possible Scenarios for CM Versus Real Meat

If CM costs more than real meat, there are several negative implications. First, there are many studies that associate plant-based foods with disempowered social groups such as women and people of colour because meat is often more expensive. Second, does this mean only the haves can pay for the privilege of a guilt-free conscience while not changing their actual eating habits? Would this be considered virtuous? This echoes Shaunaka Das' criticism. Third, if CM is too expensive, then maybe there are tiers of CMs where less nutritious CMs are cheaper, which means the lower class will have no option but to buy the less nutritious CM.

But most would argue that the costs of CM will continue to decrease so that it'll become cheaper than real meat. If CM costs less than real meat, there are several possible consequences. First, CM would then become the cheapest option to the disadvantaged groups. Real meat then would become a luxury item, like Kobe and Wagyu beef are now today. Second, fast food vendors (McD, KFC etc.) would use CM because it's cheaper, but most likely less nutritious. Third, livestock farmers in rural communities would lose their jobs. The path for a developing country to become developed is through agriculture, which means developing countries will remain behind, especially since CM requires high-skilled labour.

To avoid either of the aforementioned scenarios, many have argued for a government-regulated CM industry. Currently Singapore has invested the most ($108m) for the development of CM. India has been creating government-industry infrastructure to support CM production. Unfortunately, if CM were cheaper and climate crisis is inevitable, governments might unilaterally provide only CM in government food aid. Since CM composition can be engineered precisely, national healthcare could provide surveillance to monitor the effects of CM but also to propose specific CMs for specific population groups. We would then be concerned with individual freedom to choose what we eat.

Another Narrative of Climate Change from the Sea

CM claims to solve climate change by reduction of land use, water use and carbon footprint. This is largely due to the increasing temperature of land surfaces which cause loss of agriculture and food production. Such a narrative of climate change leaves us little room to disagree that CM would solve the problem. But as an Indonesian, the largest archipelago nation in the world, I would like to start a different narrative of climate change that is sea-based.

If we step back and look at it on a global basis, there is a really important factor that we need to take fully into account. The sea covers three-quarters of the earth's surface, containing 97% of the earth's water, and representing 99% of the living space on the planet by volume. According to the World Register of Marine Species, there are now 240,470 accepted species, but this is believed to be just a small proportion of the species that exist, with new marine life being discovered every day. Of all the extra heat from global warming, 93% is absorbed by the oceans.[18] The oceans provide and regulate our rainwater, drinking water, weather, climate, coastlines, 15% of our food, and even the oxygen in the air we breathe. The ocean produces at least 50% of the planet's oxygen. Due to global warming, oceans now also contain less oxygen, while acidity has increased by over 25% since pre-industrial times. Due to acidification, the deteriorating condition of marine ecosystems will have a wide range of consequences for human societies, including substantial revenue declines and loss of employment and livelihoods. For example, ocean acidification is affecting important marine species, thus undermining coastal communities' livelihoods and food security.

Almost 98% of the Pacific region is ocean. With 25,000 islands lying within it, the Pacific Ocean has more islands than anywhere else on the planet. The Pacific is wider than the moon. At its widest point, from Indonesia all the way to Colombia, the Pacific Ocean is 12,300 miles across, which is more than five times the diameter of the moon. But how are the oceans connected to the stability and security dynamics in the Pacific? By a rise in the sea level. Sea-level rise has various impacts that affect coastal communities in the Pacific. First of all, coastal erosion and saltwater intrusion negatively impact coastal communities and areas crucial for food production making land unproductive, thus affecting food and water security. The region is suffering irreversible food source degradation where between 70% and 90% of Pacific populations' access to healthy foods and livelihoods are threatened. Diminishing freshwater supplies for low-lying atolls from inundation droughts and saltwater intrusion are affecting key food crops. As a result, there is increasing dependency on low-nutrition imports as alternatives in a region producing some of the highest non-communicable disease (NDC) rates in the world (70–75% of deaths due to NDCs)[19] and 1 in 3 children suffer from stunting because of malnutrition.[20]

Fish ranks as one of the most highly traded food commodities and fuels a $362 billion global industry.[21] Millions of people, mainly in developing Small Islands Developing States, depend on the fishing industry for their livelihood. When fish disappear, so do jobs and coastal economies. To address the above-mentioned ocean-driven and climate security challenges in the Pacific, the UN Secretary-General's Peacebuilding Fund (PBF)-funded Climate Security in the Pacific project is taking decisive climate action to build resilience and secure a sustainable future.

Implemented by the United Nations Development Programme and the International Organization for Migration (IOM), the initiative is focusing on empowering low-lying atoll nations, in particular Tuvalu, the Republic of the Marshall Islands and the Republic of Kiribati. The scheme describes itself as 'working in close partnership with the Governments of the three countries and regional actors, it helps set the direction to manage climate-related security risks and strengthen the capacities of Pacific SIDS, supporting the coastal and indigenous communities that depend on the ocean and its ecosystem services, including fisheries, recreation, tourism and transport sectors.'

As the former Pacific Islands Forum Secretary General Dame Meg Taylor stated, 'the ocean requires global governance and understanding to ensure its long-term health and wellbeing and prosperity for all'. The thinking behind this project is that 'We need collaborative action to improve and understand ocean-driven security challenges, promote sustainable development and management practices, and maintain good ocean health, which are essential for us and the wellbeing of our planet.'[22]

Alternatives to CM: Approaching Climate Change from the Sea

Marine permaculture is the ocean farming of kelp and seaweeds. It is a win/win solution when it comes to taking positive steps to help the planet. It turns out that kelp and seaweed are nature's climate warriors and cultivating them at scale could counteract ocean acidification, climate change and loss of biodiversity.[23] Seaweed and kelp can also be a source of biofuel and feed for cattle and could provide food security for millions.[24] Our oceans have absorbed over 90% of the heat from global warming to date.[25] This has created a layer of warm water near the surface which acts as a barrier to upwelling, which is the movement of nutrient-rich water from the deep ocean to the surface. Plankton relies on upwelling for nutrients and, in turn, many fish rely on plankton as a food source. As a result, we have seen the collapse of a dozen major fisheries.[26]

The ocean has also been absorbing much of the carbon dioxide that we have been pumping into our atmosphere and this is causing the acidification of our oceans. It's time for us to give our oceans a much-needed leg up! Marine permaculture requires no fresh water, no deforestation and no fertilizer. It simply sets up the conditions that are needed for this natural process to take over that will help restore balance to our oceans.

Researchers estimate that if 9% of the world's ocean surfaces were used for seaweed farming, we would be removing 53 billion tons of CO_2 a year from the atmosphere.[27] The key technology required is a lightweight, latticed structure that is roughly a square kilometre in size. It is submerged about 25 metres below sea level where kelp can attach to it.[28] Kelp forests are an amazing carbon sink and draw more CO_2 from the atmosphere by area than land-based rainforests! They will even grow in ocean 'dead zones' and, remarkably, will restore these areas. Here's how it works:[29]

The floating platforms use wave energy to pump nutrients from the cooler, deep waters so plankton and kelp have the food they need to thrive. Once the kelp becomes established, it forms the basis of an ecosystem by providing habitat for forage fish who will feed off plankton. Game fish will then join the party because they eat these forage fish, and on and on, up the food chain to tuna and sharks. What was once an ocean desert, now becomes a productive and thriving community.

Marine permaculture has the potential to provide 200kg per year, per person for 10 billion people.[30] Kelp is also a fantastic food source in itself. Filled with vitamins, Omega-3s and 46 minerals, kelp contains more calcium than milk, more iron than spinach and more fibre than brown rice! Some companies are already developing fibres and bioplastics from seaweed too.[31]

Closing Remarks

There are clear advantages of CM which would reduce land use, water use and carbon footprint by around 90% compared to conventional farming agriculture. Both Hindus and Christians need to reflect within their respective traditions to engage with the CM proposal. Both want to accept CM at least as an alternative due to climate change and animal suffering. Both are against the anthropocentric dominion over animals. Both pay attention to the individual cultivation of spirituality in reducing meat intake.

However, there's a need to focus on social class issues that cut across both Hindus and Christians. There's a need to have a critical global perspective of CM business and how it affects 'Christian' and 'Hindu' nations. We need to add a sea-narrative because many disadvantaged populations live by the seas. Hindus need to reflect whether vegetarianism is attainable not only in India but for the rest of the world, and whether it would be sufficient for climate healing. Christians need to reflect whether the holy war against obesity and adopting vegetarianism are the best way to engage with CM and climate change. We need to engage the CM proposal not only through various interreligious dialogues but also through economic critiques. CM is a product of American capitalism which causes economic injustices. CM arises from a land-based narrative of global warming and food shortage which cause injustice to developing countries. Upon re-evaluating the sea-based narrative of climate change, we become more aware of potential solutions from the sea. Complicated science can sometimes be masked as justice, but when we delve into it, science is often used to preserve food preferences dictated by the powerful, rather than to guide us in choosing healthier and more sustainable food sources.

Notes

1 Lewis Ziska et al., 'Climate and Health Assessment Chapter 7: Food Safety, Nutrition, and Distribution' (US Global Change Research Program, 2016), https://health2016.globalchange.gov/food-safety-nutrition-and-distribution (accessed 21/02/2024).

2 Ibid.

3 Damian Carrington, 'Climate change making food crops less nutritious, research finds', *The Guardian*, 7 May 2014, https://www.theguardian.com/environment/2014/may/07/climate-change-food-crops-nutrition (accessed 21/02/2024).

4 R. P. Singh et al., 'The Emergence of Ug99 Races of the Stem Rust Fungus is a Threat to World Wheat Production', *Annual Review of Phytopathology* (Vol. 49, 2011), 465–81, https://www.ars.usda.gov/ARSUserFiles/34883/Singh-AnnRePhytopath.pdf (accessed 24/03/2024).

5 Kagondu Njagi, 'Extreme weather increasing level of toxins in food, scientists warn', *Reuters*, 31 May 2016, http://www.reuters.com/article/us-climate-change-food-toxins-idUSKCN0YM0AH (accessed 21/02/2024).

6 'Inflation Reduction Act: Agricultural Conservation and Credit, Renewable Energy, and Forestry', *Congressional Research Service* (10/08/2022), https://crsreports.congress.gov/product/pdf/IN/IN11978 (accessed 24/03/2024); https://www.noaa.gov/news-release/statement-from-noaa-administrator-on-signing-of-historic-inflation-reduction-act (accessed 24/03/2024).

7 Ted Peters, 'To Eat No-Kill Cultivated Meat. Part 3: Hindu? Jain?', https://www.patheos.com/blogs/publictheology/2022/09/to-eat-no-kill-cultivated-meat-part-three-hindus-jains/ (accessed 11/06/2023).

8 Rachel E. Gross, 'Test-Tube Burgers: Holy Cow?', https://momentmag.com/test-tube-burgers-holy-cow/ (accessed 11/06/2023).

9 Krista M. C. Cline and Kenneth F. Ferraro, 'Does Religion Increase the Prevalence and Incidence of Obesity in Adulthood?', *Journal for the Scientific Study of Religion* (Vol. 45, 2, 2006), 269–81.

10 Don Colbert, *What Would Jesus Eat Cookbook* (Nashville, TN: Thomas Nelson, 2011); Rex Russell, *What the Bible says about Healthy Living* (Grand Rapids:

Revell, 1996); Richard Mays, *The Bible Diet* (Bloomington, IN: AuthorHouse, 2006); Rick Warren, *The Daniel Plan: 40 Days to a Healthier Life* (Nashville, TN: Zondervan, 2013).

11 Colbert, *What Would Jesus Eat Cookbook*, x.

12 Patricia B. Kremi, *Slim for Him: Biblical Devotions on Diet* (Plainfield, NJ: Logos International, 1978; Bridge Publishing, 1994); Gwen Shamblin, *The Weigh Down Diet* (New York: Doubleday, 1997; Waterbrook Press, 2002).

13 Lisa Isherwood, *The Fat Jesus: Christianity and Body Image* (New York: Seabury Books, 2008); Lynne Gerber et al., eds, *Fat Religion: Protestant Christianity and the construction of the fat body* (Abingdon: Routledge, 2021).

14 Deepak Choudhury, Ting Wei Tseng and Elliot Swartz, 'The Business of Cultured Meat', *Trends in Biotechnology* (Vol. 38, 6, 2020), 573–7.

15 'Daily Meat Consumption Per Person, 2020', *Our World in Data,* https://ourworldindata.org/grapher/daily-meat-consumption-per-person (accessed 21/02/2024).

16 Choudhury et al., 'Business of Cultured Meat'.

17 Xin Guan et al., 'Trends and ideas in technology, regulation and public acceptance of cultured meat', *Future Foods* (Vol. 3, 2021), 100032.

18 'Latest ocean warming review reveals extent of impacts on nature and humans', IUCN (5 September 2016), https://www.iucn.org/news/secretariat/201609/latest-ocean-warming-review-reveals-extent-impacts-nature-and-humans (accessed 25/03/2024).

19 'Noncommunicable Disease', WHO (16/09/2023), https://www.who.int/news-room/fact-sheets/detail/noncommunicable-diseases (accessed 21/02/2024).

20 'Malnutrition prevalence remains alarming: stunting is declining too slowly while wasting still impacts the lives of far too many young children', *UNICEF,* https://data.unicef.org/topic/nutrition/malnutrition/ (accessed 21/02/2024).

21 'Overfishing', Worldwildlife.org, https://www.worldwildlife.org/threats/overfishing#:~:text=Fish%20ranks%20as%20one%20of,a%20major%20source%20of%20protein (accessed 21/022024).

22 UNDP, 'Ocean-driven security challenges in the Pacific', 8 June 2021, https://www.undp.org/pacific/news/ocean-driven-security-challenges-pacific (accessed 12/04/2024).

23 'Kelp forests and keystone species', *The Liquid Earth*, https://theliquidearth.org/2013/10/kelp-forests-and-keystone-species/ (accessed 21/02/2024).

24 Fahmida Sultana et al., 'Seaweed farming for food and nutritional security, climate change mitigation and adaptation, and women empowerment: A review', *Aquaculture and Fisheries* (Vol. 8, 5, 2023), 463–80.

25 'Why ocean heat matters', NASA (December 2022), https://climate.nasa.gov/vital-signs/ocean-warming/#:~:text=Why%20Ocean%20Heat%20Matters&text=Covering%20more%20than%2070%25%20of,heat%20as%20Earth's%20entire%20atmosphere (accessed 21/02/2024).

26 Stephanie Uz and Leann Johnson, 'El Nino: Disrupting the Marine Food Web', NASA (13/10/2015), https://svs.gsfc.nasa.gov/4387 (accessed 21/02/2024).

27 Climate Council, 'How seaweed can kelp us tackle climate change', 31 March 2016, https://www.climatecouncil.org.au/seaweed-climate-change/#:~:text=What's%20the%20potential%3F,carbon%20during%20the%20growing%20process (accessed 21/02/2024).

28 Francesco Curto, Michael Lewis and Murray Birt, 'Oceans & Climate –

Exploring the Nexus', *DWS* October 2021, https://download.dws.com/download?elib-assetguid=416ece57eacc4b51b5e36f661fa6abfe (accessed 21/02/2024).

29 Regenerators, *2040* (film), https://whatsyour2040.com/marine-permaculture/ (accessed 21/02/2024).

30 Climate Foundation, 'Marine Permaculture', https://www.climatefoundation.org/marine-permaculture.html (accessed 21/02/2024).

31 Jewel S. Cabrera, 'Innovators develop seaweed-based alternatives to plastic food wrappers', *Mongabay* (17/01/2023), https://news.mongabay.com/2023/01/innovators-develop-seaweed-based-alternatives-to-plastic-food-wrappers/ (accessed 21/02/2024).

15

Discussing Human Dignity from the Peripheries: A Dialogue between *Buddhagotra* and *Imago Dei*

PATRICIA GUERNELLI PALAZZO TSAI

Introduction

Neoliberalism divides the world into winners and losers. It accomplishes this task through its ideological linchpin: the individualization of all social phenomena.[1]

This statement by Ronald Purser is as true as it gets. Societal systems created by humans to humans (also non-humans) have changed rapidly, turning into a neoliberal artificial world that measures every single person through consumption standards. Life, nature and even human dignity are severely maimed by this system.[2] Neoliberalism has, as its focus, the consumer – an individualized human person that has rights if, and only if, they have money to consume. The person becomes rights-less the moment he or she loses the capability to keep up with the system, turning into a non-consumer. However, neoliberalism does not only segregate consumers from non-consumers but offers different shades of each category. Consumers from countries known for their active part in colonialism are not the same as the ones from the peripheries of the world. This also can be analysed by the differences between rights in colonial countries and in peripheral ones.

Theoretically, each person is equal. But in reality, we are not the same – a Brazilian human being (or from any other peripheral country) is inferior to a European. The outrageous violence against the Yanomami in Brazil, and examples of equally horrendous crimes against the Rohingya, the Yazidi, and others in the African continent, Pakistan, Palestine, Iraq, Afghanistan and other places, violence against refugees etc. do not cause the same uproar as if they were occurring in Europe or the US.[3] In another example, Europe is moving towards carbon-zero emissions, having investments in electric cars. But where do the batteries come from? Many of them come from the so-called 'third world' – South American countries and many others, where inevitably ecosystems are preyed upon to extract the lithium ore these cars require.[4] It seems that in a neoliberal world, 'human dignity' can only apply to those who matter most to the system, as in Judith Butler's discussion on lives worthy of grief.[5]

But this issue also hits a soft spot: the role religions play in this discussion on human dignity. The scope of this chapter will be a dialogue between Mahāyāna Geluk Buddhism and Latin American Liberation Theology. It will be divided into three parts: a) The (Un)Human Dignity Issue; b) Becoming a Buddha and Fully Human in God's Image; c) Dialoguing Dignity from the Peripheries – when Buddhism and Christianity Meet. I have used these two dialogue partners to argue that we are facing new waves of dehumanization, reinforced by national and international policies, implemented by sinful structures and sinful systems, based on neoliberalism and its blind faith in the market.

The need to rediscuss human dignity is more than urgent, from an inter-religious and also secular dialogue, but also to unite efforts to act against the horrors we are experiencing on a daily basis. For this to happen, the global North must give room for the global South to help and lead the way, since there are many contributions to be made from the ones who were (and still are) silenced and colonized.

The (Un)Human Dignity Issue

What is the definition of human dignity? The most basic answer can be found in the UN's Universal Declaration of Human Rights, Article 1, that states 'All human beings are born free and equal in dignity and rights.' But what can be considered human and what should be understood as dignity? Even though biologically every being in the *Homo sapiens* species is considered human, regardless of any other characteristics, historically (and also today) there have been times when not everyone has been considered human; some have been treated and recognized as animals.[6] The dehumanized being is no longer seen as *imago Dei* or as having the *Buddhagotra* (or *tathāgatagarbha*)[7] but is a mere creature to be used and disposed of. By this logic, 'humans' could enslave 'animals' as they please. Colonialism thrived by this logic, and it still subsists in different forms to this very day – in neoliberal garments.

Losing the status of a human implies the rupture of any ties that could link this person to his or her previous relations. In the eyes of the society surrounding this person, it is the same as having died, becoming nothing more than an object or a tool; as Patterson says, '[t]he slave was natally alienated and condemned as a socially dead person.'[8] Social death imposes on a human person a non-human or animal status, forcing the loss of identity and social relations. Neoliberalism confers social death when the person is no longer productive to the system and is unable to consume. Králová points out this relationship between social exclusion and the person's status in the system:

> these concepts of the 'non-person' (Goffman, 1961), 'homo-sacer' (Agamben, 1998) and 'ex-human' (Biehl, 2004) suggest a loss of social identity and of social integration, triggered by a person's inadequacy in the eyes of others. Here the person's characteristics go hand in hand with their low socio-economic status, leading to social exclusion.[9]

To uphold their social ties and rights, one has to submit to the neoliberal system and live by its guidelines. This means living in constant fear of not being able to maintain one's status. Since human beings are social animals, the sense and need of belonging to a community are used perversely to keep people under the yoke of the market.

As noted by the Latin America liberation theologian Jung Mo Sung, regarding neoliberal ideology, 'the question at stake is whether all human beings have the right to live or is this right only applicable for consumers …?'[10] In the neoliberal capitalist system, the only way to have the right to live is by being productive (i.e. being exploited by the capitalist system) and having access to buy things (from the same capitalist system that is exploiting you). The ones who do not make it, do not deserve or have the right to live. According to this mentality, dignity refers only to those who 'deserve it', those who follow what the market demands.

In a world in which people are labelled as winners or losers – the winners being the ones who can buy products, and the losers being the ones who cannot – the road to happiness is one of wealth accumulation. The existence of a gap between rich and poor is understood not as sin, but as a right. This produces another gap, related to the ability to put oneself in another's shoes. Daniel Goleman, a psychologist and researcher on emotional intelligence, in a *New York Times* article, mentions that '[r]educing the economic gap may be impossible without also addressing the gap in empathy.'[11] Goleman refers to the US, but this is replicated on a global scale, where 'third world' citizens are worth less than the lowest individual in a 'first class' country. Immigrants or even citizens of less developed countries suffer grave violations to their dignity since the immigrants are nuisances to foreign governments,[12] and the citizens are completely ignored. Even though there is occasional information, it is as if the peripheries of the world are so distant that they do not matter. There is little solidarity for the 'third class' countries unless the developed world wish to profit from them.

This need to belong, allied to the insensitive culture of consumerism,[13] can create a cascade effect, bringing large numbers of desensitized and non-solidary individuals (and collectives)[14] while further destroying the environment. As noted by Wilczynska et al., 'The need to belong is a strong interpersonal motive influencing human behaviour, emotions, and thoughts.'[15] Fuelling this discussion, Matthieu Ricard says that our natural sociability 'is rarely taken into account by public policy and is neglected by most economists'.[16] It is also noteworthy that this sociability happens in an actual place – it is earthbound. As Hannah Arendt, one of the most influential political theorists of the twentieth century, stated, 'The earth is the very quintessence of the human condition.'[17]

Similarly, Ailton Krenak, a Brazilian indigenous leader and environmentalist, affirms that, 'I cannot imagine ourselves separated from nature.'[18] It is impossible to theorize about human dignity when it is devoid of the conditions required for all life to thrive. The concept of human dignity – and the right to live – is intertwined with the earth. There is no possibility of understanding it apart from the physical environment in which people and all sentient life exist. Human dignity is linked with the right to live, but also with many other aspects that involve quality of life and identity, and of being accepted in a community. This is central to understanding Arendt's poignant statement regarding human dignity as 'the right to have rights'.[19]

Even though neoliberalism affirms that it is the only option for a better world, the earth and all nature are not guided by the logic of this system, nor governed by financial institutions and huge enterprises. Therefore, human dignity cannot be seen with this restrictive neoliberal lens that divides us from the earth that gives us life.

This treatment can also be found inside religious communities and religious leadership. As a disease, neoliberalism spreads and corrodes the solid foundations of the very religious principles that were once fiercely defended by the founders and their disciples. It is time for religions to fight back, reassessing what is crucial, to avoid being devoured by the neoliberal beast. If the priorities are money and power, then the battle is already lost, for our hearts have turned to stone.

Becoming a Buddha and Fully Human in God's Image

For human dignity to be considered from a Buddhist perspective, there needs to be a foundation, a soil from which all other principles derive. The richness of this soil depends on the four immeasurables (Skt *catvaryapramāṇāni*; Tib. ཚད་མེད་བཞི་), which are equanimity, compassion (Skt *karuṇā*; Tib. སྙིང་རྗེ་), loving-kindness (Skt *maitrī*; Tib. བྱམས་པ་) and sympathetic joy (Skt *muditā*; Tib. དགའ་བ་). Equanimity is the most significant for our purposes (Skt *upekṣā*; Tib. བཏང་སྙོམས་).[20]

Upekṣā can have multiple meanings, but here it is used in the sense that it enables one to see every being on the same level as oneself, and also to assume responsibility for caring for them.[21] But this cannot be achieved if individuals and/or groups attach themselves to identity markers; as the Dalai Lama and Thubten Chodron warn,

> Emile Bruneau ... has found that the strength of our identity with a group affects our empathy and thus our equanimity. The more we identify with a particular group – be it racial, ethnic, religious, political, and so on – the less we can empathize with the situation and feelings of those from another group ...[22]

If the limit of heartlessness is crossed, identity becomes a pulling force for belligerence between groups, communities and even countries. For instance, the extreme right-wing *Bolsonarismo* movement in Brazil, where the excessive identification with hate speech, which dehumanizes the other, opens the door to horrendous acts that the world has seen (and remained silent). The destruction of the Amazon forest, Pantanal, and others; the death of more than 600,000 people from the pandemic; the genocide of indigenous communities; stirring a mob of people into destroying the Brazilian Congress. After all those hideous actions, Bolsonaro enjoyed a three-month vacation in the US and so far has not been held accountable.

The notion of equanimity is reinforced by the concept of Buddha nature – *Buddhagotra* (Tib. སངས་རྒྱས་ཀྱི་རིགས་)[23] or *Tathāgatagarbha* (Tib. དེ་བཞིན་གཤེགས་པའི་སྙིང་པོ་)[24]. In Thubten Chodron and Dalai Lama's words, *Buddhagotra* is 'the latency, seed, or potency that has existed since beginningless time and has the potential to give rise to the three bodies of a buddha'.[25] This potential to become a Buddha, an awakened one, is also found in the noble Asaṅga's *Mahāyanottaratantraśāstravyākhya*: 'Therefore, it is said: all beings possess *tathāgata* essence.'[26] By 'all beings' we should understand not only human beings but all sentient beings. This implies that all beings should be considered as having the same potential as human beings. So, the notion of dignity from a Buddhist view is related to this equal potential that all sentient beings have, and thus, all forms of sentient life should be protected, for all of them have the seed for becoming fully awakened.

All conditions for human (and all non-human) existence depend on the earth, in an intricate complex relation. Thus, to establish any dialogue on human dignity it is important to mention the relation between dignity and interdependence[27] (Skt *pratītyasamutpāda*; Tib. རྟེན་འབྲེལ་) from a Buddhist perspective. Tsai defines interdependence:

> The network of interdependent connections of the world is what guarantees conditions for the existence of the aggregates, the environment, the elements that constitute nature, the planet, the planetary systems, etc., which are part of the general network or world network, while the network of the five aggregates is what grounds and makes possible the sentience and the knowledge of oneself, and from that, of the network of the world ...[28]

Pratītyasamutpāda links all beings that have the same potential together but also relates to all conditions for life to be sustained. Putting it simply, it is interdependence that implies that there is no being that can live by itself, isolated from others and the world. This indicates that human action has consequences not only for oneself but also for the entire structure.

Considering all sentient beings as equal means not only recognizing their natural rights but also assuming the responsibility of making this potential flourish, until the final goal is achieved. By assuming this responsibility one becomes a Bodhisattva.[29] This responsibility does not come top-down, but by inviting people from every walk of life to engage in benefiting others: as Bodhisattvas all of us can inspire a down-top revolution, using as the main argument universal responsibility (Tib. སྤྱི་སེམས་) as an ethical option.

When a select group profits – forcing the vast majority of people to submit to unjust wages, precarious living conditions and also exploiting animals and nature to a point of no return, it is not an example of success, but rather a tragic loss. Human dignity from a Christian perspective comes from the fact that it 'is a gift that comes from God for all eternity. What Christ offers is the acknowledgment of this dignity.'[30] Also, while reflecting upon Gutiérrez – the acknowledged founder of Liberation Theology – Mario Aguilar summarizes:

For Gutiérrez, God is at the centre of that social and religious change that allows human beings to be liberated from their own personal sin, but most importantly from sinful structures that do not allow them to be fully human and in God's image.[31]

If human dignity is understood from Gutiérrez and Aguilar's viewpoint, then it can be seen as the potential to be fully human, as a reflection of God's image. Also, by being God's image this means humans can and must act to report and condemn sinful structures. Hence, human dignity is not only the potential of being fully human, but it relates to the capacity of denouncing injustice and proclaiming justice, in the image and likeness of Jesus.

In a system in which some are recognized and others are not, there is no possibility of such a thing as human dignity truly existing. It can exist, but only as a mere name, devoid of actual meaning. This is why, returning to Isaiah 58.7, it is important to understand the practical dimensions of human dignity, the sharing of food with the less favoured, hospitality and care towards the afflicted and the ones torn down by sinful structures. The passage still mentions the importance of not turning our backs on people in need. With 1.2 billion people living in acute multidimensional poverty[32] – most of them in underdeveloped countries – and concurrently, with 2,668 billionaires in the world,[33] we are in a scandalous situation.

In Matthew 25.35–36, it becomes quite clear that Jesus is found with the excluded, the unseen and the unwanted. By putting together this crucial point in the Sermon on the Mount and the data before, 1.2 billion Jesuses are living in unfathomable conditions due to sinful structures. The potential to become a Buddha and the possibility of a fully human status – as in God's image – is crucial in understanding that human dignity implies affirming the individual that cares for everyone and everything surrounding her or him.

Since religion and politics can (and should) be put together, how can we overcome this? It seems there is a need to restore the sense of human dignity more than ever. But this cannot become a reality if the education system continues to pursue neoliberal goals and subject people to it. This is exactly why the Dalai Lama often speaks of the need for educating hearts:

Modern education is premised strongly on materialistic values. Yet ... it is vital that when educating our children's brains we do not neglect to educate their hearts, and a key element of educating their hearts has to be nurturing their compassionate nature.[34]

Also, as Jennifer Chan affirms, 'Neoliberalism is 'undemocratic, inequitable, imperialist, and unsustainable ... It is intolerant not only of diverse human cultures and value systems but also of biodiversity.'[35] Because of an entire global system focused on competition and profit, education became a lucrative business to distinguish the rich from the poor. The neoliberal idea is to select the best and leave the rest behind, for it is their fault if they can't succeed.[36]

Neoliberalism affects and infects the UK education system as well, as stated by Hall and Pulsford:

> The restructuring of primary education, in particular in the global North, repositions that sector of education against a need to map the lives of individuals as a whole around ordered liberties that prioritize the economy or the market, through the development of human capital (Bruff and Tansel, 2018). Democratic, political rights are secondary to the efficient provision of educational services for value-driven ends.[37]

The neoliberal agenda in education seeks to destroy the innate sense of collectivity and diversity our children have – building concrete walls between people, in the attempt to control and segregate for maximum profit and efficiency.

> Thus, central to the neoliberal re-engineering of the primary school terrain is the import of market-based logics that pit members or factions of communities against each other in pursuit of improved standards and efficiency: pupils, teachers, parents, and schools must compete. Such competitive individualism and individuation instilled in contemporary educational cultures weaken social ties and limit the possibilities for a shared sense of purpose and collaboration ...[38]

Accordingly, the alternative to this neoliberal education system is the education of hearts, which exists in both Buddhist and Christian traditions. For this to work an effort must be made not only from all religions but also from non-religious sectors.

The lack of nurturing humane values and warmheartedness from early childhood has an immediate effect on the rise in excessive individualism, which leads to an increase in violent behaviour towards others. Intolerance towards social and welfare systems, desire to dominate the *other*, imposition of brute force against the excluded, and also consumption as a form of numbing people, are all part of the core values in a neoliberal system.

Inspired by Brazilian liberationist educator Paulo Freire's *Pedagogy of the Heart*, FitzSimmons states,

> the dominating elites of neoliberalism know ... that their own neoliberal ideology is a collective enterprise on behalf of and for a select minority of neoliberal ideologies. As such, the pedagogy of neoliberalism is placing the student outside the learning process by equating education and schooling as exchange value for profit and individualization.[39]

Education is at the forefront of the battle, in which neoliberalism seeks to dismantle social justice and human rights movements. There can be no human dignity outside a *humane* system. Social and collective rights are targeted as enemies. Yet, all major religious systems have at their roots humane values, their founders having defended these principles of justice. So, religions are also at the forefront, even if their role is unacknowledged. Will they succumb to the (false) promise of prosperity or will they maintain coherence with their roots?

Dialoguing Dignity from the Peripheries – when Buddhism and Christianity Meet

The potential that every sentient being has to achieve the state of awakening – be it *Buddhagotra* or *Tathāgatagarbha* – is a revolutionary concept. But this concept needs to be implemented, which is why the educational system must change. Also, if this potential is the same for everyone, this means that human dignity also should be analysed through an intersectional lens to enable each person to reach that potential. Kimberlé Crenshaw, a leading scholar on critical race theory, says that intersectionality is:

> basically a lens, a prism, for seeing the way in which various forms of inequality often operate together and exacerbate each other. We tend to talk about race inequality as separate from inequality based on gender, class, sexuality or immigrant status. What's often missing is how some people are subject to all of these, and the experience is not just the sum of its parts.[40]

This lens is valid also for the notion of human dignity present in Christian traditions, with the example of the Gospel of Matthew. If Jesus is to be found in each human, then it is necessary to implement a huge shift from the mentality of 'human capital' to 'human being'. And further, the needed shift from favouring 'first-class' countries and allowing all forms of injustice towards people from 'third-class' countries. There is no profit if the entire world suffers for the temporary gain of a select few. This means rethinking 'green' policies that fit the US and Europe but sink Latin America and all peripheral countries even further into poverty.

Until now all policies are made top-down, allowing little or no space for the common people to rise. The will of oligarchies – neoliberalism's crème de la crème – subdues democracies to their will. But their money and power are illusions, just like the horns of a rabbit.[41] Camila Vergara discusses the possibilities for a bottom-up revolution:

> To achieve equal liberty, the many need to perform their own emancipation in action, and therefore the institutionalization of equal access to political action – which according to Arendt can be experienced only collectively in the realm of appearances – is the proper end of revolution.[42]

If we can promote interreligious and non-religious dialogues on human dignity, it is possible that a new concept might arise, not only a theoretical one but one that encompasses theory and practice together.

Buddhism has developed theories – and practical advice – for more than 2,500 years and can offer contributions to advancing lenses of equality. Yet that can only happen if seats are offered for this tradition to join the discussion and decision-making. The same needs to occur with other religious traditions, especially the ones coming from the global South. For too long the global South has been ignored and denied a seat at the global decision-making table. It is up to the new generations to correct the wrongs previously done, and the time is now.

A Buddhist and Christian Response Against Neoliberal Injustice

The notion of human dignity has been under direct attack since the rise of the empire of the market, and in recent years with the development of new ideas for transforming an already ruthless and sinful system, neoliberalism is even more voracious in terms of sacrificing people and devouring communities. Because of neoliberal policies, individualism became a core value, and thus insensitivity was promoted as a virtue, for some lives are worthy, while others are not.

Dehumanization is central to a neoliberal way of life since solidarity, kindness and any religious or ethical, humanistic value is an obstacle to achieving efficiency and the profits the god-market has promised. Therefore, the idea of human dignity must be completely obliterated for this neoliberal kingdom to come. The conversion of hearts to neoliberal faith takes its toll on societies, since only a select few will have what it takes to keep up with the system, and all the rest can be discarded. This protocol of demanding efficiency and success, along with all other neoliberal impositions, destroys the sense of collectivity, altruism and care, leading to injustice and unjust structures, environmental destruction and also a mental health crisis.

Discussing human dignity from the peripheries in a dialogue between Mahāyāna Buddhism and Latin American Liberation Theology is vital to highlight neoliberal agendas from different worldviews, but also to promote dialogue between all religions, as well as non-religious institutions, uniting to denounce injustice and build a better world not only for future generations of humans but all sentient beings. For all sentient beings can become fully awakened Buddhas and the whole world the space in which Jesus is incarnated, and which God proclaimed was 'good'.

Notes

1 Ronald E. Purser, *McMindfulness: How Mindfulness Became the New Capitalist Spirituality* (London: Repeater Books, 2019), 25.

2 For the ethical and spiritual inversion of neoliberalism see Jung Mo Sung, *Idolatria do Dinheiro e Direitos Humanos: uma crítica teológica do novo mito do capitalismo* (São Paulo: Paulus, 2018), https://www.paulus.com.br/loja/appendix/4948.pdf (accessed 25/03/2024).

3 Even though Palestine has been for many years suffering brutal violence, the war in Ukraine gets more support and media, proving that some lives matter less. Mohammed Mhawesh, a Palestinian journalist, wrote: 'We fight our oppressors, and we get branded terrorists. Ukrainians do the same, and they get applauded for their courage', https://www.aljazeera.com/opinions/2022/3/6/what-the-war-in-ukraine-thought-us-palestinians (accessed 21/02/2024).

4 The degradation and impact are immense, as reported by R. B. Lakshmi, https://earth.org/environmental-impact-of-battery-production/ (accessed 25/03/2024).

5 Judith Butler, *The Force of Nonviolence: An Ethico-Political Bind* (London: Verso, 2020), 28.

6 Achille Mbembe, *Necropolitics* (London: Duke University Press, 2019), 77.

7 This refers to the potential that all sentient beings have to become a complete Buddha. They are sentient because of possessing the five aggregates (Skt *pañca-skandha*; Tib. ཕུང་པོ་ལྔ་), and are not limited to human beings, as the Christian sense

of *imago Dei* implies. The Sanskrit and Tibetan terms will be preserved during the entire chapter, in order to avoid misinterpretations based on translation.

8 Orlando Patterson, *Slavery and Social Death* (Cambridge, MA: Harvard University Press, 1982), 337.

9 Jana Králová, 'What is social death?', *Contemporary Social Science* (Vol. 10, 3, 2015), 235–48, at p. 239.

10 Sung, *Idolatria do Dinheiro e Direitos Humanos*, 48.

11 Daniel Goleman, 'Rich People Just Care Less', *New York Times*, June 2013, SR12.

12 Like the US and UK policies on 'illegal' immigrants, denying a safe haven for human beings, employing humiliation, mass deportation and even criminalization of a basic human right.

13 Regarding this topic there are many liberation theologians who debate the culture of insensitivity such as Jung Mo Sung, Mario I. Aguilar, Joerg Rieger etc.

14 Concerning insensitivity and a society of consumers, see Zygmunt Bauman and Leonidas Donskis, *Moral Blindness: The Loss of Sensitivity in Liquid Modernity* (Cambridge: Polity Press, 2013); Zygmunt Bauman, *Consuming Life* (Cambridge: Polity Press, 2007).

15 Agnieszka Wilczynska, Maciej Januszek and Kamila Bargiel, 'The Need of Belonging and Sense of Belonging versus Effectiveness of Coping', *Polish Psychological Bulletin* (Vol. 46, 2015), 72–81, at p. 72.

16 Matthieu Ricard, *Altruism: The Power of Compassion to Change Yourself and the World* (New York: Little, Brown, 2015), 479.

17 Hannah Arendt, *The Human Condition*, 2nd ed. (Chicago: University of Chicago Press, 1998), 2.

18 Ailton Krenak, *A Vida Não É Útil* (São Paulo: Companhia das Letras, 2020), 30.

19 Hannah Arendt, *The Origins of Totalitarianism* (New York: Harcourt Brace Jovanovich, 1973), 296.

20 *Upekṣā* was translated into English as 'impartiality': 'By cultivating impartiality you eliminate the unevenness in attitude that comes from the bias of your attachment and hostility, and your mind becomes like a good field', Tsongkhapa, *The Great Treatise on the Stages of the Path*, Vol. 2 (Ithaca: Snow Lion, 2004), 37–8. It is important to stress that equanimity does not mean indifference.

21 Patricia Guernelli Palazzo Tsai, *Responsabilidade Universal: Dialogando Dalai Lama e Direitos Humanos* (Valinhos: BUDA, 2022), 156–7.

22 Dalai Lama, Gyatso Tenzin and Thubten Chodron, *In Praise of Great Compassion* (Somerville: Wisdom Publications, 2020), 112.

23 Buddha disposition, according to the Dalai Lama and Chodron's translation.

24 Can also be understood as Buddha nature, but the translation means the embryo or essence of a Tathāgata. A Tathāgata is someone who has gone beyond suffering.

25 Dalai Lama, Tenzin, and Chodron, *Saṃsāra, Nirvāṇa and Buddha Nature* (Somerville: Wisdom Publications, 2018), 293.

26 Pandita Asaṅga, Pandita Maitreyanātha and Darma Gyaltsap Rinchen, trans. Bo Jiang Marty, *The Sublime Continuum and Its Explanatory Commentary with the Sublime Continuum Supercommentary* (New York: American Institute of Buddhist Studies, 2017), I.27, 82.

27 Sallie B. King mentions that these concepts are frequently used in Buddhist engagement in social action: 'The Doctrine of Buddha-Nature is Impeccably Buddhist', in *Pruning the Bodhi Tree: The storm over critical Buddhism*, ed. Jamie Hubbard and Paul L. Swanson (Honolulu: University of Hawai'i Press, 1997), 174–92, at p. 191.

28 Plínio Tsai, *Sermão do Grande Fundamento* (Valinhos: BUDA, 2019), 220.

29 Bodhisattva refers to the being that pursues *bodhi*, awakening, in order to benefit all sentient beings. A Bodhisattva is not yet a Buddha, it is someone who assumes the responsibility of becoming one.

30 Jung Mo Sung, *Idolatria do Dinheiro e Direitos Humanos*, 240.

31 Mario I. Aguilar, *After Pestilence* (London: SCM Press, 2021), 134.

32 According to the UNDP's (United Nations Development Programme) 2022 Global Multidimensional Poverty Index, https://hdr.undp.org/content/2022-global-multidimensional-poverty-index-mpi#/indicies/MPI (accessed 21/02/2024).

33 According to the 36th Forbes List, https://www.forbes.com/sites/chasewithorn/2022/04/05/forbes-36th-annual-worlds-billionaires-list-facts-and-figures-2022/?sh=796d04ab7e30 (accessed 21/02/2024).

34 Dalai Lama and Tenzin Gyatso, *Beyond Religion* (New York: Houghton Mifflin Harcourt, 2011), 49.

35 Jennifer Chan, 'The Alternative Globalization Movement, Social Justice, and Education', in William Ayers, Therese M. Quinn and David Stovall, eds, *Handbook of Social Justice in Education* (New York: Routledge, 2009), 557–8.

36 Lisa Vahapoğlu, *'We are poor because I don't work hard enough': Neoliberal Self-Evaluation of Bangladeshi Microfinance Participants*, Global Health Equity Research in Translation, ed. N. S. Murshid, E. Frimpong Boamah and K. Kordas (Community of Excellence in Global Health Equity, 2020).

37 Richard Hall and Mark Pulsford, 'Neoliberalism and primary education: Impacts of neoliberal policy on the lived experiences of primary school communities', in *Power and Education* (Vol. II, 3, 2019), 241–51, at p. 243.

38 Hall and Pulsford, 'Neoliberalism and primary education', 244.

39 Robert FitzSimmons, 'Countering the neoliberal paradigm: A Pedagogy of the Heart from a Finnish Higher Learning Perspective', *Journal for Critical Education Policy Studies* (Vol. 13, 1, 2015), 210–37, at p. 232.

40 Kimberle Crenshaw, 'She Coined the Term "Intersectionality" Over 30 Years Ago. Here's What It Means to Her Today', Interview by Katy Steinmetz for *Time Magazine*, February 2020: https://time.com/5786710/kimberle-crenshaw-intersectionality/ (accessed 21/02/2024).

41 In Buddhist debate, horns of a rabbit is used as an example of something absurd, that cannot exist concretely.

42 Camila Vergara, *Systemic Corruption* (Oxford: Princeton University Press, 2020), 266.

16

A Lived Theology of Belonging

AMAR D. PETERMAN

The quest for knowledge and certainty has long been a struggle for the Christian church.[1] In different times and places, this endeavour has taken new and renewed forms of belief and practice. For much of church history, though, a throughline traced across the theological and hermeneutical (interpretation) task was an acceptance of mystery and multiplicity. Lay leaders and theologians alike did not frame Christianity as a striving for ultimate answers, but as a daily practice of faithfulness and devotion filled with mystery and wonder.

However, the rise and influence of the Enlightenment in the academy deeply transformed how certain theological traditions went about interpreting, understanding, studying, theologizing and preaching the biblical text. The theological academy's embrace of Enlightenment thought transformed the theologian's task from daily devotion to an embrace of an interpretive framework that asserts a universal and empirical method for discerning truth.[2] Deeply problematic in this method is the prerequisite of emptying oneself of bias and presupposition before approaching the biblical text to examine its history and syntax and the intent of the author. While studying context and language is not poor practice, this interpretive prerequisite functioned as a homogenizing tool as non-white scholars seemingly had many more 'biases' (language, culture, norms, experience) to rid themselves of compared to their white counterparts. A lasting consequence of this method is the false presentation of a universalized hermeneutic methodology that baptizes a single theological imagination – namely, the one formed by the white, self-sufficient man – as purest and most holy.[3]

Scholars have referred to this project and the colonial propagations of this imagination as 'whiteness'.[4] This is not speaking simply about the colour of one's skin, but an imagination of the world and one's place within it. It is not an exclusive reality of race, but an inclusive reimagining of the natural order. Whiteness, as a colonial endeavour, seeks to eliminate the particularities of both person and place.⁵ In biblical studies, the fundamental, Enlightenment-derived enterprise of whiteness is to make all things 'white' so that the idealistic and assumed universality of the biblical text might actually become reality. The underlying imaginative logic of whiteness asserts that difference and diversity are a hindrance to unity, proclamation of the gospel and the divine authority of the Bible. To have multiple or culturally subjective interpretations of Scripture, these scholars argue, is to compromise the integrity of objective truth. The goal, this tradition argues, is a 'unity in Christ', even at the expense of acknowledging vast experiences of Christians across the world and in the United States.⁶

Rejecting the lens of whiteness, this chapter will argue for a recognition and embrace of the diverse and the particular both in the biblical text and in the social locations from which interpreters approach the scriptures. The authority and autonomy to interpret the scriptures in one's particular context, I will argue, holds incredible liberative possibilities. More specifically, I will examine how both Paul's culturally located interaction at the Areopagus in Acts 17 and subsequent interpretations of this text by specific readers across social locations point Christians toward an acknowledgement – perhaps even an embrace – of a multi-vocal reading. In conclusion, this chapter will assert that necessary to the project of multi-vocal reading is a lived theology of belonging. This community-centred reality is found not only in Acts, but in the entirety of the New Testament. A theology of belonging, I conclude, is the healing balm to our ecclesial malady of division and polarization within the church.

The Particularity of Athens and Acts 17

The Acts of the Apostles records the formation and expansion of the Christian community following Christ's resurrection, specifically how this new collection of Christ-followers evangelized to various peoples in particular places, thus reimagining and reforming their growing community.⁷ Acts, then, deals with the weighty question of how Christians might find unity amid difference. That is, how can Jew and Gentile, rich and poor, slave and free, be intimately joined together in worship under the lordship of Jesus Christ? Even more, how can these diverse groups worship together without losing the traditions, languages, norms and liturgies that characterize each individual community? Luke, a master storyteller, answers this question through a series of literary episodes 'follow[ing] God on the ground, working and moving in and through the quotidian realities of struggle, of blood and pain, suffering and longing'.⁸

Acts 17.16–34 offers one of these episodes. Willie James Jennings places this encounter between the Athenian philosophers and Paul within the framework of diasporic Jews in the Gentile marketplace. The underlying Gentile question, Jennings asserts, is this: 'What will you do if I join you at the body of Jesus and fall in love with your God and with you? The Gentiles of Acts are on their way to communion with Jews while remaining Gentiles.'[9] The particularity of the Paul–Athens narrative in Acts 17, therefore, can be interpreted both religiously and ethnically. As Luke states, Paul's 'spirit was provoked (παρωξύνετο) within him as he saw that the city was full of idols' (17.16). Paul's spiritual disturbance stems from a religious idolatry located in Athens, a city well known for the creation of pagan idols, mythology and devotion to their gods. However, inherent to this religious identity is an ethnic designation: Jew (or Judaean) and Greek. The idols worshipped by the Athenians on the Areopagus created a dividing wall between Jerusalem and Athens – a locked door between ethnic and religious differences.

Even still, Paul, like Peter in Acts 10, joins in conversation with these Gentiles. He enters into the 'unclean' space of Athens and extends an invitation into a greater community. However, Paul does not do this by proclaiming the gospel in some Jewish-style polemic. No, Paul recognizes the deep particularities of Athens – its cultural heritage, its philosophy, its theological questions. Paul preaches a gospel that demands repentance (μετανοεῖν, v. 30), yet he contextualizes the gospel by proclaiming the love of God made known in Jesus Christ who is the fulfilment of their spiritual longing. He is the 'Unknown God' made known to all people through the incarnation, life, death, resurrection and ascension of Christ. This repentance is rooted in resurrected life, not death – in grace, not empire. Paul offers the Athenians a new way of being in and relating to the world around them that does not deny their particularities, but rather is a fulfilment of their distinct longings. The proclamation of the resurrection challenges the listener's reality while reorienting both to 'how we see earth and sky, water and dirt, land and animals, and even our own bodies'.[10] Paul's Spirit-filled provocation did not lead him away from these idolaters to maintain some notion of purity or exclusivity. No, the Holy Spirit leads Paul towards the Athenians in love, beckoning them to see what is already in front of them. 'The man who agreed to the stoning of Stephen now stands surrounded by stones that evoke his righteous fury, yet he must yield to the Spirit who now calls him to a new word.'[11]

Paul's discourse in Acts 17 is located in one of the most distinctly Athenian places: the Areopagus – the highest Athenian philosophical court.[12] Before the Parthenon and Temple of Nike, Paul stands before Epicureans and Stoics and locates Jesus in the dirt of Athens. Before these Greek philosophers, Paul proclaims that God is not found on Mount Olympus, but rather he is found in their own culture and inscriptions: he is the Unknown God made known through Jesus Christ. Speaking directly to the philosophical ideology of the Stoics and Epicureans, Paul proclaims God as Creator of all, not a divine essence to be unearthed through a philosophic ascent. God is holy and set apart from the world, yet God is simultaneously engaged intimately with God's creation, coming incarnate for the sake of the world.[13] In this divine nature and sacred action, God unites all people in Godself:

> 'And he made from one man every nation of mankind to live on all the face of the earth, having determined allotted periods and the boundaries of their dwelling place, that they should seek God, and perhaps feel their way toward him and find him. Yet he is actually not far from each one of us ...' (Acts 17.26–27, ESV)

'He Hath Made of One Blood Many Nations'

While we ought to affirm the particularity of Paul's ministry to the Athenians, this comprises only half of the discussion at hand. In the first section of this chapter, I highlighted the particularity of Paul's gospel proclamation in Athens. In this next section, I will turn our attention to *our* distinct social locations in the task of interpretation.[14] The task of interpretation, I will argue here, does not require the interpreter to rid themselves of all bias and presupposition (which is an impossible task), but rather requires the interpreter to acknowledge such realities and read the text through their social locations.

It is, of course, no surprise that African American slaves would reject the hermeneutical logic of whiteness embraced by their oppressors that reconciled the enslavement and dehumanization of Africans with the religion of Christianity. However, what cannot be overlooked is the constructive and liberative response that accompanied this rejection. Enslaved Africans did not dismiss Christianity altogether as the religion of the slave master, but instead 'talked back to the "talking book", and valued a hermeneutic of love superior to the Pauline commands such as "servants, obey your masters"'.[15] For the enslaved person, this was also a 'hermeneutic of survival that found the dominant Pauline word in a non-Pauline affiliated book, in which the character Paul proclaimed that God 'hath made of one blood all nations' (Acts 17.26).[16]

Read through their experience as enslaved image-bearers in the Antebellum South, Black folk relied heavily on Paul's words in Acts 17.26.[17] In what is now defined as the 'One Blood' doctrine (or tradition), enslaved African American theologians interpreted Paul's words to the Athenians as describing the pinnacle of God's original creative activity. While white oppressors claimed that dark-skinned persons were inheritors of the curse of Ham (Genesis 9), enslaved African Americans used Acts 17.26 to reject this distinction of origin and push against their oppressors' use of Paul. For example, Lemuel Haynes argued that, based on his reading of Acts 17.26, 'we may conclude that liberty is equally as precious to a Black man, as it is to a white one, and bondage equally as intolerable to the one as it is to the other'.[18] Similarly, in *The Petition of 1779 by Slaves of Fairfield County*, Black petitioners in Connecticut used the 'One Blood' doctrine to argue they were never meant to be slaves.[19] No matter how persistent white enslavers were in forcing enslaved Africans to embrace a practice of Christianity that called them to contentment in subordination, Black Christians knew that Paul and the Holy Scriptures were on their side.

Harriet Jacobs offers modern readers a memorable and poignant example of how enslaved Black women drew from their particular, intersectional and often traumatic experience to interpret the Apostle Paul. Jacobs, a freed slave residing in the North, was the first Black woman to pen her own autobiography, *Incidents in the Life of a Slave Girl* (1861), which details the first 27 years of her life before her escape from the Southern plantation to the North.[20] Rejecting the cult of true womanhood, the belief that the plantation was a place of safety and refuge for Black folk, and the notion that God-ordained racial hierarchy provided a needed order to a chaotic world, Jacobs' autobiography details the horrors of Black women in the South.

In one of her most impactful illustrations, Jacobs contextually interprets Paul's words to the Athenians as a double-entendre. She begins by describing one experience: 'The next morning a message was brought to me: "Master wants you in his study." I found the door ajar and I stood a moment gazing at the hateful man who claimed a right to rule me, body and soul.' Reflecting on this horrific experience, Jacobs observes how white slave owners 'seem to satisfy their consciences with the doctrine that God created the Africans to be slaves'. Yet, the brilliance of Jacobs' argument comes in her conclusion where she observes a perverse inversion of Acts 17.26: 'what a libel upon the heavenly father, who "made of one blood all nations of men!" ... And who then are Africans? Who can measure the amount of Anglo-Saxon blood coursing in their veins of American slaves?' From her particular social location and experience of intersectional oppression, Jacobs utilizes Paul's words in Acts 17 to affirm her own dignity while simultaneously condemning white slaveholders who, through the abuse and rape of African women, literally made 'one blood' between Africans and Anglo-Saxons.

Jacobs, and many Black interpreters like her, wrote in response to the biblical interpretations taught by their oppressors.[21] Because whiteness functions as an unnamed presupposition, presuming it holds no bias or subjectivity, white slaveholders did not consider their interpretation one among many. Rather, slaveholders baptized their interpretation as the one, clear, universal truth. Take, for example, Reverend Dr Basil Manly Sr, founding president of the Southern Baptist Seminary's board of trustees, who did not see slavery as an 'unfortunate necessity' but a divinely ordained hierarchical order of Christian society.[22] As a highly influential Christian figure, Reverend Manly unequivocally preached from the pulpit this divinely ordained racial hierarchy.

Not all Christian leaders spoke so blatantly as Manly about divine racial hierarchies, yet such ordering remained the same underlying logic for many preachers and theologians. The famed Princetonian teacher Charles Hodge, while discussing interpretations of Acts 17, affirmed the 'common brotherhood of men' and rejected the notion of an 'inferior race'. Even still, Hodge consistently argued across his writings that the enslaved were not 'equal with their masters in authority, or station, or circumstances'.[23] The two responses of Manly to Hodge reveal one of the many powers of whiteness: cultural adaptation.[24]

While interpreters like Haynes and Jacobs are only a select few of many interpretive lenses, they represent the immense influence that one's social location has upon one's reading of scripture. The particularity of Paul's discourse in Athens is illuminated when interpreted in the particularities of interpreters across diverse social locations. In diverse Christian community, Paul's words provide a foundation for liberative action. However, this multi-vocal reading apart from relationship is left susceptible to the powers of whiteness and the interpretations of white scholars such as Charles Hodge and Basil Manly. This leads to my final conclusion: in order to faithfully participate in this diverse multi-vocal reading of the text, we must embrace a lived theology of belonging.

A Lived Theology of Belonging

A lived theology of belonging recognizes diversity as, first, a God-ordained reality; and second, a catalyst for cooperation across difference. Rejecting the imaginative theological lens of whiteness that asserts Christianity offers us a universal religion and truth, a correct theology of Christian community proclaims that differences between and the particularity of believers are not a tool of division but the location of unity.[25] Rather than denying the reality of difference and thus exacerbating the problem of prejudice, a lived theology of belonging calls us, like the church in Acts, to pay attention to the importance of ethnic differences and engage with such evident diversity in a deeply theological and sophisticated manner.[26]

In his book on this very subject, Willie Jennings argues that, because we belong to each other, 'belonging must become the hermeneutic starting point from which we think about the social, the political, the individual, the ecclesial, and ... the educational'.[27] This, he argues, is the foundation for a lived theology of belonging. We must come to the text in shared community and the fullness of our social locations, not a denial of them.

If we do not cultivate this belonging, our understanding of scripture and the Triune God are distorted (like Hodge and Manly). If we only lift up God as liberator, we are prone to forget God's command for Hagar to return to Abraham. If we imagine God as the Galilean Christ on the border, we miss God enthroned above the heavens. If we imagine God only as our nation's divine protector, we fall into a destructive Christian nationalism. If God is only spoken of in warrior-like imagery, we form a toxic view of masculinity and subsequently a distorted view of femininity and queerness. While each of these perspectives is drawn from the biblical text, it is only in community that believers may lift up these divine paradoxes and mysteries: that God is liberator and yet subjected to death on a cross; that Jesus located himself in the margins of society, yet God reigns all-holy above creation; that believers may, in the same motion, raise our hands in praise of an all-mighty God and also in the comfort that our God intimately knows our suffering.

The New Testament is filled with this ethnic and racial discourse of belonging. The book of Acts records the gathering of communities who would never be brought together in this way under any other circumstance. As a record of the expansion and growth of the church, Acts begins with the gospel on the move, from Jerusalem, to Judaea, to Samaria, and to the ends of the earth (Acts 1.8). At Pentecost, God brings people of different tongues and cultures together for a grandiose proclamation of unity and belonging, a temporary lifting of linguistic confusion and cultural barriers, that points to the eschatological reality that all believers will one day be gathered together again in this way (Acts 2). Acts is filled with these Lucan episodes of gospel proclamation that record the messy work of diverse people coming together under the Lordship of Jesus Christ.

Paul's epistles, written throughout the narrative told in Acts, further inform this lived reality of belonging. In Galatians, Paul asserts that for Gentile Galatian converts (and other marginalized groups), the criterion for acceptance into Christian community is that they have already been accepted by God, as confirmed by the activity of the Holy Spirit in their lives.[28] Paul's admonitions to the church in Corinth speak of the mysteries of God that surpass the wisdom of creation. 'God's power, like God's wisdom, shares no part in the logics and measures of this world ... [Paul] does not speak of human wisdom ... he speaks of the power of God, which is beyond all possibility. He does not speak of knowledge; he speaks of crucifixion.'[29] Paul's letter to the Ephesians also is filled with language of 'unity in Christ' and encouragement to join together as 'Christ has broken down the dividing wall, that is, the hostility between [believers]' (Ephesians 2.14). Scripture abounds with a theology of belonging.

While the colonial enterprise of whiteness has sought to eliminate the particularity of communities and peoples, a multi-vocal reading of the text through the social locations of faithful believers across time and geographical space manifest the mysteries of God, who has brought the people of God under his Lordship that we might 'see what great love the Father has lavished on us, that we should be called children of God!' (1 John 3.1). The New Testament records a gospel that is accessible universally, but proclaimed contextually; God reigns in heaven even as we find God in the dirt of Athens, in the altar to the Unknown God. However, it is only in relationship and belonging that this particular, located reading may faithfully point to the God of both Jew and Gentile, slave and free, marginalized and powerful. Yes, the God found in the dirt of your land is the same Triune God found in the stones of mine.

Notes

1 I extended my deepest gratitude to Dr Eric D. Barreto, Frederick and Margaret L. Weyerhaeuser Associate Professor of New Testament at Princeton Theological Seminary, for the knowledge and wisdom he has so generously shared with his students. Much of this essay is inspired by the conversations and lectures we shared during my time in Princeton.

2 See Hanna Reichel, *After Method: Queer Grace, Conceptual Design, and the Possibility of Theology* (Louisville, KY: Westminster John Knox Press, 2023); also

E. Randolph Richards and Brandon J. O'Brien, *Misreading Scripture with Western Eyes: Removing Cultural Blinders to Better Understand the Bible* (Downers Grove, IL: InterVarsity Press, 2012).

3 See J. Kameron Carter, *Race: A Theological Account* (New York: Oxford University Press, 2008); Willie James Jennings, 'Caucasia's Capital: The Ordinary Presence of Whiteness', in Markus Gottwald, Kay Kirchmann, Heike Paul, eds, *(Extra)Ordinary Presence: Social Configurations and Cultural Repertoires* (Bielefeld: Transcript Verlag, 2017).

4 See Love L. Sechrest, Johnny Ramírez-Johnson and Amos Yong, eds, *Can 'White' People Be Saved? Triangulating Race, Theology, and Mission*, Missiological Engagements (Downers Grove, IL: IVP Academic, 2018); Greg Carey, 'Introduction and a Proposal: Culture, Power, and Identity in White New Testament Studies', in Greg Carey and Lozada Francisco, eds, *Soundings in Cultural Criticism: Perspectives and Methods in Culture, Power, and Identity in the New Testament* (Minneapolis, MN: Fortress Press, 2013), 1–14.

5 Whiteness as a colonial endeavour is exemplified in the systems of European and American colonization wherein racial(ized) logics were placed upon the lands of indigenous peoples, allowing for colonizers to 'discover' a new land and bring it under their responsibility and governance. See J. Kameron Carter, 'Excremental Sacred', in Christina Sharpe, *In the Wake: On Blackness and Being* (Durham, NC: Duke University Press, 2016), 75.

6 For a longer discourse on this tradition, see Merold Westphal, *Whose Community? Which Interpretation?: Philosophical Hermeneutics for the Church* (Grand Rapids, MI: Baker Academic, 2009); Kevin Vanhoozer, *The Drama of Doctrine: A Canonical Linguistic Approach to Christian Doctrine* (Louisville, KY: Westminster John Knox Press, 2005).

7 Benny Tat-siong Liew, 'Acts', in Daniel Patte, ed., *Global Bible Commentary* (Nashville, TN: Abingdon Press, 2004), 419–20.

8 Willie James Jennings, *Acts*, Belief: A Theological Commentary on the Bible (Louisville, KY: Westminster John Knox Press, 2017), 1.

9 Jennings, *Acts*, 8, 175–8.

10 Jennings, *Acts*, 178. Also Norman Wirzba, *This Sacred Life: Humanity's Place in a Wounded World* (Cambridge: Cambridge University Press, 2021).

11 Jennings, *Acts*, 176.

12 N. T. Wright provides some clarity on what exactly the Areopagus is: 'You can see the Acropolis to excellent effect, displaying the Parthenon, the Temple of Nike, and all the rest, from another steep hill a few hundred yards to the northwest. This is the Areopagus, the "Hill of Mars" – Mars was the god of war – where from early times the senior council of Athens used to meet. Athens was in that period ruled by "archons" (the word simply means "the ruling ones"), nine of whom were elected each year. When their term of office was over, they automatically became members of the Areopagus, the hill giving its name to the body that met there. Though the status and role of the body changed as political reforms came and went, it continued to be a powerful influence in Athenian public life, and it also functioned as a court to try serious offenses, including homicide, arson, and some religious cases.' N. T. Wright, *Paul: A Biography* (San Francisco, CA: HarperOne, 2018), 193–4.

13 For a longer discussion on how Paul's message in Acts 17 directly refutes the philosophy of the Stoics and Epicureans see Wright, *Paul: A Biography*, 204–6.

14 I will use 'social location' in this paper as shorthand for that which makes the individual or community distinct from others. That is, 'social location' speaks to one's personal experience based upon their race and ethnicity, cultural heritage, gender, ability, physical location and the like. One's social location is that which formulates their biases and presuppositions.

15 See Allen Dwight Callahan, *The Talking Book: African Americans and the Bible* (New Haven, CT: Yale University Press, 2008).

16 Emerson B. Powery and Rodney S. Sadler, *The Genesis of Liberation: Biblical Interpretation in the Antebellum Narratives of the Enslaved* (Louisville, KY: Westminster John Knox Press, 2016), 169–70.

17 See Demetrius Williams' excursus, 'The African American Protest Tradition and the "One Blood" Doctrine', in 'The Acts of the Apostles', in Brian K. Blount et al., eds, *True to Our Native Land: An African American New Testament Commentary* (Minneapolis, MN: Fortress Press, 2007), 236–8.

18 Lemuel Haynes, 'Liberty Further Extended', in Richard Newman, ed., *Black Preacher to White America: The Collected Writings of Lemuel Haynes, 1774–1833* (Brooklyn, NY: Carlson Pub, 1990), 17–30.

19 See Lisa M. Bowens, *African American Readings of Paul: Reception, Resistance, and Transformation* (Grand Rapids, MI: Eerdmans, 2020).

20 Harriet Jacobs, 'Incidents in the Life of a Slave Girl', in Yuval Taylor, ed., *I Was Born a Slave: An Anthology of Classic Slave Narratives*, Vol. 2 (Chicago, IL: Lawrence Hill Books, 1999), 545–93.

21 Black scholars continue this work today. For example, see Esau McCaulley, *Reading While Black: African American Biblical Interpretation as an Exercise of Hope* (Downers Grove, IL: Intervarsity Press Academic, 2020); John M. Perkins, 'One Blood' (Chapel Lecture, Biola University, 22 February 2019).

22 Robert P. Jones, *White Too Long: The Legacy of White Supremacy in American Christianity* (New York: Simon & Schuster, 2019), 35.

23 Charles Hodge, *Commentary on Ephesians*, quoted in Powery and Sadler, *The Genesis of Liberation*, 93.

24 See Derrick A. Bell, *Faces at the Bottom of the Well: The Permanence of Racism* (New York: Basic Books, 1992).

25 See Denise Kimber Buell and Caroline Johnson Hodge, 'The Politics of Interpretation: The Rhetoric of Race and Ethnicity in Paul', *Journal of Biblical Literature* (Vol. 123, 2, 2004), 235–51.

26 Eric Barreto, 'Negotiating Difference: Theology and Ethnicity in the Acts of the Apostles', in Francisco Lozada Jr and Greg Garey, eds, *Soundings in Cultural Criticism: Perspectives and Methods in Culture, Power, and Identity in the New Testament* (Minneapolis, MN: Fortress Press, 2013), 98–9.

27 Willie James Jennings, *After Whiteness: An Education in Belonging* (Grand Rapids, MI: Eerdmans, 2020), 10.

28 Brad R. Braxton, *No Longer Slaves: Galatians and African American Experience* (Collegeville, MN: Liturgical Press, 2002). 57.

29 Jacob D. Myers, 'Wise Speech: 1 Corinthians 2:1–16', in Eric D. Barreto, Jacob D. Myers and Thelathia Young, *In Tongues of Mortals and Angels: A Deconstructive Theology of God-Talk in Acts and Corinthians* (Lanham, MD: Fortress Academic, 2018), 78.

17

Technological and Theological Visions, Desires and Practices

MICHAEL MORELLI

The question 'What does theology have to do with technology?' is like Tertullian's famous question, 'What has Athens to do with Jerusalem, the Academy with the Church?'[1] Although both questions tend to be asked to imply with rhetoric that they have nothing to do with each other, they have a lot to do with each other. They have power, for example. As far as theology and technology are concerned, globalization and climate change indicate there are few if any spaces in our world untouched by technology's power, including religious spaces. Acknowledging such similar degrees of power reveals another commonality: religion, which includes theology, and technology, both affect the vision of people: what people see, what they do not see, what they want to see, and what they do not want to see; all of which generate desires and practices, just as desires and practices generate visions.

In what ways, then, do technological and theological visions overlap and/or diverge? What desires and practices do these overlapping and/or divergent visions produce? And how do such desires and practices produce overlapping and/or divergent visions?

In this chapter I examine these questions from a Christian theological perspective because I am a Christian theologian who thinks such questions are of critical importance for the world's present and future. With that said, I do not speak only to Christians. I want to engage people who do not identify as Christian given the overlaps and divergences in technological and theological visions, desires and practices that can and do have consequences for all people. Furthermore, it is evident to me, just as it likely is evident to the people reading this book, that the willingness (or lack thereof) of older generations to take seriously these overlaps and divergences and respond intentionally, responsibly, imaginatively and compassionately, irrespective of their religious inclinations or lack thereof, will have significant implications for the present and future for younger generations.

In short, for better or for worse, justice, whatever it means today and tomorrow, cannot be properly defined or pursued without giving due consideration to the ways in which technologies shape our conceptions and expressions of justice. With that in view, I will compare three visions in this chapter – two theological, one technological. As I offer this comparison, I conclude, contrary to typical technological visions, desires and practices, the Apostle Peter, Augustine and Paul Virilio help us to see genuine *visiones Dei* (visions of God), that cultivate *frui Deo* (enjoyment of God), which in turn cultivate desires and practices that lead to the kind of whole-person happiness essential for ensuring the planet, and everything and everyone in it, will have a promising future. But I need to clarify what I do and do not mean when I use the term *enjoyment* and/or *happiness*. As Michael P. Foley puts it in *On the Happy Life*, 'Contrary to our strong visceral tendencies to identify happiness as a good feeling or emotion, the sages of both Athens and Jerusalem taught that happiness was an activity determined by one's whole character.' In other words, for someone like Augustine, happiness was less an elusive state of emotion that one sought and clung to for as long as one could and more an enduring state of one's being that could be achieved through living one's life in a particular, particularly focused way. Or, one might say Augustine associated happiness with being content, at peace with self, other people, the world and God, whereas the average person today associates happiness with their desires being gratified at any given moment. In this essay, the two classic sages and one modern sage I engage allow comparison between technological and theological visions, desires and practices. The Apostle Peter and Augustine (both 'classic' theologians) are the former sages and Paul Virilio (a modern phenomenologist-philosopher who happened to be Christian) is the latter sage.[2]

I look at Augustine's *visiones Dei* (visions of God) and their mutually reinforcing desires and practices to establish what such *visiones Dei* mean for my chapter. I conclude with a consideration of the universal creaturely stillness and silence Augustine and his mother Monica encounter during their visions of God described in the *Confessions*. In the second section I engage with Paul Virilio's understanding of (late) modern technological visions, desires and practices to show where they overlap and diverge from Augustine's *visiones Dei* (and by extension, a good many other *visiones Dei* given Augustine's influence on Christian traditions, especially Western expressions). I conclude with an examination of the ubiquitous creaturely agitation caused by rampant technological visions in a globalized world constantly experiencing threatening changes to its climate. In the third and final section, I examine in the light of the preceding sections, the Apostle Peter's Pentecost sermon in Acts 2.14–24 to construct a theology and ethic of creaturely stillness and silence that fosters prophetic, creative visions of God's justice. This is a theology and ethic that asserts, along with Peter and the prophet Joel referenced in Peter's sermon, that the most promising present and future visions of God are given to the young, the elderly and the powerless – not the middle-aged with money and power – and this prophetic promise, which is being fulfilled today and will be fulfilled tomorrow, should be taken seriously – intentionally, responsibly, imaginatively and compassionately – by all people, including and especially the people who are neither young nor elderly and have money and power.

The Stillness and Silence of Augustine and his Mother Monica's *Visiones Dei*

There is a lot of literature that describes the *visio Dei* and what it means for anyone who experiences it. On the one hand, the abundance of vision of God literature shows how difficult the term is to define. On the other hand, the abundance and attendant difficulty captures the degree to which an unmediated glimpse of God is indescribable.

Experiencing a sublime vision of God is like becoming simultaneously unconscious and conscious; is like disappearing into, but not being consumed by, the God upon whom one gazes; and, most who experience such visions return from such encounters with poetic words and images that stretch the capacities of prosaic language to plumb the depths and measure the heights of unmediated encounters with the Divine God who is at once infinitely distant and intimately close. Such visions occur infrequently for most people. But the punctual moments of divine self-disclosure tend to happen at critical spatial and temporal junctures, provoking alterations of life trajectories and inspiring lifetimes of reflection on the significance of the event(s).[3]

I engage Augustine's treatments of the *visio Dei* in this section because his work represents a genus of this species of beautiful, mysterious literature in the Christian tradition. Also, given the context in which I am embedded, I think it is useful to engage with a thinker who is writing to Christians who are acclimating and/or acclimated to social, political and economic power and decadence. I do for the most part, however, pluralize the word *visions* throughout this chapter because I want to make clear there are various visions of God that people can and do have.

Augustine first offers readers *visiones Dei* in his *Soliloquies*. He is post-conversion, pre-baptism, and reflecting on the present and future implications of becoming a Christian at this point in his life.[4] Elsewhere, and later in life, Augustine offers more *visiones Dei* in his *Confessions*, the (in)famous post-baptism reflections on his conversion written to convert people to Christianity, especially sceptics.[5] Here, I examine Augustine's descriptions of the *visio Dei* in *Confessions* to establish what it means to experience an unmediated encounter with God. Later, I examine descriptions of such encounters with the divine in Augustine's *Soliloquies* to outline the degree to which technological visions align with the theological visions shared throughout this essay. Augustine writes the following about his and his mother Monica's *visio Dei* in his *Confessions*:

> We raised ourselves up and with hearts aflame for the One we made our gradual ascent through the physical world and even heaven itself, where sun and moon and stars shine upon the earth. And now we were climbing still further by pondering, discussing and marveling at your works. We entered into our own minds and transcended them, to reach that place of unfailing abundance, where you feed Israel for ever with the food of truth [Ezekiel 34.14]. There, life is the wisdom by which all other things come to be, both past and future – wisdom that is not created but rather exists just as it always has been and always will be. In fact it does not have the capacity either to *have* existed, or to *come* to exist. It simply is, because it is eternal. While we spoke, we also gazed upon wisdom with longing; we reached out and touched it as best we could, with every beat of our heart. Then we sighed and left behind us, where they belonged, those first fruits of the Spirit.[6]

He continues, speaking of internal, universal stillness and silence brought about by his and his mother's vision of God. Augustine writes:

> So we went on conversing: 'Imagine that someone experiences within themselves the stilling of the commotion of the flesh, the stilling of every image of earth and sea and sky, the stilling even of heaven, and the soul itself. Imagine that dreams grew silent, and symbolic revelations, every tongue, and every sign; and that anything which comes into being through transition grew silent to that person ... Then suppose that those things fell silent after their declaration, because they turned their attention to him who made those things and then he alone spoke, not though

them, but by his own self, so that we heard his Word not by means of a tongue of flesh, nor by the voice of an angel nor by the thundering of a cloud nor by the mystery of a mental image; so that we heard the Word himself, the one we love in all these things, yet heard him without them, created as they are. In this way my mother and I now reached out, and, in the witness of our thought, we touched eternal Wisdom which lasts beyond all things. Imagine that all other visions (so greatly inferior) were removed, and that this alone were to remain: would this vision by itself seize us and absorb us and restore the beholder to those inner joys, so that eternal life would be just what that moment of understanding had been (the one for which we sighed)? ... In any case, Lord, on that day when we were conversing in this fashion, and the physical world, with all its particular pleasures, became cheap in our eyes as we were speaking.[7]

Among the many facets I want to focus on the outcome of Augustine and Monica's vision: stillness and silence – not only the stillness and silence of Augustine and Monica, but the stillness and silence of everything and everyone in the heavens and the earth as this mother and her son observe their Creator. *All* flesh; *all* images of the earth, sea, and sky; *all* of the heavens; *all* souls; *all* dreams; *all* symbolic revelations; *all* tongues; and *all* signs are stilled and silenced as this mother and her son transcend their senses to gaze upon God directly, and experience a momentary glimpse of what the saints will see in full and forever in heaven: the face of God (1 Corinthians 13.12).

With this stillness and silence in sight, a practical but critical question arises for me: if this is what can happen when two people gaze upon God in this way, what happens when more people gaze upon God in this way (cf. Ecclesiastes 4.9–12)? This question will be left open for now, but I will return to it in the final section. For now, I will move to the second section that compares Augustine and Monica's stilling and silencing visions of God with the phenomenologies of agitated and agitating technological visions offered by philosopher Paul Virilio, framed first by Augustine's descriptions of the *beatific vision (beata visio)* in his *Soliloquies*.

Technological Grievances and Disturbances

In *Soliloquies*, the conclusion to the *Cassiciacum Dialogues* tetralogy, two characters, *Augustine* and *Reason*, engage in a classic philosophical dialogue. This staged back-and-forth treatise creates the dramatic conditions for the first use of the term *beatific vision* (*beata visio*) in Latin (a synonym for the *visio Dei*) featured throughout Augustine's writings.

Augustine intended the *Soliloquies* to summarize with constructive critique the three preceding *Cassiciacum Dialogues* that were edited transcripts of actual discussions with his family and friends on a retreat in Cassiciacum, Italy, outside of Milan. On this retreat Augustine recovered from poor health and in his company prepared for baptism and its quiet secret, rigorous teachings and rituals.[8] At this point in *Soliloquies*, Reason says to Augustine:

> When the soul has seen that unique and true Beauty, it will love all the more; and unless it fixes its eye with unbounded love and never ceases from looking, it will not be able to remain in that most beatific vision. But as long as the soul is in this body, even if it were to see God most clearly – that is, understand Him – nevertheless, because the body's senses make use of their proper function (there is, indeed, nothing about them that leads to doubt), that by which the senses are rested and that by which something else is believed to be true instead can still be called faith. Likewise, because in such a life the soul still endures many bodily grievances (even though, when it understands God, it is now happy), it needs to hope that all those inconveniences will not longer exist after death.[9]

The reason why Augustine and Monica's visions of God described in *Confessions* do not last for ever is given in *Soliloquies*: the earthly body is subject to 'grievances' and 'disturbances' that cause *visiones Dei* to be powerful, but fleeting. For this reason, faith, hope and love are essential for pre-eternity life on earth because 'bodily grievances' and various 'inconveniences' interrupt *visiones Dei* until the full *beatific vision* appears at the Eschaton, the return of the Messiah Jesus Christ, and with him the new heavens and new earth where no created lights will be needed because God will be the light of the new, Heavenly City (Revelation 21.1–8). Practically speaking, on this side of the Eschaton, holding onto beautiful, divine, mystical visions like Augustine and Monica's is like trying to catch a wild pony by the tail in the undulated meadow of a 'groaning' world (Romans 8.22). Consequently, virtuous faith, hope and love can plant people in fertile love of God, neighbour and self that sows and harvests peace in the world; that helps make real, lasting and devastating bodily grievances and inconveniences easier to bear until the Eschaton is fully realized.

Turning to Paul Virilio and technological visions, one of many gifts given by this late French, Catholic philosopher-phenomenologist is his descriptions of how our overly technologized (late) modern world multiplies the 'bodily grievances' and epistemological 'inconveniences' that Augustine brings into view in the passage previously cited. For the purposes of this chapter, Virilio's cryptic analyses of 'the vision machine' concisely capture the causes and effects of these technologically enhanced grievances and inconveniences.[10] Virilio writes:

> To manage at last to 'bring to light' an over-exposed world, a world without dead angles, without 'areas of shadow'... this is the objective of the technologies of synthetic vision. Since *a picture is worth a thousand words*, the aim of multimedia is to turn our old television into a kind of domestic telescope for seeing, for foreseeing (in a manner not unlike present weather-forecasting) the world that lies just around the corner. The aim is to make the computer screen the ultimate window, but a window which would not so much allow you to receive data as to view the horizon of globalization, the space of its accelerated virtualization ... Here the computer is no longer simply a device for consulting information sources, but an automatic *vision machine*, operating within the space of an entirely virtualized geographic reality.[11]

Elsewhere in his work, Virilio describes how this ubiquitous vision machine produces 'a new fusion-confusion of perception and object';[12] produces a 'fusion/confusion of the factual [and] the virtual; the ascendancy of the "reality effect" over a reality principle';[13] where 'the delineation between past, present, and future, between here and there, is now meaningless except as a visual illusion';[14] because they are 'replaced by two tenses, *real time* and *delayed time*, the future having disappeared meanwhile in computer programming, and on the other hand, in the corruption of this so-called "real" time which simultaneously contains both a bit of the *present* and a bit of the *immediate future*'.[15] This phenomenon, Virilio says, is generated by a particular, enduring desire: 'the will to universalized illumination';[16] the desire to see all and know all; and, due to such a desire, to desire to become like God and act accordingly.

Therefore, if the classic Christian *visio Dei* is one in which the person looks upon God without mediation, the (late) modern technological visions generated by the ubiquitous vision machine reverses the direction of the gaze towards people who desire to be gazed upon as if they are divine beings. With such reversals, the power of mediation offered by vision machines are venerated for their abilities to make a person feel like they are a god being gazed adoringly upon by the world and everything and everyone in it. This feeling of being gazed upon with all the world's adoration produces the feeling of being able to gaze back at the world omnipresently and omnipotently – and in some cases, it actually gives a person (or people) the power to exert control in and over the world.[17]

As mentioned in the introduction, this desire, and the technological visions and practices it generates, cause relentless, exhausting, damaging agitation. The intoxication brought about by these synthetic visions of omnipresence and omnipotency pushes users to dismiss the damage as they increasingly desire what continually is delivered: the rush of power and the seizure of control for a fleeting moment. Consequently, pervasive turning away from *visiones Dei* to these technological visions causes a steady eclipsing of the adage *seeing is believing* by the idiom *I can't believe my eyes*.[18] That is to say, the more people use their vision machines to play at being gods in the online world, the more the categories of true and false erode. In a time like our own, when power-hungry people are being gazed upon like gods, there is an ever-decreasing trust that written, audio *and* visual media can render anything true or false for us – especially if what is being rendered contradicts the god(s) to which one pledges allegiance.

To be clear, those who identify as Christian are not exempt from this mass turning away from visions of God, towards seductive vision machines. In fact, in many respects, Christians constitute the vanguard of this kind of mass turning away from visions of God. As examined in Nathan Dever's chapter in this volume, and applied to the discussion at hand, the emergence of Christian nationalism in North America indicates dangerous 'epistemic closure' effected by prolonged use of everyday technologies.[19] As Burke, Juzwik and Prins point out, 'The White Christian nationalist movement seeks social control through any means necessary, it has a vested interest in citizens not learning critical media literacy so they are more easily manipulated by those they trust, whether state officials (e.g., former president Trump, Governor DeSantis, Chancellor Perdue), ethnoreligious leaders (e.g., pastors in White Christian or Catholic churches), or media sources (e.g., Newsmax).'[20] It is clear, then, that Christians can just as easily have their visions of God eclipsed by technological visions of power just as much if not more than those who are not Christian. Nevertheless, whoever is turning, when visions of God are lost and technological visions increase without ceasing, people not only turn away from God, they turn away from sensed reality altogether because trust in what is true and what is false, good and evil, and life and death are eroded by powerful vision machines.[21] Then, significant damage results.

If we have eyes to see the flames, this world is on fire.[22]

But there is hope. If mass-scale turns towards vision machines are possible, so too are mass turns away from agitated and agitating vision machines, towards stilling and silencing visions of God.

To propose the latter kind of turn, the next section begins with the Apostle Peter's vision in Acts 2.14–24, and returns to the question asked at the conclusion of the previous section to formulate an answer in response to the unlikely Apostle's visionary sermon.

Hope, and the Apostle Peter and the Prophet Joel's prophecies, visions, and dreams for the young, the elderly, the powerless, and the poor

After the promised Holy Spirit of God descends like tongues of fire during Pentecost, the good news of the gospel is preached in ways intelligible to the people present at the divine descent (Acts 2.1–13). The preaching of this goodness is so passionate and overwhelming that there are some who conclude the preachers must be drunk, not filled with the Holy Spirit. Then, the Apostle Peter steps up to preach the following sermon, to correct the poor vision of the onlookers as he engages a past prophecy to offer a present prophetic word to the people assembled at Pentecost:

> But Peter, standing with the eleven, raised his voice and addressed them, 'Men of Judea and all who live in Jerusalem, let this be known to you, and listen to what I say. Indeed, [we] are not drunk, as you suppose, for it is only nine o'clock in the morning. No, this is what was spoken through the prophet Joel:
> 'In the last days it will be, God declares,
> that I will pour out my Spirit upon all flesh,
>   and your sons and your daughters shall prophesy,
> and your young men shall see visions,
>   and your old men shall dream dreams.
> Even upon my slaves, both men and women,
>   in those days I will pour out my Spirit;
>   and they shall prophesy.
> And I will show portents in the heaven above
>   and signs on the earth below,
>   blood, and fire, and smoky mist.
> The sun shall be turned to darkness
>   and the moon to blood,
>   before the coming of the Lord's great and glorious day.

Then everyone who calls on the name of the Lord shall be saved.'
You that are Israelites, listen to what I have to say: Jesus of Nazareth, a man attested to you by God with deeds of power, wonders, and signs that God did through him among you, as you yourselves know – this man, handed over to you according to the definite plan and foreknowledge of God, you crucified and killed by the hands of those outside the law. But God raised him up, having freed him from death, because it was impossible for him to be held in its power (Acts 2.14–24, NRSV).

Two critical aspects of this passage stand out to me in regards to the discussion at hand. First, the remarkable, hidden-in-plain-sight detail that the person doing the preaching in this passage is not counted among the religious authorities of his day. Quite the opposite. Peter and his Apostle compatriots are a mixed bag of religious misfits who, by the standards of their day, had little authority to speak. But, the authority they receive from God bestows authority and the responsibility to be creative and peaceful carriers of God's good news in a world filled with bad news, lack of imagination, and violence. Of course, this otherworldly authority and responsibility terrifies and enrages the religious leaders who, up until that point, perceived themselves as chosen, set apart from, and privileged in contradistinction to people like Peter. Nevertheless, Peter preaches fearlessly because God has changed Peter. And people hear and are changed by what Peter and his friends preach: the life, death and resurrection of Jesus Christ the Messiah, and the reconfiguration of all visions in the light of this good news.

Second, and building on the first detail, the radicality of Peter's sermon is that he prophetically reminds listeners that the visions and dreams promised by God through the Prophet Joel will come, and they are coming, to the young, the elderly, the powerless and the poor – not the middle-aged people with power and money. For some, this is good news. For others, this is bad news.[23] The critical question for all listeners, then, is how do we hear Joel's prophecy and Peter's sermon as good news ... and respond (live) accordingly?

To return to the question posed earlier – if universal stillness and silence emerges when Augustine and Monica catch a temporary vision of God, what can happen when more than two people gaze upon God in this way? – the answer to this question, as it seems to be the case with any true vision of God, exceeds the limits of literal words and images. Yet, with the content of Peter's sermon in one's sightline, it becomes clear that it is not only scripturally appropriate, it is theologically and ethically constructive, to ask and answer the following question: what if the Pentecost event was not and is not only about the universal clarification of *verbal* language? What if the Pentecost event also was about and is about the universal clarification of *visual* language? Or, more simply: what if the promise of Pentecost being realized today is that we not only have our speech about God clarified, we also have our visions of God clarified?

If Pentecost is about both – and I think it is – that means the good news of the gospel can be preached and received by all people, and prompts a micro- to macro-level turning away from agitated, agitating vision machines, and micro- to macro-level stilling and silencing turns toward God, either again or for the very first time.[24] Phrasing the question in this way, my answer is as follows: Pentecost *is* about both, and it locates for us a promising source of hope in a world rife with seductive, poisonous, agitated and agitating technological visions. If that is the case, then it is possible to say that present and future justice will emerge with a reconfigured and reinvigorated understanding of what happens when people, especially the overworked and the underpaid, rest and sleep: they can meet a Holy Spirit who brings radical, world-changing visions and dreams. For those who are overworked and underpaid, this simple, powerful truth can cultivate concrete, enduring hope that past, present and future conditions in our world, many of which are unsustainable in the broadest and deepest sense of the word, can and will change. For those who are overpaid because they overwork and underpay other people, this simple, powerful truth is a prophetic challenge to alter unsustainable conditions in our world so that more rest and more sleep are offered to the prophets of today and tomorrow: the young, the elderly, the powerless and the poor in the world today who *are* having revolutionary dreams and visions of God. Space and time simply need to be made and stillness and silence need to be received in relationship with such people for such dreams and visions to be received and practically engaged. To conclude, as Willie James Jennings comments on this passage in Acts,

> The famous Joel passage noted here could never be fully captured with our conceptions of egalitarianism. It proclaims a new world order energized by the movement of the Holy Spirit, breaking through on all flesh and destroying social orders that find slavery useful, stable, capable of making fundamental differences of identity between would-be masters and would-be slaves. These slaves, men and women, prophesy. God speaks through them and they are to be obeyed. This new world order begins with collapse. God shakes foundations, especially ones that wrongly claim divine imprint. However, it is only as Peter makes the christological turn that he connects the overturning of the social order

with the new order of the Spirit. Only as he speaks of Jesus does he begin really signifying the present. Now Peter sets the template through which future preaches' words will be spoken about the real God in real time who is working in the concrete histories of people. Jesus of Nazareth is the history foretold by Joel. We must not lose sight of the storyteller at work here, because this will become the legacy for the many that will follow Peter. He presents the life of Jesus as reachable, attainable, and one who has been among us. This Jesus was murdered, and in his journey toward death, Peter declares the sameness of Jesus with all human beings. Like us he faced the powers of empire and death. But now he has risen from the dead.[25]

In conclusion, it is possible for people of all ages to turn away from their vision machines and turn toward the stillness and silence created by visions of God. With such a turn, the promised visions and dreams of the young, elderly, powerless and poor are encountered, and the most promising visions of God can cultivate faith, hope and love that plants us in a love of God, neighbour and self; that heals, rather than harms, the planet and everything and everyone in it.

This is not to say that the healing of the planet depends entirely on any one person or group of people. Rather, it is to say that participation in God's healing of the world depends on our willingness to reject the agitations of technological visions and embrace the abundant, stilling, rest-inducing, transformative visions of God now, and in the days to come.

Notes

1 Tertullian, 'On the Objection of the Heretics', in David Ayerst and A. S. T. Fisher, eds, *The Records of Christianity*, Vol. 1 (Oxford, UK: Basic Blackwell, 1971), 95–6.

2 'Introduction', *On the Happy Life: St. Augustine's Cassiciacum Dialogues*, Vol. 2, trans. Michael P. Foley (New Haven, CT: Yale University Press, 2019), 4.

3 I am not a specialist in this area of theology, but I have been enriched by what I have encountered. Three texts that immediately come to mind (in the order I encountered them): Teresa of Avila, *The Life of Saint Teresa of Avila by Herself*; Julian of Norwich, *Revelations of Divine Love*; Hildegard of Bingen, *Book of Divine Works*.

4 Augustine, *Soliloquies: St. Augustine's Cassiciacum Dialogues*, Vol. 4, trans. Michael P. Foley (New Haven, CT: Yale University Press, 2020), 33. Translator, annotator and commentator Foley helpfully comments in a corresponding footnote on page 289: '"*Beatissima visio*". This is the first instance in Latin of the expression

"beatific vision" (*beata visio*), the term used to designate the saints' seeing God face to face in heaven and the ineffable bliss that results (see 1 Cor. 13.12; Augustine, *Literal Meaning of Genesis* 5.14.32; *Explanations of the Psalms* 147.24). Augustine, as we see from the "Vision of Ostia" later in his life, had an abiding interest in "what the eternal life of the saints could be like" (*Confessions* 9.10.23–24).'

5 Augustine, *Confessions*, 9.10.23–25. In this essay I use the following translation: Augustine, *Confessions: Books 9–13*, ed. and trans. Carolyn J.-B. Hammond (Cambridge, MA: Harvard University Press, 2016). I write *(in)famous* here because I struggle with the implications of Augustine's problematic renderings of women in his writing. With this acknowledged, it is important to say any theologian engaged with past and present voices should critically censure the bad and constructively engage the good. I try to do this with Augustine in this chapter by focusing on the good, which happens to include a positive portrayal of his mother Monica.

6 Augustine, *Confessions*, 9.10.23–25.

7 Augustine, *Confessions*, 9.10.23–25.

8 Providing helpful context for the state of Augustine's theology and faith at this time, Foley, 'Introduction', xxiv writes, 'The Cassiciacum dialogues [were] written by a mere catechumen, a candidate for baptism. Because of the early Church's so-called *disciplina arcani*, or "discipline of the secret", being a catechumen in the late fourth century meant not experiencing all of the Church's practices and teachings. Augustine the catechumen may have engaged in advanced theological speculation at Cassiciacum, but he probably did not know the wording to the Apostles' Creed which was taught to catechumens only a few weeks before their baptism. And he may have known that the Eucharist was the bread of life, but he had probably never seen the Eucharist, since catechumens were dismissed from Mass after the homily.'

9 Augustine, *Soliloquies*, 33. Resonances with 1 Corinthians 13.12–13 are strong here: 'For now we see in a mirror, dimly, but then we will see face to face. Now I know only in part; then I will know fully, even as I have been fully known. And now faith, hope, and love abide, these three; and the greatest of these is love.'

10 Paul Virilio, *The Information Bomb*, trans. Chris Turner (New York: Verso Books, 2005), 15–16. See also Paul Virilio, *The Vision Machine*, trans. Julie Rose (Bloomington, IN: Indiana University Press, 1995), 59, 64, 70, 72–3 and 76.

11 Virilio, *The Information Bomb*, 15–16. Author's emphasis.

12 Virilio, *Vision Machine*, 29. See also 53, 68 and 70.

13 Ibid., 60.

14 Ibid., 31.

15 Ibid., 66. Author's emphasis.

16 Ibid., 70. See also 14, 33 and Virilio, *Information Bomb*, 13. The risks? Virilio writes in *Open Sky*, trans. Julie Rose (New York: Verso Books, 1995), 139: 'To tamper with light, with the illumination of the world, is thus to attack *reality*. Illumination's lack of place gives place to time, to that tangible duration without which no reality of events can exist. As for *truth*, that is quite a different thing from the much-vaunted effectiveness of the sciences and technologies of information.' Author's emphasis.

17 See, for example, M. J. Riedl, J. Lukito and S. C. Woolley, 'Political Influencers on Social Media: An Introduction', *Social Media + Society* (Vol. 9, 2, 2023), https://doi.org/10.1177/20563051231177938.

18 Elinor Carmi, Simeone J. Yates, Eleanor Lockley and Alicja Pawluczuk, 'Data citizenship: Rethinking data literacy in the age of disinformation, misinformation, and malinformation', *Internet Policy Review*, ISSN 2197-6775, *Alexander von Humboldt Institute for Internet and Society*, Berlin (Vol. 9, 2, 2020), 1–22, https://doi.org/10.14763/2020.2.1481.

19 K. J. Burke, M. Juzwik and E. Prins, 'White Christian Nationalism: What Is It, and Why Does It Matter for Educational Research?' *Educational Researcher* (Vol. 52, 5, 2023), 286–95. https://doi.org/10.3102/0013189X231163147.

20 Ibid.

21 Admittedly, these are difficult terms to define. But I do not think I need to define them to point out the obvious: our planet is in a precarious state, and the collapse of these categories into one another are apparent to anyone paying close enough attention.

22 Note, there are different kinds of fire to be seen, and their import is relative. Here I have in mind the fire of the Holy Spirit and the kinds of forest fires currently raging in Kelowna, British Columbia, Canada, as I write these words. Kelowna is about a four-hour drive from my home.

23 Willie James Jennings, *Acts* (Louisville, KY: Westminster John Knox Press, 2017), 76–7. Jennings writes, 'Our Christian readings of this text often fly past the iconic element found in verse 14 that shapes the entire speech. Immediately after the ears have heard the new, the eyes will see it. Standing in front of all those who had heard their tongues are the twelve disciples, now becoming apostles of Jesus. This is Israel speaking to Israel, calling to their own with the good news of the intensification of their election and of the personification of the free grace that shaped their existence from its beginning. This is precisely where the scandal that was Jesus of Nazareth, Mary's baby with all the tensions he created and all the theological, social, and political contradictions that religious and civic leaders associated with his ministry, began to spread over many bodies. This is a strange image, an unappealing icon – twelve men, none with exceptional credentials, no fabulous educational pedigrees, none with reservoirs of immense cultural capital to draw from, all standing in front of Israelites with nothing more than a message. We live in times when images create and carry so much power. For us, image and word, body and text, are inseparable, merging together, mutually constituting. Yet in this primordial moment the image standing before these gathered does not carry gravitas. It can never match its message. Nor will it ever. This is the eternal imbalance that will mark preaching, a message far more powerful than its messengers. Indeed, image emerges here fully encased in witness.'

24 Speaking of which, it is noteworthy that lockdowns during the Covid-19 pandemic caused noticeable reductions in pollution and improvements in air and water quality as well as the livelihood of wild animals. See Koushik Sen, Tanmay Sanyal and Susanta Roy Karmakar. 'COVID-19 forced lockdown: Nature's strategy to rejuvenate itself', *World J. Environ. Biosci* (Vol. 10, 2021), 9–17.

25 Jennings, *Acts*, 79.

18

The Fallacy of Hopelessness: Constructing a Metamodern Theology of Hope

IONA CURTIUS

Tell me we'll be alright
Say that we'll be fine
Lie to me it's alright, right?
Say that we'll be fine
Just a little bit of tenderness
It's a little bit of tenderness
Say that we'll be alright, right?
Even if it's lies.

This generation, our people, young people, *people* yearn for hope. We long to be told that it is going to be OK.[1] At the same time, we reject platitudes and the easy comfort of those who would tell us to close our eyes to the outside world and forget our troubles. Our world is burning, literally and figuratively. It's not OK. Nothing is OK. We are afraid. We are angry and scared, paralysed by the overwhelming need. Where do we even begin?

Yet, this generation do not give up. Crippled with climate anxiety they take to the streets on Fridays. They proclaim boldly 'I can't breathe,' holding clenched fists aloft. They confront late-stage capitalism in bright, pink plastic commercials.[2] They undermine cisgender, heteropatriarchal power structures with *quirky*[3] and dark art.

All these actions are bound together by a similarity. Yes, they are all acts of resistance characterized by a determination grown out of desperation. But more than that, they are riddled with contradiction. They swing between extremes, often holding two contradictory ideas, emotions or actions in the same space.

Such oscillation is one of the things that characterizes a 'structure of feeling' which is arising around us: metamodernism.[4]

We are still on the cusp of discovering what metamodernism is. How do we act and interact with this cultural moment? What does it mean for how we do theology? What does it mean for how we do justice? Can theology learn from it, work with it, help to shape it, even? This chapter attempts to construct a metamodern theology of hope, seeking to show how metamodern thinkers and doers, artists and activists, ardent Gen Zers and bewildered Millennials 'expose the fallacy of hopelessness'.

Everyone's First Question: What is Metamodernism?

In 2010, cultural theorists Timotheus Vermeulen and Robin van den Akker confidently declared that 'The postmodern years of plenty, pastiche, and parataxis are over.'[5] They went on to herald a new cultural moment, a new 'structure of feeling'. This they called 'metamodernism'. In order to understand (maybe 'get a feel for' would be a more appropriate expression) *meta*modernism, however, one must first understand both modernism and postmodernism. The challenge shall be to keep this brief.

For the purposes of this chapter, modernism might best be understood as characterized by *certainty*. Modern thinkers challenged the idea that tradition ought to be the highest epistemological (as well as moral) authority. Rather than simply trusting that the ancients knew best, these modern philosophers had the 'courage to use their own reason'.[6] We cannot know that anything is really real, as René Descartes so famously observed. Except, that is, the fact of our own thoughts. For Descartes and his fellow modern thinkers, only human reason could be relied upon completely as the source of objective truth. There were objective, ultimate truths to be discovered out there in the world and it was the privilege and duty of the responsible citizen to use their reason to explore them. This certainty gave birth to an optimism and hope that came to define this cultural epoch. The universe was no longer a mysterious place, governed by dark, capricious gods. It operated according to laws that could be uncovered and understood. In this world, progress was inevitable. Such grand metanarratives provided a frame and gave meaning to the artistic and scientific endeavours of the modern era.

The twentieth century saw radical shifts in these tendencies. In the shadow of the horrors of two world wars, bloody revolutions, and devastating economic crises, the authority of human reason was eroded, leading to the inevitable decay of the neat metanarratives that modernism had provided. The world that had previously seemed so reasonable had become incomprehensible. Human reason had proved itself capable of conjuring unspeakable and 'unreasonable' evil. Doubt took over. Where modernism had been determined by certainty, postmodernism was characterized by scepticism. 'Deconstruction' dominated discourse. Postmodernism is about questioning previously held and cherished beliefs. It is about taking apart what we know. Neither tradition nor human reason allow us to discover (objective) truth. Its very existence is doubtful. Postmodernism is cynical, ironic, sceptical, nihilistic, apathetic.

For some years now though, a growing number of cultural theorists have declared this period to be over. A few different thinkers have attempted to name this new structure of feeling, following Linda Hutcheon's challenge to do so in *The Politics of Postmodernism*.[7] Gilles Lipovetsky suggests that we find ourselves in *Hypermodern Times*, hyperindividualized and lost to intrinsically meaningless cultural practices.[8] Alan Kirby proposes a 'digimodernism' arising out of the new digital technologies of the late twentieth and early twenty-first centuries.[9] Similarly emphasizing technological developments, Robert Samuels argues that our new cultural epoch is best understood as a 'combination of technological automation and human autonomy', which he names 'automodernism'.[10] Each of these theories focusses on a particular area of cultural or social development that they see as critically relevant. They also, as Vermeulen and van den Akker point out, 'appear to radicalize the postmodern rather than restructure it'. Vermeulen and van den Akker suggest that such a restructuring is vital and posit the idea of 'metamodernism' as an alternative to these ways of understanding our current cultural moment.

Vermeulen and van den Akker parse their chosen prefix 'meta' as referring to 'such notions as "with", "between", and "beyond"'.[11] Thus they argue that metamodernism 'should be situated epistemologically *with* (post) modernism, ontologically *between* (post) modernism, and historically *beyond* (post) modernism'.[12] Metamodernism is often conceptualized in terms of oscillation between the modern and postmodern. 'It oscillates', they write, 'between a modern enthusiasm and a postmodern irony, between hope and melancholy, between naïveté and knowingness, empathy and apathy, unity and plurality, totality and fragmentation, purity and ambiguity.'[13] Metamodernism is both at once and neither. It never settles in one place or reaches an equilibrium, always maintaining its pendulous motions between two or more opposite extremes. 'Each time the metamodern enthusiasm swings toward fanaticism, gravity pulls it back toward irony; the moment its irony sways toward apathy, gravity pulls it back toward enthusiasm.'[14]

This chapter works closely and primarily with Vermeulen and van den

Akker's definition of metamodernism, as set out in their seminal text on the topic: 'Notes on Metamodernism'. The term has also been used by others and in varying ways. Jason Ananda Josephson Storm, for instance, uses the concept of metamodernism to argue for a new approach to Theory, which, he says, is in desperate need of an overhaul after decades of postmodern decay.[15] Storm himself distances himself from other uses of the term, such as Vermeulen and van den Akker's.

It is also worth noting that much, if not most, of the current scholarship on metamodernism is situated in a western European context. This is very much the background for this chapter. Neither the scope of the chapter nor the author's expertise unfortunately allow for a broader exploration of the topic from differently situated global perspectives, for instance.

Where modernism had confidently bet on human reason and received certainty, postmodernism had questioned the possibility of knowledge, and received scepticism. Metamodernism seems to acknowledge that it may not be possible to know anything for certain. Human reason definitely does not seem like the (only) way to arrive at truth. And yet, unlike the postmodern, the metamodern still values the pursuit of knowledge and truth. There is space for such endeavours. Commitment and faith are not ridiculed. Instead, the desire, even need, for them is acknowledged and sympathized with. Hope is not futile.

Hope

While hope is not futile, it is difficult to grasp – both actually and conceptually. It seems to have something to do with the future, with how things ought to be, with how we long for them to be. It is related to faith and justice. It is connected to optimism. There is a temptation to call it naïve. Paulo Freire talks about hope as an 'ontological need'.[16] Caron Gentry calls hope the 'antithesis of ... anxiety'.[17] For Emily Dickinson it is a delicate but resilient little bird.[18] Caitlin Seida replies that it is a sewer rat,

> an ugly thing
> With teeth and claws and
> Patchy fur that's seen some shit.

It carries diseases such as 'Optimism, persistence, / Perseverance and joy'.[19] How are we to begin to understand this multifaceted, amorphous phenomenon?

It is almost impossible to write about hope in a theological context without engaging with Jürgen Moltmann (introduced on the back cover of his *Ethics of Hope* as the 'father of the theology of hope'). Moltmann writes that 'eschatology [is] the doctrine of the Christian hope, which embraces both the object hoped for and also the hope inspired by it.'[20] Caron Gentry puts it thus:

> While hope may be basically defined as an aspiration for something (better) to happen, it is also, in this context, a determination for the world to be a better place. For Christians, hope is grounded in the person of Christ, whose death and resurrection make possible a hopeful life now and the promise of life after death.[21]

This adds another layer to what we know about hope. It is inscrutable, appears flighty yet exhibits great resilience. It takes grit and perseverance. It is future-oriented, yes, but it is also concerned with the present. Crucially, hope is concerned with creating a world that is better, with striving towards justice.

Freire writes that, while hope is an ontological need, 'hopelessness is but hope that has lost its bearings, and become a distortion of that ontological need'.[22] Moltmann writes that it can take two forms: 'presumption' and 'despair'.[23] 'Presumption', according to Moltmann (who is borrowing here from Joseph Pieper), 'is a premature, selfwilled anticipation of the fulfilment of what we hope for from God'.[24] Meanwhile, 'despair is the premature arbitrary anticipation of the non-fulfilment of what we hope for from God.'[25] Both are forms of hopelessness that lead away from God; however, Moltmann seems to judge despair the greater evil.

Despair is an attempt to pre-empt disappointment, to protect ourselves from the vulnerability of our ontological need for hope. Such an attempt, however, is misguided, even dangerous. For, in 'this so-called realism dictated by the facts we fall victim to the worst of all utopias – the utopia of the *status quo*, as R. Musil has called this kind of realism'.[26] 'Realism' (or, despair) accepts the status quo. It declares it immutable, asks us to give up ideas of a better world and thus prevent us from taking action against injustice. Hope stands against this. Gentry writes that 'Hope must be an active resistance to injustice anywhere and at any time, to be determined by those with need, not by those with power.'[27] In *Ethics of Hope* Moltmann writes that it is not tragedy or disappointment that destroy hope (as 'realism'/despair would suggest), but that 'Lethargy is the real enemy of every hope.'[28]

Thus, defending hope from the charge of meaningless optimism (which leads to apathetic despair) is crucial to Moltmann. Hope is important, not just because it provides personal comfort and warmth, like Emily's bird, but because it makes action possible. He writes, 'Hope finds in Christ not only a consolation in suffering, but also the protest of the divine promise against suffering.'[29] Such hope is not naïve or unrealistic. In fact, he insists it is far more realistic than the (post)modern 'realists': 'Hope alone is to be called "realistic", because it alone takes seriously the *possibilities* with which all reality is fraught.'[30] Hope sees possibilities realistically, despises apathy, and motivates towards justice.

James Cone pointed out that 'Black people in their sermons, prayers, and songs of the nineteenth and twentieth centuries were talking about the politics of hope long before the appearance of hope theology in Germany.'[31] Nonetheless, he appreciates the moves made by Moltmann and other such 'theologians of hope'. In contrast, he heavily criticizes much of white (American) theology's discourse on hope. He warns that, unless a theology of hope 'begins and ends with the liberation of the poor in the social existence in which theology takes shape', it is 'alien to the gospel of Jesus'.[32]

He contends vehemently that talk about hope cannot be an abstract endeavour, removed from the actual struggles of the oppressed and marginalized in the specific society in which the conversation is taking place. He writes,

> When connected with the person of Jesus, hope is not an intellectual idea; rather, it is the praxis of freedom in the oppressed community. To hope in Jesus is to see the vision of his coming presence, and thus one is required by hope itself to live as if the vision is already realized in the present.[33]

'Hope in Christianity, then, is multifaceted,' writes Gentry. 'It springs from and is sustained by the life promised to Christians by God and through the resurrection of Christ, but it also speaks into the reality of life in a world where corruption, oppression and harm occur.'[34] Hope is not only or merely the promise of a better future – perhaps postponed until the next life – but a protest against specific and concrete injustice in the present.

The Fallacy of Hopelessness

Activism

Having described hope in a way that emphasizes a resistance to despair and apathy, it is possible to see how theological accounts of hope intersect with metamodernism. Such hope, which advocates a clear-eyed, 'realistic' appraisal of possibilities, and inevitably leads to action, is particularly clearly visible in the work of many activist organizations. Especially movements led by young people (such as Fridays For Future),[35] exhibit realistic analysis of the situation, recognition of possibility, and resilient action. The Black Lives Matter foundation's 2020–2021 global impact report recognizes 'that we are in a moment ... full of *promise and peril*'.[36] Extinction Rebellion write on their website that 'We acknowledge that we are in the midst of a massive crisis', but also that 'Our hearts tell us a different world is *possible*.'[37] Just Stop Oil use visceral language, evoking brutal climate disasters that will cause societal collapse. 'If we continue down our current path,' they warn that we '... will face the starvation and the slaughter of billions of the poor – and the utter betrayal of our children and their future.' However, they are hopeful that a different future is possible. 'We can do it now, in an orderly manner – creating millions of proper skilled jobs and protecting the rights of workers.'[38] Fridays For Future describe themselves as a movement founded on frustration at 'society's unwillingness to see the climate crisis'. At the same time, they most explicitly declare that 'we have hope'.[39] These activists embody the kind of hope that we have described above, the idea that 'too often conceived of as a sentiment, hope is better understood as an action'.[40] They also embody metamodernism.

Metamodern Hope

The pattern of cynicism and hope expressed by these activists is exactly the kind of oscillation that characterizes metamodernism. Author and cultural critic Maria Popova gives voice to this pendulous movement. In a 2016 interview she said that 'Critical thinking without hope is cynicism, but hope without critical thinking is naïveté. I try to live in this place between the two, to try to build a life there.'[41] Vermeulen names this phenomenon: 'this modernity that is at once critical and naïve may be called metamodernism.'[42] Andrew J. Corsa writes (quoting Vermeulen and van den Akker's 'Notes on Metamodernism') that

Those who experience metamodernism choose to live according to grand narratives that describe humanity collectively moving toward a far better world. And by doing so, they might, at least sometimes, better collaborate with others to make social improvements in the short term: 'Humankind, a people, are not really going toward a natural but unknown goal, but they pretend they do so that they progress morally as well as politically.'[43]

The metamodern actor recognizes the artifice of the story they are telling, knows that meaning is arbitrary, and yet believes the myths and rejoices in the purpose anyway. As we see in the various founding myths, manifestos, goals and demands of the movements discussed above, the metamodern response to tragedy and atrocity, to climate disaster and racism is not merely certain belief in progress or apathetic surrender to the status quo, but hopeful action.

Theology and Metamodernism

The stated aim of this chapter was to construct a metamodern theology of hope. Hopefully (yes, I know), this has been achieved. However – and maybe it is slightly duplicitous to only state this explicitly at this late stage – it also seeks to serve as an exemplary case of a meeting and collaboration between metamodernism and theology.

At this juncture, let me make this piece truly metamodern by doing an about-turn and swinging in the opposite direction. Here, I lift the veil of impassive, distanced academic writing and reveal a human being with a personal agenda. I hope (yes, again) to show with this piece how theology and metamodernism (even culture more broadly) can come together productively. I believe that, as theologians, we must understand the culture in which we find ourselves, if we are to have a hope of being even remotely relevant (and therefore important). We can also learn from our culture and, crucially, from other disciplines, such as cultural theory, to broaden and strengthen our work. Equally, we can, in turn, give to other disciplines and begin to play a part in shaping cultural developments.

Metamodernism holds a great deal of potential for theology. Whenever it gets too close to nihilistic apathy, it swings away again towards action and optimism. It does assert that there may not be any objective, unconstructed truths and metanarratives (though I feel it is more agnostic and open to being positively surprised on that front than postmodernism was). However, it strongly insists that stories matter, nonetheless.

That they are not 'true' in the way we used to construe that term is of no concern. What matters is that we live by them. Some of these ideas, and particularly the sentiments behind them (the *vibes*, one might say), may appeal to theologians after decades of fighting for truth and hope in postmodernism. However, I would like to issue a warning. If we are to embrace metamodernism (and I believe we have much to gain from doing so), we must go through postmodernism first. We cannot jump from modern certainty to metamodern hope. If we do not go through the process of deconstruction, or 'wintering', we will not understand metamodernism and therefore will not be able to learn from or contribute to it. We will fail to understand young people and, worst of all, we will continue to betray them (us) by misinterpreting and undermining their (our) hopes and passionate charges towards a better, more just world.

Conclusion

Over the last few pages, we have come on a journey. From modern certainty and optimism, via postmodern scepticism and irony, we are tentatively easing into a movement that oscillates between the two. We have explored the idea that hope is not naïve or unrealistic. As Rebecca Solnit commented in 2016,

> It is important to say what hope is not; it is not the belief that everything was, is or will be fine. The evidence is all around us of tremendous suffering and destruction. The hope I am interested in is about broad perspectives with specific possibilities, ones that invite or demand that we act.[44]

We have found that hope is about seeing the world for what it is, recognizing oppression and suffering, and nevertheless seeing possibilities for a better future, taking action, seeking justice.

As touched on briefly above, this chapter is situated rather narrowly in a western European/Anglo-American context. It is primarily this context that I have commented on, from which and to which I speak. There is, of course, a much broader conversation to be had here and I look forward to hearing and learning from various voices from backgrounds different to my own on how hope is expressed there. I wonder whether the philosophical-cultural framework of metamodernism will be useful to resource other resistance communities and how that will in turn shape metamodernism?

There is no way we can go back behind postmodernism, no matter how much we long for a simpler, naïve conception of the world where there is little to fear and metanarratives explain the mysteries away. However, if we simply surrender to dejection and cynicism we will be paralysed into apathy. Metamodernism resists this temptation. If modernism is certainty and postmodernism is scepticism, maybe metamodernism is HOPE. It acknowledges the real terrors of the world, the meaninglessness of it all. But it does not stop there. It goes through the valley of the shadow of nihilism and emerges out the other side. Maybe not into sparkling sunlight and wide meadows. Maybe into parched desert or flood-scarred barrenness. But into light. And where there is light, we can see a path forward. And where we can see a path, we can have hope.

Notes

1 I find the song 'Plug In ...' by the British indie pop band Bastille to be an arresting expression of this sentiment.

2 Yes, I *am* referring to the *Barbie* movie.

3 'Quirky is a sensibility that can be recognised most easily by its tone, which we might broadly describe as walking a tightrope between a cynically "detached" irony and an emotionally "engaged" sincerity.' James MacDowell, 'Quirky | Notes on Metamodernism', 13 August 2010, https://www.metamodernism.com/2010/08/13/quirky/ (accessed 26/03/2024).

4 Timotheus Vermeulen and Robin van den Akker, 'Notes on Metamodernism', *Journal of Aesthetics & Culture* (Vol. 2, 1, January 2010), 5677, https://doi.org/10.3402/jac.v2i0.5677.

5 Vermeulen and van den Akker, 'Notes'.

6 The Latin phrase 'sapere aude' is widely proclaimed as the motto of the enlightenment: Immanuel Kant, 'An Answer to the Question: What Is Enlightenment?', in *Practical Philosophy*, The Cambridge Edition of the Works of Immanuel Kant (Cambridge: Cambridge University Press, 1996), 17.

7 Linda Hutcheon, *The Politics of Postmodernism* (London: Routledge, 2002), 181.

8 Gilles Lipovetsky, *Hypermodern Times*, 1st ed. (Cambridge; Malden, MA: Polity, 2005); Vermeulen and van den Akker, 'Notes'; Brian Longhurst, 'Review: Hypermodern Times Gilles Lipovetsky, Polity, Cambridge, 2005, £13.99, 90pp', *The Sociological Review* (Vol. 53, 4 (n.d.)), 777–9, https://doi.org/10.1111/j.1467-954X.2005.00595_2.x.

9 Alan Kirby, *Digimodernism: How New Technologies Dismantle the Postmodern and Reconfigure Our Culture* (New York: Bloomsbury Publishing, 2009). A new cultural paradigm has taken center stage, displacing an exhausted and increasingly marginalized postmodernism. Alan Kirby calls this cultural paradigm digimodernism, a name comprising both its central technical mode and the privileging of fingers and thumbs inherent in its use.

10 Robert Samuels, 'Auto-Modernity after Postmodernism: Autonomy and Automation in Culture, Technology, and Education', in *Digital Youth, Innovation, and the Unexpected.*, ed. Tara McPherson (Cambridge, MA: The MIT Press, 2008), 219, doi: 10.1162/dmal.9780262633598.219.

11 Vermeulen and van den Akker, 'Notes'.
12 Vermeulen and van den Akker, , 'Notes', italics original.
13 Vermeulen and van den Akker, 'Notes'.
14 Vermeulen and van den Akker, 'Notes'.
15 Jason Ananda Josephson Storm, *Metamodernism: The Future of Theory* (University of Chicago Press, 2021), https://doi.org/10.7208/chicago/9780226786797.001.0001.
16 Paulo Freire, *Pedagogy of Hope: Reliving Pedagogy of the Oppressed.*, trans. Robert R. Barr (New York: Continuum, 1996), 8.
17 Caron E Gentry, 'The Politics of Hope: Privilege, Despair and Political Theology', *International Affairs* (Vol. 96, 2, 1 March 2020), 373, https://doi.org/10.1093/ia/iiaa011.
18 Emily Dickinson, *The Complete Poems*, ed. Thomas Herbert Johnson (London: Faber, 1975).
19 Caitlin Seida, *My Broken Voice: Poetry From the Edge and Back* (Lulu Press, 2018).
20 Jürgen Moltmann, *Theology of Hope* (London: SCM Press, 1967), 16.
21 Gentry, 'The Politics of Hope', 372.
22 Freire, *Pedagogy of Hope*, 8.
23 Moltmann, *Theology of Hope*, 23.
24 Moltmann, *Theology of Hope*, 23.
25 Moltmann, *Theology of Hope*, 23.
26 Moltmann, *Theology of Hope*, 23.
27 Gentry, 'The Politics of Hope', 372.
28 Jürgen Moltmann, *Ethics of Hope* (Minneapolis, MN: Fortress Press, 2012), 3.
29 Moltmann, *Theology of Hope*, 21.
30 Moltmann, *Theology of Hope*, 25, italics added.
31 James H. Cone, *God of the Oppressed*, rev. ed. (Maryknoll, NY: Orbis Books, 2008), 141.
32 Cone, *God of the Oppressed*, 141.
33 Cone, *God of the Oppressed*, 142.
34 Gentry, 'The Politics of Hope', 369.
35 'Fridays for Future – How Greta Started a Global Movement', Fridays For Future (accessed 17/10/2023), https://fridaysforfuture.org/what-we-do/who-we-are/.
36 '2020–2021 Global Impact Report' (Black Lives Matter Global Network Foundation, 2021), 2, italics added.
37 'What Is XR', Extinction Rebellion, https://rebellion.global/about-us/ (accessed 17/10/2023), italics added.
38 Roger Pielke Jr, 'What if We Just Stop Oil?', https://rogerpielkejr.substack.com/p/what-if-we-just-stop-oil (accessed 11/06/2023).
39 'Fridays for Future – How Greta Started a Global Movement'.
40 Caron Gentry, 'Hope from Despair: How Young People Are Taking Action to Make Things Better', The Conversation, 29 June 2022, http://theconversation.com/

hope-from-despair-how-young-people-are-taking-action-to-make-things-better-184859 (accessed 26/03/2024).

41 Maria Popova, 'Mapping Meaning in a Digital Age | Maria Popova | Becoming Wise', The On Being Project, https://onbeing.org/programs/mapping-meaning-digital-age-maria-popova/ (accessed 29/09/2023).

42 Timotheus Vermeulen, 'As If', in *Beyond the Aesthetic and the Anti-Aesthetic*, ed. James Elkins and Harper Montgomery (University Park, PA: Pennsylvania State University Press, 2013), 170, http://ebookcentral.proquest.com/lib/abdn/detail.action?docID=6224173.

43 Andrew J. Corsa, 'Grand Narratives, Metamodernism, and Global Ethics', *Cosmos and History: The Journal of Natural and Social Philosophy* (Vol. 14, 3, 2013), 256.

44 Rebecca Solnit, '"Hope Is an Embrace of the Unknown": Rebecca Solnit on Living in Dark Times', *The Guardian*, 15 July 2016, sec. Books, https://www.theguardian.com/books/2016/jul/15/rebecca-solnit-hope-in-the-dark-new-essay-embrace-unknown (accessed 26/03/2024).

Conclusion: Disengaging our Disengagement and Disconnections

Justice is just a posh term for revenge. (Graham, 16)

This understanding was collected by Phil Wall, a chaplain at a young offenders institute in England. The young Graham, Phil explains, perceived the 'justice system as stacked against some people'.[1] Another one of the children that Phil works with exclaimed, 'I reckon I'll be in hell.'[2] Phil has noticed the children in custody aligning soteriology to the system of 'judgement, reward, and punishment' that they experience in the prison[3] and explains the difficulty of moving them away from didactic, individualist, limiting comprehensions of faith.

The absence of grace and redemption results in further psychological damage for the child.[4] Theology, instead of inspiring another way, cultivating imagination, or dreaming of transformation, becomes another system to navigate, a set of rules to follow, a hopeless, sticky predestination.

Tackling limited approaches to justice was the aim of Part 1 of this book, 'Questioning Western Epistemological Hegemony: Rethinking Approaches to Justice'. The topics in this section explored limited ideas of time and progress, exclusive ownership of justice agendas and solutions, the injustice of legacies of colonial impositions of 'right' relations between people and people and the land, and gave a counter to restrictive ideas of justice that focused on the individual in the wrong rather than healing in and for the community. It also wondered how we tackle injustice when it becomes normative, such as in the context of settler communities, and how indigenous knowledge and practices restore wisdom and wholeness.

Sam Efrain Murillo Torres criticized the obsession with chronological time. The building up of good deeds, or the constant working towards something in the future, the proving-yourself logic that burns people out. How can we live outside this acceleration of time that 'gives only emptiness', he asked.[5] Sam prompts a noticing of the irruption of chronological time, as Christ becomes every day anew in the most human of daily encounters – whether they be the highest point of grief or the tummy-hurting kind of laughter in community. These special moments of living are where we encounter God's love with and through each other.

Capitalism's acceleration of time was explored also in Michael Morelli's chapter in Part 3, but these ideas of progress were teased out in Part 2 of the book: 'Insiders and Outsiders: Struggling through History and Context'. The two chapters situated from the context of the UK thought about how diversity sits alongside solidarity. By looking at the 'progress' in Britain through the eyes of the homeless we see that social improvements in the UK have bypassed some of the most vulnerable in society. A focus on trade unions also reminded us how solidarity necessitates a keen awareness of intersectionality when thinking about justice. Moving to the US, a seemingly positive narrative that moderate evangelicals are withdrawing from politics is exposed as a dangerous avoidance which not only disempowers some but gives power to others. A historical approach to church history also demonstrated how radical and long-term approaches to justice work hand-in-hand. Finally, in Palestine, the voices of the doubly invisible are highlighted to show an excellent example of a bottom-up fight for self-emancipation from occupation.

The rigid structure of a prison, or of the 9-to-5 working week, shift work or the management and routine of home, are no longer allowed to be regarded as demanding. As explored in the Introduction, our current form of capitalism moulds all time into potentially productive time.[6] Dave Korn attempted to write his haunting and touching essay while trying to be a witness in a place of heightened trauma (the location might be uncovered from the essay with close reading). Dave found the atmosphere (or vibes to use Iona's language) too heavy, too real, too layered, to begin to unpack while there. His essay, influenced by Morrison's novel *Beloved*, allows the disruption of trauma to break through his deep theorizing. The attempt to bury trauma, flashbacks – or maybe in the positive, our dreams and visions – fails us. Our overstimulation from the vision machine, as explored by Michael Morelli, distorts our place in the world and our responsibilities towards, and relationships with, others. We're restricted when we do not communicate. Arvin Gouw's chapter in Part 3, 'Disrupting Theology, Theory and Thinking', gives a practical example to Daniel Jara J.'s noticing where people of the global South, or, more specifically, those who live in close proximity to the sea, see the immense potential of the sea for environmental help that land-based scholars and scientists overlook.

How might our world look if we followed the prophetic words of the Apostle Peter:

and your sons and your daughters shall prophesy,
and your young men shall see visions,
and your old men shall dream dreams.[7]

How might it be if we took seriously the UN Convention on Rights of a Child (UNCRC) that children have a right to play?[8] How is it possible that, in the bleakness of Gaza during the attacks from Israel, the children still play? This section also touched upon the raw necessity of hope – a hope that scoffs at simple optimism but also sees the dangers of despair and non-action. A hope that is embedded in all beings in our Buddhagotra, or through the incarnated Christ. A hope that can be seriously distorted through scriptural reading that forgoes its evolutionary nature and adopts exclusive, rigid classifications. Amar Peterman demonstrates how the wisdom held in the Bible is continually revisited anew with our particular contexts, lenses, oppressions, struggles, joys and forthrightness.

This project was supported by Westminster College, Cambridge, SCM Press and CTPI Edinburgh. These organizations allowed us to put on a small conference to meet each other and present our ideas in their embryonic forms. We cannot thank each organization enough. This collection has explored ideas of justice from emerging scholars who use their particular context and creative fuel to contribute to envisioning a more just future for all. A justice that does not belong to the 'posh' people, but a graspable justice that is sparked when the beauty of the everyday unexpectedly seeps through the mundane. A justice that can be dreamt in community with an understanding of our connectedness and reliance on one another. A justice that may flow through a world that truly believes in the strife to fight for the flourishing of every living thing, because every living thing is made by, and is loved by, our generous, grace-filled, good, good God.

Blessed are those who hunger and thirst for righteousness,
for they shall be satisfied. (Matthew 5.6).

Notes

1 Phil Wall, 'The fragility of grace in a law focused land: Reflections on ministry with young offenders', *International Journal for the Study of the Christian Church* (Vol. 24, 1, 2024), 70-80.
2 Ibid.
3 Ibid., 74.
4 Ibid., 77.

CONCLUSION

5 Chapter 1, p. 25.
6 Chapter 1, p. 6.
7 Acts 2.17, quoted by Michael Morelli on p. 230.
8 https://www.unicef.org.uk/wp-content/uploads/2010/05/UNCRC_PRESS200910web.pdf (accessed 12/06/2024).

Index

Acceleration of time/life 22, 23, 24, 25, 26, 30, 31, 33fn
Activism 12, 16, 111, 113, 119, 241–2
Acts 1 218
Acts 17 213–17
Acts 2 219
Advaita 177, 182
Afro-communitarianism (see Ubuntu)
Althaus-Reid, Marcella 60, 64
American Evangelical identity 141
Ancestors 51, 93, 95–6, 102
Animal suffering 51, 185, 188, 191, 195, 204
Apostle Paul 22, 214–19
Apostle Peter 214, 223, 224, 230–3
Art 6, 236, 114, 163–4, 167–9
Augustine 21, 225–8

Beatific vision 226–7
Belonging 25, 27, 30, 32, 57, 70, 201, 213, 218–19
Black Lives Matter 242
Body image 190
Boesak, Allan A. 11
Bonhoeffer, Dietrich 14, 25, 29, 30–1, 77–80, 82–7
Botho (see Ubuntu)
British Empire 55, 77, 80–2, 90fn
Buddhagotra 199, 200, 203, 204, 205, 207, 209

Buscando nos Encontramos 31

Capitalism 4, 23, 28, 79, 83, 84, 156, 185, 196, 199, 236
Carbon footprint 185, 192, 195
Carey, William 82, 90fn
Cassiciacum dialogues 226–7
Children 3, 9–10, 24, 27–8, 31, 51–2, 72, 101, 104, 133, 148, 186, 190, 193, 206, 219, 242
Chomsky, Noam 4, 11–12
Christianity 21, 29–30, 49, 54, 56, 77, 78–84, 87–8, 111–14, 122, 126, 185, 190, 200, 212, 215–16, 218, 225, 241
Chronos/chronological 21, 22, 23, 25, 26, 27, 31, 32
Church history 122, 131, 212
Church law 126, 130, 132
Church Missionary Society (CMS) 81, 88
Class struggle 3, 13, 40, 41, 79, 83–4, 105, 117–18, 154, 192, 195, 202
Climate change/emergency 13, 14, 93–6, 118, 185–8, 192–6, 222, 236, 242–3
Colonialism 42, 43–4, 49, 52, 57, 77–8, 80, 82, 102–3, 199, 200
Settler-colonialism 77–8, 82, 86–7
Community 5–8, 11–14, 22, 25, 27–8, 30–5, 46, 49, 50–4,

INDEX

56–9, 61, 64–5, 67–75, 82, 84, 93–6, 113, 115, 119, 126, 129, 130–4, 139, 146, 150, 152–3, 157, 166–7, 169, 171, 174, 195, 201, 202, 211, 213–14, 217–19, 221, 241
Consumerism 96, 115, 202
Cosmos 93
Cosmology/cosmologies 175, 176, 183
Cosmotheandric/cosmotheandrism 176, 181
Cross 27–8, 48–9, 53, 58–61, 83, 85–6, 218
Cultural theory 237–8
Cultured meat 185, 187–8, 189–92

Decoloniality 8, 36, 58, 79, 100
Deconstruction 42, 139, 238, 244
Dehumanize/d 48, 52, 60, 99, 148, 200, 203
Delayed time 228
Demythologization 38
Desire 142, 164, 206, 228–9, 239
Deverell, Garry Worete 85–6, 91
Dreams 7, 164, 225, 226, 230, 231–2, 233

Economy 3, 4, 8, 104, 153, 156, 157, 191, 206
Edelmann, Jonathan 177, 178
Education 2–3, 4, 6, 35fn, 79, 82, 104, 118, 205, 206, 207
Enforced disappearances 22
Enlightenment 79, 212–13
Epistemology 7, 13, 21, 36, 39, 40–2, 46, 100, 144, 228, 237–8
Erasure 48, 53–5, 57, 61
Ethics 95, 116, 240

Evangelical-Republican Alliance 141–2
Exploitation 56, 82, 83, 87
Extinction Rebellion 242
Exvangelical 139

Faithless 24, 29
False-peace 2
Feminism 8–9, 40, 99, 100–1, 105–7, 113, 129
Feminist Theology 40
Fridays For Future 242

Gaudium et Spes 115
Gay 56, 57, 61, 63, 129–34, 137, 146, 155, 157, 159
Gaytari Chakravorty Spivak 100–10
Gaza 9–10, 27–8, 34fn, 99, 101, 105
Globalization 42, 78, 222, 228
Grace 8, 10–11, 60–1, 131, 133, 214, 235fn
Gutiérrez, Gustavo 28, 39, 78–80, 82, 84, 89, 91, 116, 204–5

Happiness 24, 25, 201, 223
Harmony 67–74
Helen Crawfurd 113
Hell 248
Hijra 53–4, 56–7, 63–4
Hinduism 54–5, 64fn, 115, 175–83, 189, 195–6
Holistic 93, 95, 177
Holy Spirit 2, 11, 45, 128, 214, 219, 230, 232, 235fn
Homelessness 13, 148, 149, 150, 157, 158
Homosexuality 48, 54, 63, 154, 155, 159

INDEX

Hope 9, 12, 13, 22, 25–32, 39, 116, 227, 230, 232–3, 239–41, 242
House building 152, 156, 157
Housing Act, 1996 150
Housing associations 152
Housing shortage 156
Human dignity 31, 39, 69, 96, 170, 199, 200, 201, 202, 203, 204–5, 207, 209
Human rights 24, 39, 55, 108fn, 170, 199, 200, 201

Imagination/imagine 6, 84, 163–4, 212, 231
Imago Dei 199, 200, 203, 205, 209
Immanentism 112, 115
Incarnation 8, 10, 115–17, 214
India 48, 53–5, 62–4, 175–7, 179, 180, 182, 189, 191, 192, 195
Indigenous 31, 39, 42, 48–53, 55–8, 60–4, 65, 67, 77, 79, 80, 81, 82, 85–8, 91–2fn, 93, 93, 95–6, 194, 202, 203, 220fn
Indigenous Theology 80, 85–7, 91–2
Indra 175, 176, 181, 182
Intercultural Theology 36, 42, 46
Intifada 103–4, 107
Invisibility 53, 55, 144

Jennings, Willie, James 81, 214, 218, 232
Judgement 84, 142, 158, 248
Just Stop Oil 242
Justice 2, 8, 9, 11, 13–14, 16, 21, 24, 46, 49, 58–60, 65–74, 77, 78, 79–80, 85, 86, 87, 93, 100, 103, 106, 110–11, 115, 117–19, 123, 127, 134–6, 139, 144, 149, 171, 179, 185, 196, 205, 207, 223, 224, 232, 237, 239, 240–1, 244, 248

Kairos/kairological 8–9, 10–11, 22, 25, 26, 27, 31, 32
Koyama, Kosuke 3, 5

Labour churches 112–14
Legal reforms in the UK 154, 155
Lesbian 56, 129, 131, 137
LGBTQIA+ 49, 122, 130–2, 136
Liberal Theology 37, 128
Liberation Theology 36, 38, 39, 40, 41, 42, 116, 176–7, 179, 181–3, 200, 204, 209
Literature 6–7, 163–5, 169, 172, 224
Local government/councils 148, 149, 150, 151, 152, 156, 158
London, England 148, 149, 150, 153, 154
Love 2, 6, 9, 25–6, 28–9, 54, 59, 93, 115–16, 133–4, 142, 214–15, 219, 226–7, 233

Malu 93–6
Māori 80–1, 88, 90
Marriage 52, 122–3, 130, 132, 136, 155, 159
Marsden, Samuel 81, 85, 87–8, 90
Marxism 39
Mediation 2, 6, 16
Memory 23, 24, 25, 27, 39, 53, 164–6, 169
Metamodernism 237, 238, 242–4
Míguez-Bonino, José 11

255

INDEX

Mission 36, 37, 38, 41, 42, 81–2, 126, 142–3
Moderate Evangelicals 140, 142, 145
Modernism 237
Moral majority 141
Multi-vocal reading 213, 217, 219
Munther, Isaac 9
Mutuality 5

Naga 49–58, 60–4
Nationalism 218, 229
Necropolitics 21, 22, 23, 24, 25, 27, 28, 30, 31, 209fn
Neoliberalism 94, 114, 115, 199, 200, 201, 202, 205, 206, 207, 208, 209

Ordination 122, 123, 125, 128, 129, 130, 131, 136, 137
Organizing 104, 110, 112, 125

Palestine 8, 32fn, 99, 100, 102–9
Panikkar, Raimon 175, 176, 178, 179, 180, 181, 182, 183
Patriarchy 2, 13, 51, 52–3, 57–60, 57, 102–4, 111, 133, 177, 179, 190, 236
Pentecost 218, 224, 230–2
Pentecostalism 40, 41, 110
Personhood 7, 14, 69, 71, 72, 73, 74, 93, 107
Politicization 104, 140–6
Polity 123, 128, 130, 131, 136
Poor 8, 10, 11, 28, 39–41, 84, 112, 116, 153, 186, 201, 206, 213, 230, 231–3, 241–2
Pope Francis 115, 118
Post-colonial 36, 39, 45, 53
Postmodernism 237–9, 243–5

Postwar consensus 155, 156
Power 2, 9, 11, 15, 31, 45, 55, 59, 61, 78–9, 84, 85–6, 103, 110–12, 115, 117–19, 134, 138, 140, 142, 144, 149, 151, 156, 165, 167, 176, 181, 202, 208, 219, 222, 224, 228–9, 231, 235fn, 236, 240
Practical politics 122, 130, 131
Presbyterian/Presbyterianism, 122–37, 145
Private rented sector/market 152, 153
Proletariat 40, 82–5, 86
Prophecy 230–1

Queer 7, 14, 48–64, 122–37, 218, 219

Racism 15, 43, 78, 114–15, 132, 145, 154, 155, 243
Rambachan, Anantanand 177, 178, 179, 182
Ram-Prasad, Chakravarthi 178
Reconciliation 7, 65, 71, 72, 73, 74, 76, 95, 10
Redemption 60–1
Religion 8, 15, 21–24, 27–31, 43, 55, 57, 83, 111, 113, 118, 144, 179, 182–3, 190, 205, 215, 218, 222
Religionless 29, 30, 31, 79
Religious Right 140, 141
Renewal 95
Responsibility 3, 14, 15, 45, 93–4, 138, 143–4, 158, 203–4, 231
Rest 227, 232–3
Restorative justice 70, 72
Revolution 39, 96, 103, 116, 204, 208

INDEX

Right to buy 152
Robinson, John 124, 136
Rooster 58–9, 61
Rough sleeping 150
Rudolph Bultmann 37, 38

Schleiermacher, Friedrich 37, 38
Sexuality 52, 54, 56, 57, 63, 64, 118, 129, 133, 135, 137, 157, 207
Silence 31, 223–6, 231–3
Sindt, David Baily 129, 131, 134, 135
Slavery 58, 89fn, 115, 124, 126–7, 132–4, 144, 165, 201, 215–17, 219, 232
Sleep 8, 149, 232
Society 3–5, 11, 24, 32, 39, 49, 51, 52–3, 56, 59–60, 66, 68, 73–4, 79, 83, 99, 100, 102, 104–6, 108, 127, 141, 149, 150–1, 153–8, 163, 170–1, 175, 179, 183, 201, 217–18
Sofa surfing 151
Solidarity 2, 8–13, 56–7, 59–61, 65, 69–70, 74, 104, 110–19, 134, 170, 202, 209
Spirituality 93, 95–6, 127, 140, 145–6, 195
State of exception 23, 27
Stillness 223–6, 231–3
Sturt, Charles Napier 82, 90
Subaltern 102

Taboo 48–52, 54–6, 58, 60–4, 95
Tal'at movement 105–6
Tathāgatagarbha 200, 203, 204, 207, 209
Technology 23, 28, 175, 180, 185, 187, 191, 195, 222–9, 232–3, 238

Temporary accommodation (TA) 150, 151, 152
Thatcherism 156, 157
Time 4–6, 21–32, 228–9, 232–3
Tolpuddle Martyrs 111–13
Trade Unions 104, 110–19, 156
Transitional Justice xi, 65, 66, 67, 68, 69, 71, 73, 74, 75, 76
Trauma 36, 96, 163–70, 172, 216
Trump, Donald 138–42, 145–6, 229
Truth and Reconciliation Commission 65, 71, 72, 76
Two Kingdom Theology 142–3, 147

Ubuntu 7, 14, 39, 65, 66, 68, 69, 70, 71, 72, 73, 74, 75
Unity 73, 128, 138–40, 145, 213, 218–20, 238
Universal credit 153
Universal responsibility 204
Unmerited grace 60–1
Upolu Lumā Vaai 79–80, 95

Vashum, Yangkahao 58, 60, 64
Violence 11, 24, 33–4fn, 52, 55, 59, 73–4, 78–9, 85, 87–8, 105–6, 134, 150, 157, 164, 167, 169–73, 199, 231
Virilio, Paul 33fn, 223, 226–8, 234fn
Visio Dei 224–8
Vision machine 228
Vision(s) 21, 61, 78, 106, 140–1, 169, 178, 222, 224–34, 241

Ways of thinking 3, 36, 38, 41, 42
Whakapapa 80, 82, 87, 89

Whiteness 2, 212–13, 215, 217–19
Woosley, Louisa Maria Layman 125, 126, 131, 134
Work (labour for pay) 4–5, 8, 54, 56, 104, 110, 114, 117–18, 155

Wright, Theodore Sedgwick 126, 127, 131, 134, 136

Young, Woke and Christian (2021) 12, 132

1960s Britain 154, 155, 156, 157

www.ingramcontent.com/pod-product-compliance
Lightning Source LLC
Chambersburg PA
CBHW022043290426
44109CB00014B/969